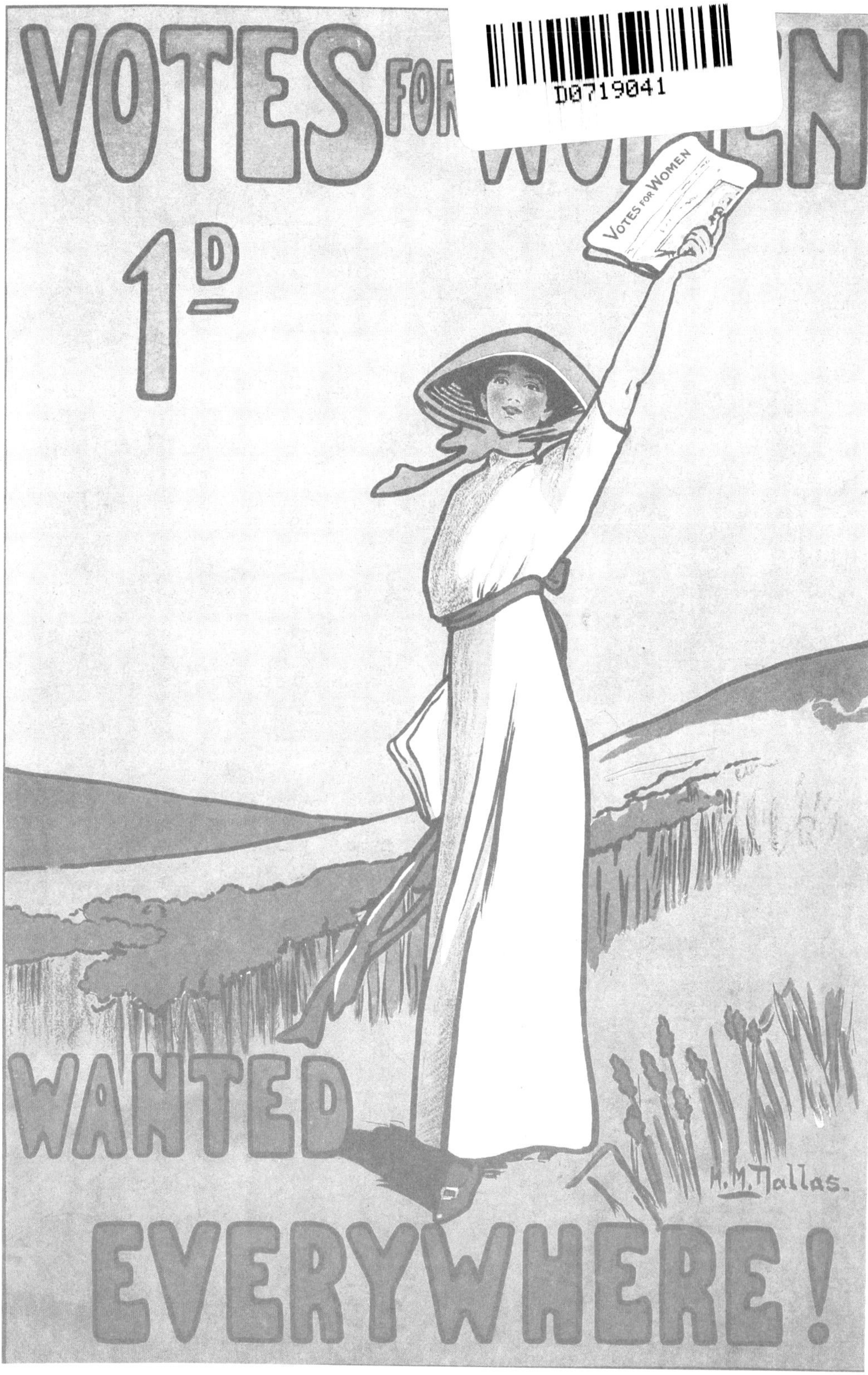
VOTES FOR
1D
VOTES FOR WOMEN
WANTED
EVERYWHERE!
H. M. Dallas.

Votes for Women

Votes for Women

The Virago Book of Suffragettes

Edited by

JOYCE MARLOW

A *Virago* Book

First published by Virago Press 2000

This collection and introduction
copyright © Joyce Marlow 2000

Acknowledgements on pp 277–280 constitute
an extension of this copyright page

A CIP catalogue record for this book is available from
the British Library

ISBN 1 86049 840 X

Typeset in Berkeley by M Rules
Printed in Great Britain by Clays Ltd
St Ives plc

Virago Press
A Division of
Little, Brown and Company (UK)
Brettenham House
Lancaster Place
London WC2E 7EN

For Emma and Adam

Contents

THE VOTE GIRL

I WANT THE VOTE, AND I MEAN TO HAVE THE VOTE, THATS THE SORT OF GIRL I AM

Introduction

'Promise me you'll always use your vote,' my mother said. 'Too many women suffered too much for you to waste it.' It's not a promise many mothers would ask of their daughters today, but that was in 1951 and aged twenty-one I was newly eligible to vote. Half a century later my mother's insistence does not surprise me because in 1951 British women had only had the full right to vote for twenty-three years.

Throughout the westernised world the suffrage struggle was long and bitter. Of nowhere was this more true than in Great Britain and Ireland where the 'Votes for Women' campaign produced acts of heroism, courage, violence and brutality unknown in any other land. The particular virulence of the British experience perhaps stemmed from both proponents and opponents being infused with the confidence and righteous indignation of the daughters and sons of the British Empire. The struggle lasted nearly one hundred years, from the first woman's petition presented to the House of Commons in 1832, until 1928 when women were finally entitled to vote on the same terms as men.

There is no shortage of books about the suffragists and their organisations, but my aim in this anthology is to let the women speak for themselves. To pass beyond the obvious, and particularly beyond London, I have delved into diaries, pamphlets, newspapers, letters, journals and memoirs, using the voices of the women (and men) who were out there, marching through the streets, climbing on their soap-boxes, being pelted by rotten eggs, assaulted by yobs and, as frustration mounted, who battled with the police, went to prison and suffered the abomination of forcible feeding. Pieced together year by year theirs is an inspiring story of ordinary women who, by standing up to be counted, became extraordinary – and ultimately triumphant.

In comparison to the final phase leading up to the outbreak of the First World War in 1914, to the dramatic images of these years that have come down to us, the first forty years of the struggle may seem singularly uninspiring. Yet, for Victorian women to pen pamphlets advocating their political rights, and to tour the country 'spouting' about them on public platforms, demanded tremendous courage. Particularly when their beloved Queen Victoria was among those fulminating against 'this mad, wicked folly of Woman's Rights' and privately declaring that Lady Amberley (one of the vanguard known to her) deserved a good whipping.

To this day, many people equate the British women's suffrage struggle and the final victory with the famous Pankhurst family – Emmeline and her daughters Christabel and Sylvia – and their militant cohorts in the Women's Social and Political Union. In its early years the Union was a bold, innovative, imaginative organisation, among the first to appreciate the value of publicity. Not without justification, its members regarded themselves as the Praetorian Guard of the 'Votes for Women' campaign. But for every suffragette (a term coined by the *Daily Mail* in 1906 to denote these new style militants) it's fair to say there were always dozens of non-militant suffragists. Some would argue – including me – that it was the constitutionalists of the National Union of Women's Suffrage Societies, led by Millicent Garrett Fawcett, who actually won the vote. In 1912, while the militants embarked on arson and bombing, the constitutionalists forged a successful working alliance with the burgeoning Labour Party. It was this group, with other non-militant societies, which successfully lobbied for the inclusion of women in the 1918 Franchise Act. The suffragist and suffragette arguments for and against the use of violence reflect the problems and conflicts in virtually every major reform movement.

The focus was *not*, as some disparagers claim, wholly and solely on the vote. For most activists the vote was the first essential step – but only on to the hard, high road towards greater sexual equality. Many of them worked for causes and reforms outside the suffrage arena. A cursory trawl through editions of the National Union of Women's Suffrage Societies' newspaper, *Common Cause*, produced articles on: Massacre of the Innocents – Mortality Rates in Workhouses; Anti-Sweating Bill; Child Murder; Partition of Bengal; State Registration of Nurses; Payment of MPs; Nameless Cruelties to Pit Ponies; Free Libraries; Public Nurseries; National Equine Defence League. The vote was the means, not the end.

Anorexic as opposed to thin on the ground in positions of power, women were heavily dependent on the men who supported them in and out of Parliament. Extracts are devoted to those men, known and unknown, who played a valiant part in the fight. (How much difference a pro-suffrage prime minister would have made in the pre-Great War years is a moot point. Having to deal with a man like Mr Asquith who failed absolutely and utterly to understand why any woman should want the vote was assuredly not helpful.)

It also seemed to me important to let the opponents, commonly known as Antis, have their say. The National League for Opposing Women's Suffrage had considerable clout and it was one of its female leaders, Mrs Frederic Harrison, who said, 'Our society must in the main depend on women: women have to destroy a women's movement.'

The movement has often been characterised as a middle-class enterprise which neither interested nor involved the working class. It is true that the majority of activists came from middle or upper-class families. A working woman, unless she was one of the few paid suffrage organisers or had a particularly supportive husband, could not afford to take part in demonstrations or go to prison. But more than a handful of working-class women participated in the struggle. Their voices are here, too.

Because I do not expect all readers to be over-familiar with the political complexities or with all the participants, I have provided a running commentary to indicate who was doing what to whom, where, when and why. Few people, I suspect, read anthologies from start to finish; most regard them as a literary hors d'oeuvre from which they may pick and choose; so as a checklist for them, there is a Select Dictionary of Dates.

Before she died, in her hundredth year, I persuaded my mother-in-law – born Alice Kedge in 1895 into a working-class London family – to record her memories. She said: 'Although I wasn't a brave soldier in the women's army, what the movement did was to make me think and then to believe I could do things for myself. And I did! People like me didn't write books about their experiences, so the effect on us gets forgotten. The suffragettes certainly helped change my life.'

JOYCE MARLOW, DERBYSHIRE, 2000

Abbreviations

Initials and Acronyms

AFL	=	Actresses' Franchise League
Antis	=	Opponents of women's suffrage
ILP	=	Independent Labour Party
IWSA	=	International Woman Suffrage Alliance
NUWSS	=	National Union of Women's Suffrage Societies, often simply referred to as the NU or National Union
NUSEC	=	National Union of Societies for Equal Citizenship
WFL	=	Women's Freedom League
WSPU	=	Women's Social & Political Union

Currency

The old British currency of pounds, shillings and pence was much loved and incredibly complicated. Comparisons with today's decimal currency are not very helpful but 12 pennies equalled 1 shilling and 20 shillings equalled £1. £9.5.6d meant nine pounds, five shillings and sixpence and 14/11 meant fourteen shillings and eleven pence. At decimalisation in 1971 one shilling equalled 5p.

Select Dictionary of Dates

1832 First Parliamentary Reform Bill. First woman's suffrage petition presented to the House of Commons by Henry 'Orator' Hunt.

1866 Provisional Petition and Enfranchisement of Women Committees formed in London.

1867 Second Reform Bill. John Stuart Mill presented women's petition to Parliament. Manchester National Society for Women's Suffrage founded, Lydia Becker, its driving force. Followed by London National Society which included Millicent Garrett Fawcett.

1881 Women enfranchised on the Isle of Man.

1884 Third Reform Bill. Amendment to include women rejected.

1897 Twenty London and provincial societies amalgamated into the NUWSS. Millicent Garrett Fawcett elected President.

Between 1866 and 1902 some dozen petitions, resolutions and bills for women's suffrage were presented to the House of Commons. Few proceeded beyond a second reading. Most fell by the wayside.

1903 WSPU founded in Manchester by Emmeline Pankhurst.

1905 Onset of militancy. Christabel Pankhurst and Annie

Kenney arrested and imprisoned in Manchester. Slogans 'Votes for Women' and 'Deeds Not Words'.

1906 Liberals led by Sir Henry Campbell-Bannerman returned to power in landslide victory. WSPU moved its HQ to London. Arrests and imprisonments in the capital.

1907 Split in the WSPU. Breakaway group formed WFL. Non-violent militancy spread. Men's League for Women's Suffrage founded.

1908 Campbell-Bannerman resigned. H.H. Asquith became Prime Minister.

1909 Women's frustration mounted. First hunger strike followed by forcible feeding. The National League for Opposing Women's Suffrage formed. Battles over Lloyd George's Budget. Parliament dissolved.

1910 Liberals returned to power with greatly reduced majority. Conciliation Committee to promote agreed Suffrage Bill. Militancy suspended – 'The Truce'. Conciliation Bill passed its second reading. Further Liberal battles with House of Lords. Second dissolution of Parliament. Women's march on House of Commons resulted in 'Black Friday'.

1911 Liberals re-elected. Truce reintroduced. Another Conciliation Bill passed its second reading with a large majority. Optimism high. November, the Bill 'torpedoed'.

1912 Mass window-smashing. Labour Party came out in favour of women's suffrage. NUWSS/Labour alliance. Christabel Pankhurst fled to Paris. Major WSPU split. Reform Bill capable of amendment to include women in the pipeline.

1913 January: ruling by the Speaker of the House of Commons scuppered the Reform Bill. Widespread fury. Militant bomb and arson campaigns. Prisoners' Temporary Discharge for Ill-Health Bill (the 'Cat-and-Mouse' Act) introduced. Emily Wilding Davison died from injuries received on Derby Day.

1914 Continuing violence. 4 August war declared. Suffragette prisoners released.

1915 Women's Peace Congress in neutral Holland caused NUWSS split. Pacifists resigned.

1916 Reform of electoral register to include men serving in armed forces. Speaker's Conference arranged to discuss inclusion of women. December – Lloyd George Prime Minister.

1917 House of Commons passed Clause IV of the Representation of the People Bill which entitled women aged 30 and over with household qualifications to vote.

1918 January: House of Lords passed the Bill. February: received Royal Assent. November: Armistice ended the Great War. December: 'Coupon Election'. 16 women candidates. Only Constance Markievicz elected, as Sinn Fein candidate for South Dublin.

1919 NUWSS renamed NUSEC.

1922–27 Continuing campaign to equalise the franchise.

1928 Fifth Reform Bill. Women entitled to vote on the same terms as men. Emmeline Pankhurst died.

1929 General Election. 14 women MPs. Margaret Bondfield first woman Cabinet Minister. Millicent Garrett Fawcett died.

Countries Enfranchised before the UK

1869 First women in the world enfranchised in the state of Wyoming. Over the next decades other sparsely populated western US states granted women the vote.

1893 New Zealand the first country to do so.

1902 The Commonwealth of Australia (i.e. women were entitled to vote for their Government but not yet in all the individual states. Victoria was the last in 1908).

1906 Finland.

1908 Norway limited female suffrage.

1913 Norwegian women fully enfranchised.

1915 Denmark and Iceland.

1917 Newly formed USSR.

1918 Canada (as in the USA some provinces had already enfranchised their women).

Suffrage Societies 1914

Actresses' Franchise League
Artists' Suffrage League
Catholic Women's Suffrage Society
Church League for Women's Suffrage
Clerks Union (WSPU)
Civil Service Union
Conservative and Unionist Women's Franchise Association
Cymric Suffrage Union
East London Federation of Suffragettes
Federated Council of Suffrage Societies
Forward Cymric Suffrage Union
Forward Suffrage Union
Free Church League for Women's Suffrage
Friends' League for Women's Suffrage
Gymnastic Teachers' Suffrage Society
Jewish League for Women's Suffrage
London Society for Women's Suffrage
Men's Federation for Women's Suffrage
Men's League for Women's Suffrage
Men's Political Union for Women's Enfranchisement
Men's Society for Women's Rights
National Industrial and Professional Women's Suffrage Society

National Political League for Men and Women

National Union of Women's Suffrage Societies

New Constitutional Society for Women's Suffrage

People's Suffrage Federation

Qui Vive Corps

Scottish Church League for Women's Suffrage

Suffrage Atelier

United Suffragists

Women's Freedom League

Women's Social & Political Union

Women's Tax Resistance League

Women Teachers' Franchise Union

Women Writers' Suffrage League

1825–1903

I am a working woman,
My voting half is dead
I hold a house and want to know
Why I can't vote instead

Sarah Ann Jackson 1868

The Queen is most anxious to enlist everyone who can speak or write to join in checking this mad wicked folly of woman's rights, with all its attendant horrors on which her poor sex is bent

Queen Victoria 1870

Mary Wollstonecraft's *Vindication of the Rights of Women* (1792) is rightly regarded as the first great feminist tract but it does not deal specifically with the vote. The first publication to advocate women's suffrage directly was William Thompson's *Appeal*, though its driving force is generally believed to have been the Mrs Wheeler to whom it is dedicated (she was an Irish lady who had fled to London to escape a ghastly marriage). Seven years later Henry 'Orator' Hunt presented the first woman's suffrage petition to the House of Commons. By 1832 Hunt was the maverick MP for Preston, but he had previously suffered imprisonment as a result of the mass meeting for (male) parliamentary reform held on St Peter's Field Manchester in 1819, that went into English history as 'the Peterloo Massacre'. In 1851 an Association for Female Franchise flourished briefly in Sheffield, founded by an ardent campaigner named Anne Knight who persuaded Lord Carlisle to present a suffrage petition to the House of Lords. It suffered the same fate as Henry Hunt's – 'laid on the table' and was thereafter ignored. Until the 1860s there was no concerted effort to promote women's suffrage, but the issue was kept alive by a few dedicated individuals.

Appeal of one half of the Human Race, Women, against the pretensions of the other half, Men, to retain them in political, and thence in civil and domestic slavery: with an introductory letter to Mrs Wheeler, 1825

When will you, the most oppressed and degraded of the human race – for no vice, for no crime, degraded and oppressed – see your wrongs, commune about them, break in upon the leaden slumbers of your masters, and remonstrate and petition for their removal? When will you remonstrate and demand that the same enlarged education, which ought to be afforded to all men, should also be afforded to you? that all exclusive laws restraining your exertions should be repealed? that, whether married or not, your actions, like those of men, should be regulated by your own notions of propriety and duty, restrained only by equal and just laws—

WILLIAM THOMPSON

Hansard Parliamentary Debates: 3rd Series: Vol. XIV

Friday, August 3, 1832

Rights of Women. *Mr Hunt* said he had a petition to present which might be a subject of mirth to some hon. Gentlemen, but which was one deserving of consideration. It came from a lady of rank – Mary Smith of Stanmore, in the county of York. The petitioner stated that she paid taxes, and therefore did not see why she should not have a share in the election of a Representative; she also stated that women were liable to all the punishments of the law, not excepting death, and ought to have a voice in the making of them; but so far from this, even upon their trials, both judges and jurors were all of the opposite sex—

Sir Frederick Trench said, it would be rather awkward if a jury half males and half females were locked up together for a night, as now often happens with juries. This might lead to rather queer predicaments.

Mr Hunt well knew that the hon. and gallant Member was frequently in the company of ladies for whole nights, but he did not know that any mischief resulted from the circumstances.

Sir Frederick Trench: Yes, but not locked up all night.

Petition laid on the Table.

The Rights of Women
Dedicated (By Permission) to
Miss Mary Ann Moon of Perth

Question:- Ought women to interfere in the political affairs of this country?

My Dear Mary Ann,

—Go on fearlessly advocating the right of women to interfere in the affairs of state—Tell your countrywomen it is a duty they owe to God, their country, themselves, and their posterity—tell them that bad laws will never cease to be, nor wicked legislators cease to rule, until every man of twenty-one years of age, and every woman of twenty, obtain, by their strenuous exertions a voice in the election of those whom reason and honesty qualify for law-makers and administrators. Tell them this will never come to pass until the women of Scotland, England, Wales and unfortunate Ireland, stand by and encourage their husbands, fathers, brothers, and sons, forward in the cause of freedom—I take my leave for the present; but fear not I shall ever be ready to vindicate the *Rights of Women* against the oppressors' calumny, and the despot's scourge.

R.J. RICHARDSON
State Prison, Lancaster Castle,
September 1840

Richardson had been imprisoned for his Chartist activities. Who Mary Ann Moon was remains unknown.

The Right of Women to Exercise the Elective Franchise: 1855

It is difficult for even the sweetest nature to retain its full sweetness, if constantly kept in the combative, aggressive state, I think, therefore, that continuous opposition and restriction will tend to produce a large influx of the genus, strong-minded woman—

'JUSTITIA'

The pseudonym 'Justitia' was adopted by Mrs Henry Davis Pochin, the suffragist wife of the Mayor of Salford.

Westminster Review, Vol. 55, 1851

Enfranchisement of Women

Many persons think they have sufficiently justified the restrictions on women's field of action, when they have said that the pursuits from which women are excluded are *unfeminine*, and that the *proper sphere* of women is not politics or publicity, but private and domestic life. We deny the right of any portion of the species to decide for another portion, or an individual for another individual, what is and what is not their 'proper sphere'. The proper sphere for all human beings is the largest and highest which they are able to attain to. What this is, cannot be ascertained, without complete liberty of choice.

HARRIET TAYLOR

It was Harriet Taylor who converted John Stuart Mill to the cause of women's suffrage. He averred that all that was most striking and profound in his pivotal book, The Subjection of Women, *had been contributed by her.*

The Subjection of Women (1869)

It cannot be inferred to be impossible that a woman should be a Homer, or an Aristotle, or a Michael Angelo, or a Beethoven, because no woman has yet actually produced works comparable to theirs in any of those lines of excellence. This negative fact at most leaves the question uncertain, and open to psychological discussion. But it is quite certain that a woman can be a Queen Elizabeth, or a Deborah, or a Joan of Arc, since this is not inference, but fact. Now, it is a curious consideration that the only things which the existing law excludes women from doing are the things which they have proved that they are able to do. There is no law to prevent a woman from having written all the plays of Shakespeare, or composed all the operas of Mozart. But Queen Elizabeth or Queen Victoria, had they not inherited the throne, could not have been entrusted with the smallest of the political duties of which the former showed herself equal to the greatest.

JOHN STUART MILL

The Garretts of Aldeburgh, Suffolk – then spelled Aldburgh without the middle 'e' – produced two remarkable daughters, Elizabeth, later better known as Mrs Garrett Anderson, Britain's first woman doctor, and Millicent who as Mrs Garrett Fawcett, or Mrs Henry Fawcett, led the non-militant suffragists to final victory. The anecdote is from Ray Strachey's history of the suffrage movement, The Cause.

from The Cause

The Garrett Sisters and Miss Davies

There is a story of them at this time which may not be true in fact but which is very characteristic of Emily Davies, and which perfectly illustrates the confident frame of mind in which they approached their tasks. Emily, the story runs, went to stay with the Garretts at Aldburgh, and at night the two friends sat talking together by Elizabeth's bedroom fire. Millicent Garrett, then quite a small girl sat nearby on a stool, listening, but saying nothing. After going over all the great causes they saw about them, and in particular the women's cause, to which they were burning to devote their lives, Emily summed the matter up. 'Well, Elizabeth,' she said, 'it's quite clear what has to be done. I must devote myself to securing higher education [*which she duly did*] while you open the medical profession to women. After these things are done,' she added, 'we must see about getting the vote.' And then she turned to the little girl who was sitting quietly on her stool and said, 'You are younger than we are, Millie, so you must attend to that.'

RAY STRACHEY

By the mid-1860s the suffrage cause was gathering momentum, several groups of women having reached the conclusion that the vote was the crucial right, without which they would make little progress in the wider field of sexual equality. In London in 1865 the Kensington Society was formed, initially to campaign for higher education and better employment for women; in Lancashire in 1867 Lydia Becker, following the lead of Elizabeth Wolstenholme (later Mrs Wolstenholme Elmy), became the secretary of the Manchester National Society for Women's Suffrage, the first of its kind in the country. The radical lawyer Dr Richard Pankhurst was already active in Manchester, though his bride-to-be Emmeline, later famed as Mrs Pankhurst, was not born until 1858.

Speech to the House of Commons: 27 April 1866

I say that in a country governed by a woman [*Queen Victoria, of course*] – where you allow women to form part of the estate of the realm – peeresses in their own right, for example – where you allow a woman not only to hold land, but to be a lady of the manor and hold legal courts and oversee the poor – I do not see, where she has so much to do with the State and Church, on what reasons, if you come to right, she has not the right to vote.

BENJAMIN DISRAELI M.P.

Helen Blackburn, herself a pioneer suffragist, wrote a most useful account of the early days. Its full title is Women's Suffrage: A Record of the Women's Suffrage Movement in the British Isles with Biographical Sketches of Miss Becker, *here abridged to* Women's Suffrage.

Women's Suffrage

The Kensington Society was keenly alive to the importance of the suffrage. The records of its proceedings preserved by its Honorary

Secretary, Miss (Emily) Davies, show the question, 'Is the extension of the Parliamentary franchise to women desirable, and if so, under what conditions?' amongst the subjects appointed for discussion on the programme issued in the summer of 1865—The discussion took place on 21st November, just after Mr John Stuart Mill had been elected Member for Westminster and in his election address had brought in Women's Suffrage.

A Reform Bill was before the country and the friends of Women's Suffrage had a champion in the House of Commons. Surely the time to move had come! They asked Mr Mill if he would present a petition from women. He said he would, if it had a hundred names – he would not approve of presenting one with less. Still they hesitated, lest the time might not be ripe, but when on the morning of 28th April 1866 they read in the morning's paper what Mr Disraeli had said the night before in the House of Commons [as above quoted] then all doubts were removed.

'Those words were the spark that fired the train.' Moved by a common impulse, Mrs Bodichon, Miss Boucherett and Miss Davies [all members of the Kensington Society] came together that morning; they drafted a petition, sent it for Mr Mill's approval and then set to work. Day by day a little informal committee of workers met at Miss Garrett's—The petition was quickly circulated through the groups of the pioneer workers, and through them to many beyond, and instead of one hundred, 1499 signatures were collected in a little over a fortnight—

The day came when the petition was to be taken down to Mr Mill at the House of Commons by Mrs Bodichon, but she was very unwell, and asked Miss Davies to go in her stead, who set forth not a little nervous at such a mission; Miss Garrett offered to accompany her, and they took a cab with the portentous roll, to Westminster Hall. There, to their relief, they met Mr Fawcett [*the blind MP soon to be Millicent Garrett's husband*] who went at once in search of Mr Mill. Meantime they felt ill at ease with their big roll in that great Hall thronged as it was in those days with many going to and fro to the old law courts. They made friends with the applewoman whose stall was near the entrance, and she hid the roll beneath her table. Presently Mr Mill arrived. 'Where is the petition?' he asked – then they had to confess it was hidden away beneath the applewoman's stall. But it was quickly produced thence, and Mr Mill, on seeing it, exclaimed, 'Ah, this I can brandish with effect.'

HELEN BLACKBURN

Early in 1867 Disraeli became Prime Minister for the first time. Stealing the Liberals' thunder, his administration enacted a Representation of the People Bill which enfranchised over a million more men. Despite his 1866 speech on women's suffrage, he did nothing to further its cause in either this short-lived ministry, or in his second full term as Prime Minister.

Previously, in 1850 Lord Brougham had successfully piloted a Bill through Parliament to simplify the language used in its Acts. The section of the Act cited as 13 & 14 Vict ca. 21 sec. 4 assumed great importance for women's suffrage because it stated '. . . **that in all acts words importing the masculine gender shall be deemed and taken to include females – unless the contrary as to gender is expressly provided'.** *The 1867 Reform Act contained 'no express gender provision to the contrary' as stipulated in Lord Brougham's Act, so women with the required qualifications decided they were entitled to vote. While they were considering how best to pursue their claims, a curious incident occurred in Manchester which the city's suffragists put to good use.*

Englishwoman's Review: January 1868

The Case of Lily Maxwell

Lord Byron remarked on the suddenness of his rise to celebrity 'I awoke one morning and found myself famous.' Much the same may now be said of a very different person, Mrs Lily Maxwell of Manchester. On the 25th of November there was nothing to distinguish her from the many other independent women who keep shops in that town. On the 26th she recorded her vote for Mr Jacob Bright [the local Liberal MP who became the women's parliamentary spokesman], and at once assumed a humble place in the annals of our time. We are told that Mrs Lily Maxwell is an intelligent person of respectable appearance, and that she keeps a small shop for the sale of crockery ware. Her act is likely to produce considerable moral effect, perhaps even some legal effect also.

The Times suggests that her name was put on the register by a deep-laid plot of the Women's Suffrage Society. This was certainly not the case; for neither the Secretary of the Manchester Women's Suffrage Society, nor Mrs Maxwell herself, was aware, until a day or two before the election, that her name was on the register of electors. When informed of the circumstance, Lily Maxwell at once announced her readiness to vote—It is sometimes said that women, especially those of the working class, have no political opinion at all, and would not care to vote. Yet this woman, who by chance was furnished with a vote, professed strong political opinions, and was delighted to have a chance of expressing them.

Accordingly, on the following day she went to Mr Bright's committee-room, accompanied by Miss Becker, the able and zealous secretary of the Manchester Suffrage Society, and by another lady, also a member of the Committee. From thence the ladies were escorted by several gentlemen to the polling-place, which was a large room containing several booths. Mrs Maxwell's name being on the list of electors, the returning officer had no choice in the matter, but was bound to accept her vote.

As soon as it was given the other voters in the room, whether supporters of Mr Bright's or of the other candidates, united in three hearty cheers for the heroine of the day.

The Englishwoman's Review *was the successor to the* English Woman's Journal, *the first magazine (1858) to deal with women's concerns.*

The Cause

Chorlton v Lings

Immediately after this event [Lily Maxwell's voting], Miss Becker set to work to get a large number of women to claim to be put on the register, and a house-to-house visitation of female house-holders was arranged. The consequence was that revising barristers were confronted by shoals of these ladies claiming what they believed to be their rights— In most places they were questioned, and an appeal to the courts was the natural and proper result. For this case the supporters of the women's claims took immense amount of trouble, and owing to the great importance of the result which might derive from it, attracted attention all over the country—

The 5,346 women householders of Manchester were the first to be heard, and their case, which was known as Chorlton v Lings, came on before the Court of Common Pleas on 7th November 1868. The counsel for the women were John Coleridge and Dr Pankhurst, and, as *The Times* said in reporting it, 'a number of ladies who appeared to take interest in the question were in the gallery. A lady, said to be Miss Becker, sat in the jury-box, and was, of course, much and favourably observed.'

The argument of the case need not be rehearsed here. It was long and erudite, but it was unavailing. The judges on the following Monday morning, gave against the claims, and held that 'every women is personally incapable' (in the legal sense)—There remained a large number of other cases dealing with the franchises, and with freeholders, and with women whose claims had not been objected to by returning officers. Dr Pankhurst made a desperate effort to get these cases heard. 'It is so great a subject,' he said, 'there is so much to urge, it involves so vast a mass of material.' But there was 'laughter in the court,' and the judges would not hear him. The decision was given, and the matter was at an end.

RAY STRACHEY

Leeds Express: 4 March 1868

I wonder, Mr Editor,
Why I can't have the vote;
And I will not be contented
Till I've found the reason out
I am a working woman,
My voting-half is dead,
I hold a house, and want to know
Why I can't vote instead
I pay my rates in person,
Under protest tho', 'tis true;
But I pay them, and am qualified
To vote as well as you.

SARAH ANN JACKSON

After the disappointment of the Chorlton v Lings case the pioneers soldiered on. Manchester was the hub of the movement but there were notable societies in Scotland, Ireland and the West Country. In London the young Millicent Fawcett was active in the Central Committee for Women's Suffrage. There were successes that might not have occurred without the ongoing pressure. Women were, for example, eligible for election to the School Boards which were a plank of W.E. Forster's 1870 Education Act.

Personal Memories of Mrs L. Ashworth Hallett

The Extraordinary Innovation of Women Speakers

The novelty of hearing women speakers brought crowds to the meetings. Invariably the doors were thronged with people unable to obtain seats. The tours of meetings, consisting of six or seven in a fortnight, were a great nervous effort in those early days. They were, however, a source of much interest, and even of pleasure in the retrospect, for we never failed to carry our resolutions affirming the principle of the suffrage and adopting petitions to Parliament. Occasionally an amendment would be moved, but nowhere was it ever carried.

The following extracts from newspapers during those early years may convey to the present generation something of the effect made upon the public mind by the extraordinary innovation of women speakers.

'The room was densely crowded – drawn thither by the announcement that feminine man, viz., three ladies, were to fight the cause. This they did right manfully, yet, withal, in a most clear, lucid and persuasive manner, without the least vulgarism. Few ladies have courage Amazonian enough to brave the publicity of meetings.'

Another paper says: 'Whether we agree or not, we admire the courage of the ladies, who have given an intellectual treat.'

Another paper, referring to Lady Anna Gore-Langton, says: 'Her ladyship's position in the chair, and the ladies by whom she was surrounded, was a proof of the highest moral courage.'

After conceding the intellectual capability and moral courage of the ladies, there yet lingered for a long time the doubt as to their physical capacity – viz. whether their voices were really fit for the strain. This doubt lingered so late as 1877.

FROM HELEN BLACKBURN'S *WOMEN'S SUFFRAGE*

Letters from Lydia Becker to Friends

Manchester (undated)

My Dear Sarah,

——When the 'woman question' presents itself to my mind, I do not think of the elegant ornaments of drawing rooms, but of the tolling thousands, nay millions of my country women, to whom life is no pleasant holiday matter but a stern reality whose (lot?) we are trying to soften. Fantastic notions about 'women's sphere' are unknown in a world where women gain their own bread by their own labour – and frequently have to bear the burdens of the men in addition to their own,

Manchester, April 3 1868

Dear Theo,

Is it not glorious that Florence Nightingale has joined our Society? It will take a very hardhearted M.P. to say 'No' when she wants her vote. I should think even Mr Gladstone [*already the people's hero and soon to be Prime Minister for the first time*] might be brought to reason if she were to try to convert him.

Queen Victoria's View 1870

From a Letter to Prince Albert's Biographer, Theodore Martin

The Queen is most anxious to enlist everyone who can speak or write to join in checking this mad wicked folly of 'Woman's Rights', with all its attendant horrors, on which her poor sex is bent, forgetting every sense of womanly feeling and propriety— God created men and women different – then let them remain each in their own position—Woman would become the most hateful, heartless, and disgusting of human beings were she allowed to unsex herself; and where would be the protection which man was intended to give to the weaker sex?

It is ironical that Queen Victoria, the most powerful woman in the world and one who enjoyed exercising her power, should have been so opposed. In 1908 the letter was printed as a pamphlet by the Men's League for Opposing Woman Suffrage, obviously with the permission of the late Queen's son, Edward VII.

Anonymous Letter to Millicent Fawcett

London, 11 May 1871

Madam,

Seeing you have been on a public platform again and have made some clever remarks about a certain M.P. and a special correspondent of the New York Herald being at the meeting I wish to observe that if you purchase a Bible and carefully read its (?) teaching you will arrive at a better conclusion as to the intentions of the Great Creator as to the relation which should exist between the sexes than you will by reading the writings of J.S. Mill who seems to be the chief apostle of the woman suffrage question. I can only say that in my estimation *no Christian woman who properly considered her sex and the Divine intention respecting her would take any direct part in politics nor would she be 'spouting' on public platforms—*

Depend on it if you wish to live a happy and useful life, you can only do so by keeping in the sphere God intended you to occupy and performing well your own duties—

Believe me the sincere well wisher of yourself and sex,

A FOLLOWER OF CHRIST AND OF PAUL HIS APOSTLE

It was Lydia Becker who had the splendid idea of starting a suffrage journal. From its inception in 1870 until just before her death twenty years later she edited a monthly issue.

Manchester National Society for Women's Suffrage Journal

March 1, 1870

In issuing the first number of our Journal, the Manchester Executive Committee are actuated by a desire to furnish a medium of communication among the members, and a record of the work done by the different branches of the NATIONAL SOCIETY FOR WOMEN'S SUFFRAGE—If persons interested in the movement could receive every month an account of what has been done in other places, they might be tempted to try what could be done in their own locality—This movement would receive an enormous impetus if every person who has it in his or her power to do something for the cause would resolutely determine that however little CAN be done SHALL be done.

December 1, 1870: Manchester School Board Election

The first contested election of a School Board under Mr Forster's (Education) Act, took place at Manchester, on 24th November, 1870. Miss Lydia E. Becker secured one of the seats. The number of electors who exercised was 26,513, each of whom might give 15 votes, and for Miss Becker 15,249 votes were recorded. An unusually large number of women voted.

October 1, 1878: A Lady's Experience with the Suffrage Petition

In canvassing for the woman's suffrage we find much less opposition to it than has been expressed in former times. A gradual but certain progression in its favour is going on in the public mind. Instead of the flippant remarks which used to be made when a signature was solicited we heard people say: 'Yes, I'll go for that, it's only right – why should not a woman vote as well as a man, especially if she pays rates and taxes?'—The working classes seem anxious for pamphlets, and like to read all they can on the subject.

Manchester Executive Committee Report 1875–76

Donations Received:

Anonymous: a Timid Friend Sympathiser; Popgun; Omega; Lover of Justice: Stayer at Home: Hope to Win: Mitrailleuse: Sigma: Peeress: Cape Cornwall. An Old Radical: A Lancashire Merchant: Friends in Fife, Kidderminister, Southport, Oxford, Grimsby, Burnley, Dudley and Liverpool: An Irishwoman: Father of Seven Daughters: A Mite from a White Slave: A Well-robbed, Well-crushed, and Effectually Suppressed Wife.

'Such a Meeting – It Would Have Done Your Heart Good to See'

Lydia Becker to Priscilla McLaren (President of the Edinburgh National Society)

Manchester, Oct 25, 1879

We have had such a meeting that I must write and tell you of it—the room, which will seat 600 or 700, was quite full of women only, all seemingly electors – all poor working women—How they listened – how they cheered – how strong and intelligent an interest they took in what was said to them. It would have done your heart good to see—

It has been a new life to me to know and I feel the strength there is in those women – when many fall away from us and leaders desert us; but in those women there is a force which, gathered together, led, organized and made manifest, is enough to lead us to victory.

from Women's Suffrage

Women Vote in the Isle of Man

In the summer of 1880 a movement had begun to make itself felt in the Isle of Man for a more extended franchise for election of the ancient 'House of Keys', and the Governor had given notice of a Bill for household suffrage to male persons. This was the occasion for a movement on the part of the Manchester Society to urge that the claim of women be considered. Miss Becker and Mrs Oliver Scatcherd visited the Island and held a series of meetings in August, addressing crowded audiences in Douglas, Ramsey, Peel and Castletown.

They were everywhere received with the utmost cordiality, the *Isle of Man Times* and other papers giving efficient help; and to judge by the results, their lectures proved instrumental in initiating the movement to obtain a measure for enfranchising women in this ancient kingdom, which does not send members to the British Parliament, but has its own Governor, House of Lords (the Council), House of Commons (the Keys), Bishop and Judge (the Deemsters); it enacts its laws, imposes its own taxes – the only Imperial control being the sanction of the Queen, which is necessary before a law takes effect.

The Governor, Sir Henry Brougham Loch, gave his assent on December 21st, and on 5th January 1881 Her Majesty Queen Victoria gave her Royal assent. The Act came into force on 31st January 1881, when it was formally promulgated from the Tynwald Hill. The first election under the new electoral Act began on 21st March 1881— The women voters were pronounced to be quick, intelligent and business-like in their procedure, and they always knew for whom they wished to vote.

HELEN BLACKBURN

from Women's Suffrage

The TUC Congress in Aberdeen 1884

A Resolution 'That this congress is strongly of the opinion that the franchise be extended to women ratepayers' was carried with but three dissentients. The resolution owed much to the forcible speech of Miss J.G. Wilkinson (Secretary of the Upholsterers' Union, London)— Instances of working men who have forged their way, through hard study, high up the ladder of achievement, are frequent in English history, but instances in which women have done so are comparatively rare. Jeanette Gaury Wilkinson was one of these. All too late the suffrage movement learned to know her value— She had wrought beyond her strength and passed away in August 1886— Her friends subscribed to place a marble slab upon her grave in Forest Hill Cemetery. Truly of her it might be said, 'She loved her fellow-*women*.'

HELEN BLACKBURN

By 1884 William Ewart Gladstone's second administration was prepared to extend the franchise to agricultural workers. The suffragists lobbied hard to have some women included in the Bill.

Letter to the Prime Minister

March 1884

Dear Mr Gladstone,

We write on behalf of more than a hundred women of liberal opinions, whose names we index, who are ready and anxious to take part in a deputation to you, to lay before you their strong conviction of the justice and propriety of granting some representation to women. Believing our own claim to be not only reasonable, but also in strict accord with the principle of your Bill, we are persuaded that if you are able to give any recognition to it, there is no act of your honourable career which will in the future be deemed more consistent with a truly liberal statesmanship.

We are, dear Mr Gladstone, your faithful & earnest friends,

HELEN P. BRIGHT CLARK, MILLICENT GARRETT FAWCETT, PRISCILLA
MCLAREN, ISABELLA M.S. TOD

Response from Mr Gladstone's
Private Secretary

April 1884

—He is most unwilling to cause disappointment to yourself & your friends, whose title to be heard he fully recognises; and he can assure you that the difficulty of complying with a request so referred does not proceed from any want of appreciating the importance of your representation, or of the question itself—His fear is that any attempt to enlarge by material changes the provisions of the Franchise Bill now before Parliament might endanger the whole measure—For this reason, as well as on account of his physical inability at the present time to add to his engagements, he is afraid he must ask to be excused from acceding to your wishes.

I beg to remain, Madam,

Your obedient servant E.W. Hamilton

The Nineteenth Century (Magazine): June 1889

An Appeal Against Female Suffrage

We, the undersigned, wish to appeal to the common sense and the educated thought of the men and women of England against the proposed extension of the Parliamentary suffrage to women.

While desiring the fullest possible development of the powers, energies, and education of women, we believe that their work for the State, and their responsibilities towards it, must always differ essentially from those of men, and that therefore their share in the working of the State machinery should be different from that assigned to men—To men belong the struggle of debate and legislation in Parliament; the hard and exhausting labour implied in the administration of the national resources and powers; the conduct of England's relations towards the external world; the working of the army and navy—In all these spheres women's direct participation is made impossible either by the disabilities of sex, or by strong formations of custom and habit resting ultimately upon physical difference, against which it is useless to contend—

In conclusion: nothing can be further from our minds than to seem to depreciate the position or the importance of women. It is because we are keenly alive to the enormous value of their special contribution to the community, that we oppose what seems to us likely to endanger that contribution. We are convinced that the pursuit of a mere outward equality with men is for women not only vain but—leads to a total misconception of women's true dignity and special mission—

Dowager Lady Stanley of Alderley: Lady Frederick Cavendish:
Beatrice Potter: Lady Randolph Churchill
+ 100 Others [mostly titled].

from My Apprenticeship

In the spring of 1899 I took what afterwards seemed to me a false step in joining with others in signing the then notorious manifesto, drafted by Mrs Humphry Ward and some other distinguished ladies, against the political enfranchisement of women, thereby arousing the hostility of ardent women brain-workers, and, in the eyes of the general public, undermining my reputation as an impartial investigator of women's questions—Though I delayed my public recantation for nearly twenty years, I immediately and resolutely withdrew from that particular controversy. Why I was at that time an anti-feminist in feeling is easy to explain, though impossible to justify—the root of my anti-feminism lay in the fact that I had never myself suffered the disabilities assumed to arise from my sex—Moreover, in the craft I had chosen a woman was privileged—In those days, a competent female writer on economic questions had, to an enterprising editor, actually a scarcity value.

BEATRICE WEBB NÉE POTTER

Tributes on Miss Becker's Death 1890

from Helen Blackburn's Women's Suffrage

'The woman's cause owes *everything to* her – she was the leader of the vanguard at the beginning and the chief supporter of it through all its first difficult years.'

'One has hardly time yet to think of the loss she will be to the cause of women, but it is *immeasurable*—She did so long to see the fruit of her labours and, as she once told me, to pass on to other things.'

After Lydia Becker's death the suffrage movement in general and the Manchester Society in particular slid into the doldrums, but in 1893 the latter found an energetic secretary named Esther Roper who breathed fresh life into the moribund organisation. In 1894 there was a national breakthrough of sorts when the Local Government Act extended the franchise to married as well as single women (with the requisite qualifications), enabling them to stand as Poor Law Guardians and as local and district councillors. In 1897 the National Union of Women's Suffrage Societies was formally constituted, bringing scores of societies and committees under its umbrella. Millicent Garrett Fawcett became the first and – as events turned out – only president. When Esther Roper met her lifetime partner, Eva Gore-Booth, the two of them settled in Manchester and helped set the renamed North of England Society for Women's Suffrage on a radically new road, the organisation of working-class women.

Lancashire's Monster Petition

Esther Roper, Eva Gore-Booth, Sarah Reddish and Sarah Dickenson along with other activists in the North of England Society, decided to launch a petition to be signed exclusively by women working in the Lancashire cotton mills. This would show the rest of the country how powerful the demand for the vote really was among industrial women—

The work was painstakingly slow. It involved much trudging down the cobbled back streets of the cotton towns, going from house to house in the evenings to collect signatures from women who had just come home from work exhausted and were preparing the family meal—

By the following spring, 1901, the total number of signatures on the petition had risen to 29,359 and the radical suffragists were ready to confront Westminster with the result of their campaign. On 18 March a deputation of fifteen Lancashire cotton workers took the Petition down to London, accompanied by two deputation secretaries—The petition was so large, that, according to the *Englishwoman's Review* it 'looked like a garden roller in dimensions'—

That evening Millicent Fawcett, as NUWSS President, entertained the women to dinner, and the following day Mr Taylor presented the giant petition in the House, where 'the honourable member was cheered as he carried it with difficulty to the table.'

EXTRACTS FROM *ONE HAND TIED BEHIND US* BY JILL LIDDINGTON
AND JILL NORRIS

By the dawn of the new millennium the Victorian pioneers had failed to make any breakthrough insofar as the parliamentary vote was concerned. With debates or resolutions on women's suffrage having occurred in most years and two bills having passed their second readings, they had put the issue firmly on the political map. That the Antis saw fit to issue a lengthy manifesto in an influential magazine was a tribute to forty years of dedicated effort. The pioneers had also implanted in the public mind the concept that women were, in Lydia Becker's words, 'the co-ordinate, not the sub-ordinate, half of humanity'. Their efforts had produced substantial gains in other areas and tilled the suffrage ground which the extraordinary Pankhurst women were soon to plough.

Changes to Women's Status During the Reign of Queen Victoria 1837–1901

In 1837 there were no girls' High Schools and no women were allowed to enter university. There were neither women nurses nor doctors. Married women had no right to their earnings or property; on marriage their husbands assumed control of both. Women had absolutely no rights over their children; husbands were the sole guardians. Apart from the Queen no woman was entitled to hold public office. There were no women's organisations *per se*.

By 1901 every town of any size had a girls' High School and technical schools were established in the leading cities. There were 2,000 women graduates, 1,500 certificated students, and 8 women had received honorary degrees. 400 women were registered doctors and 9,000 had trained as nurses. Married women owned all their earnings and other property. The rights of mothers remained constrained but they had won the right to share in appointing and being appointed their children's guardians. Women served on various public bodies. There was a network of women's organisations covering children's welfare, maternity, nursing, emigration, education, employment, trades unions and, of course, political work.

FROM HELEN BLACKBURN'S *WOMEN'S SUFFRAGE*

1903–mid 1909

The smouldering resentment in women's hearts burst into the flame of revolt. There began one of the strangest battles in English history

HANNAH MITCHELL
MANCHESTER BASED SUFFRAGETTE

Rise up women, for the fight is
  hard and long;
Rise in thousands singing loud a
  battle song

THEODORA MILLS
AUTHOR OF NEW WORDS TO THE TUNE 'JOHN BROWN'S BODY'

In 1893 after several years' residence in London the Pankhurst family returned to live in Manchester. Emmeline and Richard both joined the newly formed ILP. In 1896 they became embroiled in the bitter dispute between the City Council and the ILP about the right to hold public meetings in Boggart Hole Clough (a north Manchester park). Nine people including Mrs Pankhurst were summonsed for 'occasioning an annoyance'. The case against her was dismissed (probably because she was a woman) but two male ILP stalwarts refused to pay their fines and were imprisoned. Protest meetings were immediately organised. Up to 40,000 people packed the Clough for a demonstration led by the ILP leader Keir Hardie, Dr and Mrs Pankhurst and their teenage daughters Christabel and Sylvia. The released prisoners were fêted as heroes and the ILP case gained considerable publicity. (Eventually Manchester City Council had to restore the right to hold meetings in public parks.) In 1898 Richard Pankhurst died, leaving his widow in straitened financial circumstances with four children to support. Christabel born in 1880, Sylvia in 1882, Adela in 1885 and Henry – known as Harry – in 1889 (another son had died in infancy). Emotionally bereft and needing to earn a living, Mrs Pankhurst withdrew temporarily from the political arena, but in 1901 she renewed her links with the ILP. Soon disillusioned with them, she returned her attention to women's suffrage. When the time for positive action came, the memory of Boggart Hole Clough and the effect of the ILP's forceful tactics were securely lodged in Mrs Pankhurst's mind – and in her eldest daughter Christabel's.

from The Suffragette Movement

The Founding of the WSPU: Manchester 1903

Mrs Pankhurst was now declaring that she had wasted her time in the I.L.P.—She decided that the new organization, which she would form without delay, should be called the Women's Labour Representation Committee; but when Christabel returned from a meeting with Miss [Esther] Roper and Miss [Eva] Gore Booth and learnt the name her mother had chosen, she said it must be changed, for her friends had already adopted this title for the organization they were forming amongst the women textile workers. Christabel did not at that time attach any importance to her mother's project; her interest lay with that of her friends. Mrs Pankhurst was disappointed and distressed that Christabel should insist upon their prior claim to the name she wanted, but she bowed to her decision and selected instead: 'The Women's Social and Political Union'—

On October 10th, 1903, she called to her house at 62 Nelson Street a few of the women members of the I.L.P., and the Women's Social and Political Union was formed—

Katharine Bruce Glasier was then editing the *Labour Leader* in Black Friars' Street, Manchester. I called at her office with a W.S.P.U. resolution for which publication was desired. She at once commenced to scold me for the aggressive attitude of our family, declaring that since her daughters had grown up, Mrs Pankhurst was no longer 'sweet and gentle'—

SYLVIA PANKHURST

from Unshackled

The Actual Start of Militancy: Manchester 1904

Militancy really began on 2nd February 1904, at a first Free Trade Hall meeting with a protest of which little was heard and nothing remembered – because it did not result in imprisonment!

The Free Trade League—had announced its initial meeting in the Free Trade Hall to be addressed by Mr Winston Churchill [*then a young MP who had recently switched from the Tory to the Liberal party*]. I applied for a ticket and received one for the platform. This was excellent for my purpose. Mr Churchill had moved that 'this meeting affirms its unshakeable belief in the principles of Free Trade adopted more than fifty years ago'; others had seconded and supported the resolution, when, as related by the *Manchester Guardian*:

> Miss Pankhurst asked to be allowed to move an amendment with regard to Woman Suffrage. The Chairman said he was afraid he could not permit such an addition. It contained words and sentiments on a matter more or less contentious to which persons absolutely agreed on the question of Free Trade might have difficulty in giving their support. Miss Pankhurst seemed loth to give way, but finally, amid loud cries of 'Chair', she retired. The Chairman read the addition which Miss Pankhurst proposed to make to the resolution which asked that the Representation of the People Acts should be so amended that the words importing the masculine gender should include women. He was sorry, he said, that he must adhere to his decision not to put it.'

This was the first militant step – the hardest to me, because it was the first. To move from my place on the platform to the speaker's table in the teeth of the astonishment and opposition of will of that immense throng, those civic and country leaders and those Members of Parliament, was the most difficult thing I have ever done.

CHRISTABEL PANKHURST

from Unshackled

An Irrevocable Decision: Manchester October 1905

The life of the Conservative Government was ebbing fast, so we wasted no powder and shot upon them. The Liberal leaders, who were to replace them in office, must be challenged on the fundamental principle of Liberalism – government of the people by the people, even such of the people as happen to be women. If the new Liberal Government were willing to enfranchise women, the Liberal leaders would say so; if they were not willing, then militancy would begin. A straight question must be put to them – a straight answer obtained.

Good seats were secured for the Free Trade Hall meeting. The question was painted on a banner in large letters, in case it should not be made clear enough by vocal utterance. How should we word it? 'Will you give women suffrage?' – we rejected that form—'Let them suffer away!' – we had heard the taunt. We must find another wording and we did! It was so obvious and yet, strange to say, quite new. Our banner bore this terse device:

WILL YOU GIVE

VOTES

FOR WOMEN?

Thus was uttered for the first time the famous and victorious battle-cry: 'Votes for Women!'

34

Busy with white calico, black furniture stain and paint-brushes, we soon had our banner ready, and Annie Kenney and I set forth to victory, in the form of an affirmative Liberal answer, or to prison—

The Free Trade Hall was crowded. The sky was clear for a Liberal victory – save for a little cloud no bigger than a woman's hand! Calm, but with beating hearts, Annie and I took our seats and looked at the exultant throng we must soon anger by our challenge. Their cheers as the speakers entered gave us the note and pitch of their emotion. Speech followed speech— Our plan was to wait until the speakers had said their say, before asking our question. We must, for one thing, give these Liberal leaders and spokesmen the opportunity of explaining that their programme included political enfranchisement for women.

Annie as the working woman – for this should make the stronger appeal to Liberals – rose first and asked: 'Will the Liberal Government give votes to women?' No answer came. I joined my voice to hers and our banner was unfurled, making clear what was our question. The effect was explosive! The meeting was aflame with excitement!

CHRISTABEL PANKHURST

Manchester Guardian: 16 October 1905

Miss Pankhurst and the Police: Assault and Obstruction

Arising out of the scenes towards the close of the Liberal meeting held on Friday night in the Free-trade Hall, Miss Christabel Pankhurst, of Manchester, and Miss Annie Kenny (sic), the latter an Oldham lady, appeared as defendants at the Manchester Police Court, charged with assaulting the police and also with causing an obstruction in South-street— Inspector Mather said he was on duty on Friday night and was present when these ladies were ejected. They were taken into an ante-room. Superintendent Watson asked them to behave as ladies should, and not to create further disturbance. They were then at liberty to leave. Miss Pankhurst, however, turned and spat in the Superintendent's face, repeating the same conduct by spitting in the witness's face, and also striking him in the mouth—

Addressing the bench Miss Pankhurst said: —I want to explain as clearly as I can that at the time I committed the assault that is complained of I was not aware that the individuals assaulted were police officers. I thought they were Liberals— The reason I was forced to adopt the mode of assault that I did was because my arms were firmly pinned so that I could not raise them. There was no other course open. My conduct in the Free-trade Hall was meant as a protest against the legal position of women today. We have no vote: and so long as we have not votes we must be disorderly—

Miss Pankhurst said she admitted the charge—'As regards the meeting outside, evidently the witnesses who have been called do not understand the nature of an open-air meeting. Later on they may learn what it is. We mean to hold open-air meetings to protest against the treatment of English women asking for their rights.'—

The Magistrates then retired to consider their decision. Whilst they were out, a white flag, said to have been exhibited in the Free-trade Hall, and bearing the legend 'Votes for Women' in large letters, was produced, and the ladies hung it over the dock rail. It was, however, removed before the magistrates returned and announced their decision, which was that for assaulting the police Miss Pankhurst must pay a fine of 10s 6d. and costs, or seven days, and for causing an obstruction in South-street, each of the defendants must pay a fine of 5s, or three days.

Miss Pankhurst: I shall pay no fine.

Miss Kenny: Hear, hear.

A little later they were taken in a cab to Strangeways Gaol.

from The Hard Way Up

Making History

Next morning, I heard that both girls had been arrested, and on arriving at Mrs. Pankhurst's in the afternoon, it was to hear that both were in prison, having refused to pay the fine – 10 shillings for Christabel, and five shillings for Annie. 'Never mind,' said my friend, 'we are making history,' as we rose at four o'clock on a dark October morning to take the journey from Ashton-under-Lyne to Strangeways prison, to greet Christabel on her release. When we arrived at the prison gates, we found a large crowd had assembled, among whom I remember were Members of the Women's Trade Union Council, Eva Gore-Booth, and other members of the older suffrage societies, and a large contingent of the Manchester I.L.P.—This latter branch had arranged a meeting in the Free Trade Hall for the same evening—The two girls who only a week before had been flung out of the hall like criminals were now the central figures on the platform, which was filled with sympathizers, while the vast audience which filled the area and gallery showed the keen interest evoked by the treatment meted out to the women the previous week. Twenty years of peaceful propaganda had not produced such an effect, nor had fifty years of patient pleading which had gone before. The smouldering resentment in women's hearts burst into a flame of revolt. There began one of the strangest battles in all our English history. It was fitting indeed that it began on the site of Peterloo, where three-quarters of a century before a vast crowd of men and women met to demand the franchise, only to be trampled down by the Yeomanry sent out to disperse them.

The North was roused, and neither Sir Edward Grey [*the prominent Liberal MP*] nor his Party were ever able to damp down the fire they lit on that October evening in 1905.

HANNAH MITCHELL

from Up the Hill to Holloway

Early Militant Days in Lancashire and Yorkshire 1905–06

My instructions were to report at the Manchester home of Mrs Pankhurst in those last days of residence, I think, at 62 Nelson Street. In that frugal home, most carefully managed to the point of stringent economy, I sensed what past and present struggles had been the lot of the Pankhursts since the death of the father, Dr Pankhurst, in 1897 [*1898 actually*]. An almost silent absorption invested each remaining occupant, for the family was already scattered abroad, never again to unite in strict family sense.

I made acquaintance with the historic, pioneer Portland Street office of the Women's Social and Political Union—In no time I was off to meetings at Bolton piloted by Mrs Chatterton [*another activist*], meeting the be-clogged women workers in the cotton mills, those Lancashire voteless wage-earners of hardiest independence who had been struggling with strike problems for months. Of Mrs Chatterton I knew that when Liberal stewards at one of the anti-Churchill meetings, first series, had tried to throw or push her downstairs, she had carefully entwined her arms about the neck of the nearest and had thus declared her intentions: 'No my lad. It's a case of Ruth this time. Where thou goest I will go.' And at his attempted repudiation, down, literally, they had rolled, the Wospolu [WSPU] Ruth maintaining her hold to the last.

I was next sent to Liverpool to rouse and organize opinion in preparation for some visiting Congress—The Liverpool meetings over, such was life, I was off to Leeds to prepare the way for Mrs Pankhurst, for now the time had come to line up my native city in the new order—The subject now and for a long time to come would be Votes for Women and again Votes for Women.

Mary Gawthorpe

38

In the January 1906 General Election, after eleven years in the wilderness the Liberals won a landslide victory. Having switched his political allegiance, Winston Churchill stood (successfully) as the Liberal candidate for North West Manchester. Comments such as, 'They come here asking us to treat them like men. That is what I particularly want to avoid. We must observe courtesy and chivalry to the weaker sex dependent on us' and 'I am not going to be henpecked on a question of such grave importance' did not endear him to local suffragists. He became an early WSPU target.

The new Prime Minister was Sir Henry Campbell-Bannerman. Herbert Asquith, already a renowned Anti, was then Chancellor of the Exchequer. The crucial post of Home Secretary, responsible for law and order throughout the land, was given to the late Mr Gladstone's youngest son, Herbert Gladstone.

Christabel Pankhurst's and Annie Kenney's arrests had, as Hannah Mitchell wrote, ignited a long-smouldering resentment in women's hearts. With converts joining by the hour the WSPU soon made its presence felt in London. The word 'suffragette' was coined by the Daily Mail in January 1906 to differentiate the new-style 'Deeds not Words' activists from the old style, patiently persevering suffragists, but the words were interchangeable. 'Suffragette' could denote any woman campaigning for the vote, 'suffragist' the most violent militant.

Daily Mail: June 1906

Fighting Outside Mr Asquith's House:
Four Women Arrested

At an early hour in the morning some thirty women, many of them holding babies in their arms, assembled in the Square opposite no. 20 (Mr Asquith's house). Most of them wore buttons with the words 'Votes for Women' on them. There they waited some few minutes for the arrival of their leaders, Miss Billington and Miss Kenny (sic), who were due to be there at 9 o'clock punctually.

The windows of many of the houses overlooking the square framed the figures of maids-of-all-work, butlers etc. looking at the strange assembly—Mrs Asquith was seen in a black riding habit bidding her little son good-bye for his morning outing with his nurse.—An inspector came up and said to Miss Billington: 'You must not hold meetings here or allow the procession to stop in the square—If you take no notice of the warning I shall have to take you in charge.' To this Miss Billington calmly replied: 'Oh, very well then, I am quite willing to be taken in charge.'—

The climax came when four policemen barred the way and attempted to seize the banner. With cries of 'You shall not have the banner,' Miss Billington and some twenty women engaged themselves in a hand-to-hand struggle with the police—

Once she (*Miss Billington*) was safely in custody the banner was again held up, and the leaderless women marched back to the square, where they met Miss Kenny. The latter immediately ascended the steps of Mr Asquith's house, followed by some forty women, and rang the bell. The police immediately dragged her along to the station, Miss Kenny, who is a frail little woman, struggling most of the way—

In court Teresa Billington said: 'I do not recognise the authority of the Police, of this Court, or any other Court or law made by man.' Given the choice of £10 fine for assaulting the police, or prison, she chose the latter. Annie Kenney also subsequently elected to go to prison.

Daily Mirror: 23 June 1906

Miss Billington, the Suffragette who is suffering imprisonment for her cause, is engaged to be married. But she refuses to be led to the altar until her war-cry of 'Votes for Women' passes into law, so that the date of the wedding day is doubtful—

A true touch of femininity was shown by Mrs Roe [a WSPU stalwart] when asked if Miss Billington's hair would be cut on her imprisonment. 'Oh no; surely not,' she cried. 'It would be such a wicked thing to do. She has such beautiful hair.'

from Memories of a Militant

First Imprisonment in Holloway

This was the first time I saw the inside of a prison van. Barnum and Bailey's Wild West Show sums up the prison van. Each species of humanity has its little cage with the small iron grating to nose through. We were trundled along, picking up other specimens on our way to Holloway. Then we all alighted, shook ourselves out as it were, and were marshalled in a line by a prison wardress. Our names, our ages, our occupation, our addresses, our religion, our education, were all entered in a ledger, a book I have always hated. We were then locked in tiny cells not unlike a small pantry in a country house. Then we were all let out, marshalled again into another line, and each had a bundle of old clothes given to her. We all looked as though we were about to visit a shop that has as its sign three bright balls [a pawnbroker's]. Instead of that we were taken into a large room with a warm fire, burning brightly in the grate.

A stern wardress told me to undress. I did so, my hair was taken down and the wardress put it into her hands exactly as though she was about to give me a good scalp massage, but instead she told me to put it up again, though my combs would not be returned to me until I was released. I was then marched to the bath, a grubby grimy bath it looked, but the water was hot—

After climbing what looked like Jacob's ladder, we reached a cell, No. 18, which was the number on the canary-coloured medal I had to wear. When I was safely inside, the door was shut with a bang. What struck me was the lack of instructions given to 'first-nighters'. A printed programme would have been helpful. There is a programme, but it tells of punishments awaiting those who do this or don't do that, no use for either intelligent prisoners or prisoners who ought to be in a nursing-home!—

I had many tips given me by old hands, and when I became an old hand I passed the tips on to others.

ANNIE KENNEY

James Keir Hardie, the first ILP member elected to Parliament, was a friend of the Pankhurst family and a staunch advocate of votes for women. Emmeline and Frederick Pethick-Lawrence were wealthy Socialists. Clement's Inn, off the Strand, had been one of the old Inns of Chancery – in Shakespeare's Henry IV *part 2 Justice Shallow declares 'I was once of Clement's Inn' – but the building by then consisted of apartments and offices. The Pethick-Lawrences already owned a garden flat and leased further rooms as the WSPU headquarters.*

Fragment of Autobiography: Early Days in London

The change that came [*over the WSPU*] in mid-summer 1906 was a matter of wonder and delight. By introduction through Keir Hardie, the movement secured the co-operation of the Pethick-Lawrences, who, once enlisted, created a revolution. They were prepared to make us financially safe and to devote their great abilities to providing an efficient organisation with a headquarters capable of carrying out the militant policy and

42

coping with the crowding membership which the pioneer efforts had collected—

Within weeks the whole scene was changed almost beyond recognition, and we were proudly installed at Clement's Inn with a staff of organisers, clerks and secretaries that appeared to grow daily. To complete the change-over, Mrs Pankhurst who had made only flying visits to us during the earlier months now gave up her Manchester home to work wholly from the new centre, and Christabel, having taken her Law degree, also emerged upon the London scene—

The close compact centre group was broken up by the disappearance of the three who had pioneered the London work. Sylvia Pankhurst was sent into a form of retirement to write a Suffragette history, five great cases of her father's and mother's accumulated papers as her material. Annie Kenney was despatched to organise the West of England, and I myself given the like job in Scotland—

TERESA BILLINGTON-GREIG

Daily Chronicle: October 1906

Amazing Scenes at the Opening of Parliament: Shrieking Women Ejected

An organised attempt by some 100 Suffragettes to invade the Houses of Parliament during the opening of the Session yesterday afternoon led to extraordinary and unparalleled scenes—

During the afternoon about a hundred of the supporters of Women's Suffrage had reached the House by devious courses— The police were quite resolute in their refusal to admit the women in a body, a number of applicants, amounting to about thirty ultimately gained admission to the outer lobby. Their excuse was that they had business with various Members of Parliament—

While these comparatively peaceful negotiations were proceeding Mrs Cobden Sanderson and Mrs Despard – who is the sister of General French – returned from the House, to which they had obtained admission, and they and their colleagues were very much enraged because the poorer women who had come up from the East-end had been excluded from the precincts and were standing in Old Palace-yard—

After the colloquy which ensued on this all sense of control seemed to be abandoned, and Miss Gawthorpe of Leeds, who was one of the women expelled from Mr Lloyd George's meeting at Birmingham the previous evening, jumped on to the seat and addressed the excited throng—The shrieks and screams which ensued penetrated to the inner lobby and attracted us all to the scene of combat—

Inspector Scantlebury, who had kept an anxious eye on the movements of the little group, instantly cleared a lane through the crowd, and summoning a policeman or two, and a few plain-clothes detectives, ordered the suffragists to clear the hall. This they stoutly refused to do.

The first attack proved ineffectual, for the bodyguard fought with such vigour that they kept the police off their shrieking sisters on the bench—Leaving a few of his men to grapple with the group, Inspector Scantlebury hurried off for reinforcements. In another moment six stalwart policemen arrived at the double, and threw themselves into the melee. The bodyguard was quickly dispersed—leaving a trail of hatpins and hairpins behind them, and even bonnets.

The leaders proved the most refractory, and they had to be bodily carried off the bench—With shrieks and screams they were carried from the central hall down the steps into St Stephen's Hall, and so were at last ejected at the Strangers' Entrance. They fought gallantly to the last—

In all ten arrests were made, and the prisoners taken to Cannon-row Police Station. Their names follow: Mrs Cobden Sanderson, Mrs Pethick-Lawrence, Miss Irene Miller, Miss Gawthorpe, Miss Billington, Miss Adelaide (sic) Pankhurst, Mrs Martyn, Mrs Baldock, Mrs Montefiore.

Following the new militant line all ten women refused to recognise the authority of the court and chose to go to prison rather than pay their fines. Minnie Baldock was one of the two working-class women among them – Mary Gawthorpe was the other – and like Mary she threw herself body and soul into campaigning for the WSPU.

Governor of Holloway to Mr H. Baldock

November 1, 1906

Lucy Minnie Baldock requests you to forward the following articles to her:

1 new nightgown to be found in large chest of drawers: Under vest: Combinations: Black stockings: Red cape in wardrobe on landing: Handkerchiefs: Stamps and writing materials.

Letter from Prisoner 29649 Baldock

Nov 6 1906

My Dear Husband and Comrade,

—The first time in eighteen years that anything has come between the sacredness of our marriage. Not to kiss each other or shake each other by the hand or write a few lines seems to me very hard indeed. A Miss Robins, a lady from America, visited us the other day and promised she would write to Jack. I know that he does miss his mother very much indeed. Tell him that I will make it up to him—You are doing a lot for me, dear Hal. All work but this of women seems as naught to me.

All the love and affection you know I have for you always,

Your own wife Minnie.

Campers' Resolution

Leytonstone, November 4/ 06

That this meeting of campers, hearing of the voluntary imprisonment of Mrs Baldock in connection with the Women's Suffrage Movement, do unanimously express to Mr Baldock the sympathy with him, that his wife, our Camp Mother, and very dear friend, has to suffer in this way for the sake of her principles, and we trust that her health will not be weakened in consequence of her imprisonment.

The Times: 27 October 1906

The Women's Social and Political Union

I take this opportunity of saying that in my opinion, far from having injured the movement, they have done more during the last twelve months to bring it within the realms of practical politics than we have been able to accomplish in the same number of years.

MILLICENT GARRETT FAWCETT

An Invitation to Mrs Baldock

Nov 28 1906

Dear Madam

I think you have heard that a committee has been formed which desires to entertain you and the other seven ladies who were released from Holloway on Saturday last at a complimentary banquet. It gave us much pleasure a little while ago that you all regarded the proposal favourably. I now write informally to let you know at the earliest possible moment that the banquet will be on Tuesday Dec 11 at the Savoy Hotel and to beg you to keep that evening free.

Yours very truly

M.G. Fawcett

Cell Mates in Holloway

Dec 7 1906

Dear Mrs Baldock

I was so glad to have your note as I had missed you – and wondering whether I should have a chance of whispering a word to you when the jailers unlocked our doors! I wonder whether that is an experience now altogether in the past or whether we shall ever find ourselves cell by cell again. Do you know I am haunted by the thought of the people we have left behind there. I look at the clock and think ah! now they are just taking round the suppers – and I wonder how Mrs Stanley is and no. 6 & how Mrs Bury has recovered from her illness and whether the baby is a dear little chap and so on. I long to do something, oh I would be delighted to pull Holloway down – instead of all which after the excitement of the first few days I collapsed utterly & have had 4 days in bed and not been anywhere again yet. I am hoping to go into Clement's Inn tomorrow morning for a short time, to the banquet on Tuesday and then back to work at the office for there is much to be done. I am glad you are better and hope you will get quite well again

Kind regards from us both,

Yours affectionately,

Edith How Martyn

Complimentary Banquet to the Suffragists
Savoy Hotel 11 December 1906

Mrs Fawcett in the Chair

TOASTS

1. His Most Gracious Majesty the King
2. Her Most Gracious Majesty the Queen, the Prince and Princess of Wales, and the rest of the Royal Family
3. Success to the Women's Suffrage Cause, coupled with the names of Mrs Cobden Sanderson and Miss Billington
      Proposed by Miss Elizabeth Robins, Miss Isabella Ford
      Responded by Mrs Cobden Sanderson, Miss Billington
4. The 'Chair'
      Proposed by Charles McLaren M.P.
      Responded by Mr I. Zangwill

Programme of Music Kindly Provided by the AEOLIAN LADIES' ORCHESTRA

from Unfinished Adventure

Converted to the Cause in Tunbridge Wells

I was sent by the *Manchester Guardian*, in the autumn of 1906, to Tunbridge Wells, to report the annual conference of the National Union of Women Workers; and by coincidence, the customary session on woman suffrage, usually rather an academic affair unheeded by the Press, fell on the day when my friend Mrs Cobden Sanderson and several other women, including Mrs Lawrence, appeared in a London police court on charges of obstruction outside the House of Commons, whence they had been ejected for making a protest in the lobby the night before. This sensational news in the morning paper had the effect, that afternoon, of crowding the theatre at Tunbridge Wells, where the conference was meeting. No seat was unoccupied at the Press table, and Mrs Fawcett rose to the drama of the occasion with a speech in which she reminded her audience that 'if you treat women as outlaws, you must not be surprised to find them behaving as outlaws.' Discussion was invited, and the first name to be read out was that of Elizabeth Robins.

Elizabeth Robins, then at the height of her fame both as a novelist and an actress, sent a stir through the audience when she stepped on the platform—The impression she made was profound, even on an audience predisposed to be hostile; and on me it was disastrous. From that moment I was not to know again for twelve years, if indeed ever again, what it meant to cease from mental strife; and I soon came to see with a horrible clarity why I had always hitherto shunned causes.

EVELYN SHARP

By 1907 the WSPU 'Votes for Women' momentum had grown from a snowball to a mini-avalanche. Christabel Pankhurst and Emmeline Pethick-Lawrence understood that their message had to be got across, not just to politicians, but to the populace at large. While they embarked on a brilliant publicity campaign, Millicent Fawcett and the NUWSS persevered with their non-militant tactics. Some members decamped to the WSPU but the majority who remained were by no means all stick-in-the-mud dodos. What became known – due to the appalling weather – as the 'Mud March' was organised by the NUWSS.

Daily Mail: 11 February 1907

The Mud March

Forty societies were represented in the procession, including many delegates from the North and Midlands. The Metropolitan districts were very strong, and their banners were a feature. Though the clerk of the weather was as unsympathetic as a Liberal steward, the demonstrators held on bravely through the mud. They were led by such ladies as Mrs Fawcett, Mrs Garrett Anderson, Lady Frances Balfour, the Countess of Carlisle and her daughters. A long string of smart carriages and motor-cars formed part of the procession. There were two meetings, one in Trafalgar-square, the other in the Exeter Hall. At the former Miss Gore-Booth deplored the alienation of the Labour Party through the actions of certain sections of the suffrage movement. Mr Keir Hardie found himself strongly in sympathy with the resolution proposed at this gathering—He declared that those who are not prepared to act to others as they would desire others to act to them are unworthy of the rights of citizens.

One and One are Two

Speech in the Exeter Hall London: 11 February 1907

The proposition that we are here to maintain is so simple, so clear, that when one is called upon to justify it, one scarcely knows what to say. The fact is, it is not our business to justify it; the onus of proof lies on the other side. How do *they* justify their monstrous proposition that one half of the human race shall have no political rights?

When Wilberforce started his campaign against slavery, it was scarcely Wilberforce's business to defend the proposition that no man has the right to make a chattel of another. The burden of proof lay on the slave-owner—Our case is, I say, so simple, that it is like having to prove that one and one are two. Indeed, this is precisely what the opposition denies. It says that one and one are not two; that in politics one man and one woman are only one, and man is that one—

Hitherto I have kept away from political platforms; this is my maiden speech. But twenty years ago I used this very subject as the backbone of a political satire. Twenty years ago – twenty years of ladylike methods – and how much further have they brought us?—In that old novel of mine, Female Suffrage was passed by the Conservative Party. The prophecy has not yet been fulfilled. But I warn Sir Henry Campell-Bannerman that, unless he hurries up, my words will come true—

ISRAEL ZANGWILL

Novelist and playwright Israel Zangwill was a stalwart supporter. His maiden speech at the Exeter Hall following the 'Mud March' was later published as a pamphlet entitled 'One and One are Two'.

from Home Office Files

A Somewhat Hysterical Gentleman

Case of John Edward Croft: Notes of Evidence taken before H. Curtis Bennett Esq magistrate of the Police Courts of the Metropolis on 14th day of February 1907: Walter Hawkes PC 48 AR: At 9.15 last night I was in Old Palace Yard, I saw the prisoner with 200 or 300 men and women. He was shouting 'You cads' and forcing his way towards St Stephens Entrance. He had an umbrella and was flourishing it in the air. I spoke to him several times and said 'Go away'. He said 'I shan't go away; let the women have their rights.' He rushed between me and another PC, and pushed me on one side. I took him into custody.

Fined 40/- or one month for resisting the Police.

Comment on Home Office file: Evidently a somewhat hysterical gentleman. He persisted in spite of warnings—such female prisoners as spoke of the conduct of the police spoke rather in praise. Croft's indignation at the brutality of the police no doubt arose from a more masculine imagination.

Letter to Herbert Gladstone

Talbot St, Batley, Yorks.
14 February 1907

Sir,

Last night presumably under your orders mounted police rode down women on the footpaths and drove them from the islands under the (?) of the omnibuses and carriage horses. Several women were seriously injured; the abusive language of some of the police was most scandalous. It is incredible that unarmed peaceful women should have been so brutally ill-treated in any civilized & free society. Against these proceedings, last night in Westminster, I emphatically protest.

Yours faithfully

Ben Turner

Mr Croft and Mr Turner are unsung objectors to the Government's tactics.

Sylvia Pankhurst attributed the growing discontent in the WSPU ranks to 'questions of personality', but it went deeper than that. Many early members were strong-minded women who had cut their campaigning teeth on left-wing causes and believed in the practice as well as the theory of democracy in all walks of life, including their society. By 1907 Mrs Pankhurst and Christabel had decided the WSPU must be solely and wholly a women's organisation run by them, owing no allegiance to any men's parties. With the question of the WSPU's democratic constitution and control by Clement's Inn versus branch autonomy under review, matters came to a head at the autumn AGM.

from The Suffragette Movement

Differences and discontents were brewing in the W.S.P.U. which largely hinged upon questions of personality. There were two opposing groups on its executive: Christabel, Mrs Pankhurst and the Pethick-Lawrences and their supporters, *versus* Theresa (sic) Billington (who had become Mrs Billington Greig) supported by Mrs How Martyn, Mrs Despard and others. The Pankhurst-Pethick-Lawrence combination regarded Mrs Billington Greig as the prime malcontent in the opposing group. Returning to London I had received a telegram from Christabel urging me to attend a W.S.P.U. Members' Meeting, followed by a letter asking me to write her a report of it. She added:

'I feel as though some of us would have to round on the enemy. I am sorry to worry you about my affairs. You, poor child, have not had much family assistance in your worries. This is more than my affairs though – it concerns the Union as a whole. T.B. is a wrecker.'

SYLVIA PANKHURST

The Birth of the Women's Freedom League

When the (WSPU's Annual General) Conference day came it was attended by delegates and individual members indiscriminately assembled ready for discussion on constructive lines. But, instead of discussion, there was an announcement of dictatorship put forward with all the eloquence, skill and feeling of which Mrs Pankhurst was capable. The draft Constitution was dramatically torn up and thrown to the ground. The assembled members were informed that they were in the ranks in an army of which she was the permanent Commander-in-Chief. (Mostly the reaction to this challenge was the silence of stunned surprise)—

The abortive Conference was scarcely over before the original democratic spirit became vocal— On October 11, 1907, the gathering then assembled created the Women's Freedom League.

TERESA BILLINGTON-GREIG

from The Hard Way Up

During my illness, there had been a split in the W.S.P.U. The more democratic members, refusing to be ruled from the top, had formed a new organization, which they called 'The Women's Freedom League'. Mrs Despard and Teresa Billington were among the seceding members. I joined this new league as soon as I was able to do so. I was so deeply hurt by the fact that none of the Pankhursts had shown the slightest interest in my illness, not even a letter of sympathy. I felt it would be impossible to work with them again. I did not realize that in the great battle the individual does not count and stopping to pick up the wounded delays the fight.

HANNAH MITCHELL

Charlotte Despard was elected President of the WFL.

Votes for Women: October 1907

Leader in the First Issue

If you have any pettiness or personal ambition you must leave that behind before you come to this movement. There must be no conspiracies, no double dealing in our ranks. Everyone must fill her part. The founders and leaders of the movement must lead, the non-commissioned officers must carry out their instructions, the rank and file must loyally share the burdens of the fight. For there is no compulsion to come into our ranks, but those who come must come as soldiers ready to march onwards in battle array.

ALMOST CERTAINLY WRITTEN BY CHRISTABEL PANKHURST

After Lydia Becker's death in 1890 the non-militant suffragists failed to carry on with a suffrage journal. It was a curious mistake, or perhaps they could not find anybody to undertake the editing job. Emmeline and Frederick Pethick-Lawrence understood the propaganda value of such an organ, the way in which it could make the branches feel part of the whole. Under their joint editorship the monthly paper, entitled Votes for Women, *was launched.*

The North v South Divide

Dear Mrs Baldock,

May I remind you of your kind promise to come to Kensington for our Town Hall meeting on Thursday October 24th at 8 p.m. We are relying on you to tell our people something about the lives of Working Girls & Working Women & about the difficulties and dangers as you see them as a Poor Law Guardian. We cannot have Mrs Baines of Manchester to tell Kensington how the Working Women in the North live so there will only be yourself to make the rich & idle women realise the difficulties that drive poor women to demand the vote.

Yours sincerely,

Louisa M. Eates

The Vicissitudes of Campaigning for the WSPU, WFL and NUWSS

(i) from Life's Fitful Fever
'Go it, old gal!'

At first, I refused to speak at street corners and in the open; I could not overcome my Victorian prejudices; it seemed such a vulgar thing to do, and I shrank from the rudeness and violence, the rotten eggs and the garbage.

I made my debut outside some gas-works in South London, in 1906, and I remember the dizzy sickness of terror, with which I stood up in the cart and heard the shouts of derision as the men, leaving their work, crowded round us in their hundreds, I had been instructed 'to speak up and get ahead. Never stop and never mind talking nonsense, as long as they can hear you.' I obeyed and got ahead, though I have not a notion what I said, but I reflected with satisfaction in my agony, that with this terrible din the worst nonsense would not be audible.

Then a sharp terror seized me – they were listening – some phrases had caught their attention, and in the hushed silence I heard a voice, surely not my own, talking strange nonsense at a long distance. I nearly broke down with stage fright when a rough but friendly voice whispered encouragement: 'Go it, old gal, you're doing fine, give it 'em.' I kept my crowd, which was the test of success, and from that day I preferred outdoor speaking in spite of the roughness and physical strain.

Roughness we certainly met with. Ours was not a popular cause and at many a meeting we risked life and limb; like St Paul, 'We fought with beasts at Ephesus.'

At one of our first W.F.L. meetings at Sutton, in 1907, wild pandemonium reigned; rats were let loose amongst the audience— I have a horror of rats but being in the chair I had to endure and 'sit tight'—

Perhaps, those of us who went out with the caravan to preach our gospel in remote villages, had the worst experiences. Sometimes, the hostility of the people was so great that the police were alarmed. Occasionally, we were taken to the police station and kept there for safety till far into the night. Sometimes the caravan was attacked, windows broken, attempts made to smash it up by letting it run violently down hill—

Mrs Despard once had a rotten egg landed full in her face, but quietly continued her speech. The filth and garbage thrown at us, was most destructive to the limited wardrobe we took on tour— Fortunately, we kept the sight of our eyes, largely by the big hats then in fashion; a strong, coarse straw, tipped well over the face, was a great protection and saved us from hard missiles and the cayenne pepper blown at us from bellows. This last argument was dangerous to the audience, as the wind frequently blew it back into the eyes of unoffending listeners, and I remember, with disgust, the

57

screams of a little child, who was carried away in pain to the nearest hospital—We were all warned against the danger of speaking from chairs. Several of our members had been injured through such platforms being seized from under their feet. A soap box, generally willingly lent by the nearest grocer, was far the safer.

MARGARET WYNNE NEVINSON

(ii) from Unfinished Adventure
'I admire your pluck, mum'

It was very nerve-racking to travel down to some provincial town, to mingle with the crowd outside the meeting hall and speculate with them as to whether 'any of those dreadful women will get in this time,' to sail past the scrutineers at the entrance door, with or without a forged ticket, often quite easily because, like the crowd, they expected the dreadful women to look like nothing on earth – or like the *Punch* cartoons of them. Waiting in the audience for one's turn to come, for we were all numbered in order to spread out the interruptions as much as possible, was a time of such agonising suspense that ejection came almost as a relief, though the process was unnecessarily prolonged owing to the indecision on the part of the ejectors as to which door they intended to use for the purpose. Little details, like the tearing of a lace cuff or the rending of gathers in a skirt – our unpractical prewar clothes added considerably to the indignities of ejection – seemed often to matter more than real injuries, which in most cases were not discovered until later.

We often met with sympathy from the crowds we addressed afterwards in the market-place. It was a passer-by, a working man with his tools, who caught me as I came hurtling down the steps from a meeting in Norwich, and set me on my feet with the words, 'I admire your pluck, mum' – almost the most cherished compliment in my repertoire of compliments.

EVELYN SHARP

58

(iii) from I Have Been Young
'Don't yer wish yer was a man?'

I did cordially hate walking up the streets of a strange town ring-ing a dinner-bell to announce a meeting. I hated to stoop and chalk the time and place of a meeting on the pavement. But per-haps my most fervent detestation was for the diabolical device which sent us to polling stations, there to stand all day and collect the signatures of the voters for our Voters' Petition. The cold! The weariness! The drunken loafers and impish children! The smug platitudes served out to us! It was difficult not to retort. One young woman of my acquaintance was asked by a wastrel 'Don't yer wish yer was a man?' 'No,' she retorted briskly, 'do you?' In bitter sleet and snow we stuck it out for whole long days. At country stations and in working-class districts it was not so bad, but at one station at least, in the business centre of Manchester, the 'gentlemen' hit upon the charming device of pretending that they took us for prostitutes, and answering us as I suppose pros-titutes are answered by such gentlemen.

HELENA SWANWICK

(iv) from The Hard Way Up
'Here's one of 'em'

We got all sorts of receptions. Once in Stockport about half a dozen of us were holding a meeting on the Armoury Square, when we were attacked by a crowd of roughs. Their conduct was so terrify-ing that we fled for safety to the railway station, where the officials shut all the gates when we were safely inside. Before our train left, someone handed in through the railings a bouquet of red roses.

One of the men with us on that occasion was Leonard Cox of the I.L.P., destined many years later to become Lord Mayor of Manchester. Leonard shared many of our worst experiences. One memorable night we had planned an outdoor meeting at

Middleton. Either we had become well known or the public had an uncanny gift of witch finding, for we were always recognized at once. As soon as I got off the tramcar, I heard shouts:

'Here's one of 'em.'

I was immediately surrounded by a gang of youths, who pushed and jostled me all the way to the Market Place. Here the local women were waiting by the two lorries intended for the platform. We managed to get together, but were not allowed to mount the lorries. That was the most menacing crowd I ever saw—Leonard Cox, trying vainly to protect us, said I was so ghastly pale and spoke so firmly that the foremost hooligans fell back a few paces. But they wrecked our meeting, and chivvied us about so badly – the police were standing by – that at last we took refuge in a shop whose owner invited us inside, threatening to drench with water any youth who dared to follow—

In spite of my unpopular views, I had many good friends among my neighbours, some of whom had large families who were never allowed to shout after me in the street as many boys did. One woman used to whistle to summon her brood. If she heard the cry 'Votes for women' she would come to the door, and sound a shrill blast, which her own boys dare not disregard.

HANNAH MITCHELL

Rise Up Women!

Tune: John Brown's Body

Rise up, women, for the fight is hard and long;
Rise in thousands singing loud a battle song.
Right is might, and in its strength we shall be strong,
And the cause goes marching on
Glory, glory, hallelujah! Glory, glory, hallelujah!
Glory, glory hallelujah! The cause goes marching on.

The Women's Battle Song

Tune: Onward, Christian Soldiers

Forward, sister women!
Onward ever more,
Bondage is behind you,
Freedom is before,
Raise the standard boldly,
In the morning sun;
'Gainst a great injustice,
See the fight begun!
Forward, forward sisters!
Onward evermore!
Bondage is behind you,
Freedom is before.

THEODORA MILLS

Theodora Mills wrote new words to several well-known tunes. Her 'Women's Battle Song' won an IWSA sponsored competition for an international suffrage anthem.

Daily Express: 18 January 1908

Suffragist Raid on Cabinet: Women Chained to Railings

The militant women suffragists made another raid on No. 10 Downing-street, the official residence of the prime minister. Two of their number, Mrs Drummond and Miss Mary Garth, succeeded in reaching the swing-doors leading into the historic council chamber—While these women were being ejected two others – Miss New and Nurse Chew – chained and padlocked themselves to the railings outside the premier's residence. It was

61

some time before police inspectors could break the chains and escort the released suffragists to Cannon-row Police Station—

Each suffragist wore round her waist a long, steel chain – not unlike a very heavy dog chain—Each took the loosened end of the chain, threw it round the railings, and fixed it to the rest of the chain. This was done so deftly that it was not until the police heard the click of the lock that they understood the clever move by which the suffragists had outwitted them, and prevented for a time their own removal. 'Votes for women!' shouted the two voluntary prisoners simultaneously. 'Votes for women!'

Chaining to railings has become symbolic of the pre-Great War phase of the suffrage struggle, though very few women actually did so. The WSPU may have regarded itself as an army with Christabel Pankhurst its chief strategist and tactician, but members had the leeway to act on their own initiative. Most knew what would, and would not, meet with Christabel's approval. The chaining was almost certainly sanctioned by Clement's Inn – Flora Drummond, known as 'General' Drummond due to her abilities as a marshal and fondness for fancy uniforms, was a Pankhurst devotee from the Manchester days. Who thought up the idea of enchained women is not known.

Recollections

A Trojan Horse: February 1908

There came a time when the Authorities, hoping to escape the embarrassment of refusing to interview women who came to present petitions, placed police on the watch to prevent any body of women from reaching the doors of the House. To overcome this difficulty Christabel Pankhurst arranged that twenty of us should be hidden in a Pantechnicon [*the old word for a furniture removal*

62

van] which on passing the House of Commons should open like the Trojan horse and let us fly to the door. My sister and I were among them. Silently we slipped, one at a time, into a yard in Theobald's Road. There we found our van and disappeared into it.

The doors were shut and the twenty sat quietly in this queer dark hole. Presently we were aware of a great clattering of horses, and a sense of jolting and rumbling which lasted for what seemed to us an age. Suddenly the van stopped, our hearts beat fast, the doors swung open, we saw the House of Commons before us, and out we all flew—

When the police found that our duty and theirs were in absolute conflict and that, although exhausted, nothing would make us give in and go away, they arrested us one by one, and next day we were brought before the Magistrate who sentenced us all to six weeks' imprisonment in the second division—We were driven to prison in that terrible vehicle 'Black Maria', each one locked into what seemed like an upright coffin with a small hole for one's face to look through. Two days after our disappearance into Holloway Gaol, the following lines appeared in the 'Daily Mail' written by one of the prisoners who had managed to smuggle in a pencil in spite of the stripping and searching ordeal which we all went through.

Sing a song of Christabel's clever little plan,
Four and twenty suffragettes packed into a van,
When the van was opened, they to the Commons ran,
Wasn't that a dainty dish for Campbell Bannerman.
Asquith was in the Treasury, counting out the money,
Lloyd George among the Liberal women speaking words of
    honey,
And then there came a bright idea to all these little men,
'Let's give the women Votes they cried, and all be friends again.'

Marie Brackenbury

An Arrest warrant

Take notice that you *MINNIE BALDOCK* are bound in the sum of TWO pounds to appear at *WESTMINSTER* Police Court, situated at *ROCHESTER ROW at ten* o'clock *a.m.* on the *14th* day of *February* 1908, to answer to the charge of *wilfully obstructing Police in the due execution of their duty at Victoria Street 13.2.08* and unless you appear there, further proceedings will be taken.

Dated this *13th* day of *February* One Thousand Nine Hundred *eight*

(Signed)

OFFICER ON DUTY

Letter to Master Baldock

February 14th 1908

Dear Master Baldock,

I have not the pleasure of your acquaintance but I am a Suffragette & know your dear Mother. I met her yesterday at the Woman's Parliament & she told me she might be going to prison, so I promised her I would send you some toys & cheer you up & that cheered her up very much & she is going quite brightly to prison for the sake of the cause. You see, if we can get the vote we shall be able to vote for men to go to Parliament & make some decent laws for us poor women.

Well now, I am sending you toys. Three white mice because they always let loose mice on the suffragettes. Three little megaphones because it seems very suitable as I caught sight of your dear mother shouting out 'Votes for Women' through the megaphone & had a good old laugh at her. Then I have sent you a policeman's chain and whistle because when I was arrested last year I broke one!

Then a money box to save up yr. farthings for the cause. Now be sure to write to me when the weather gets finer and before yr. dear mother comes out of Gaol – I shall try to set aside one day – get yr. father to bring you up to me & take you to the zoo.

Yours very sincerely,
Maud Arncliffe Sennett

The Times: 13 June 1908

The Feminist Movement in France

The suffragist movement in France is both less boisterous than that in England and more harmoniously subordinated to the great feminist movement of the century. The French woman is extremely practical, and she has, perhaps, a sense of measure which it would be prudent for her English comrades in the struggle for equality of political rights to emulate. Conversations with one of the leading champions of feminism in this country shows that the demonstrations at Westminster which followed from Mr Keir Hardie's proposal for the extension of the suffrage to women were regarded in France as 'untimely manifestations of over-zealous suffragists'. The French methods have been more discreet. Even quite recently, the candidature of a lady to the Paris municipal council attracted sympathy, rather than raillery, owing to the dignity, spirit, and good humour, and the lack of all noisy self-assertion, with which in public meetings she defended the feminist cause.

The Times: 19 June 1908

M.P.s Harangued from the River: Terrace Surprise

The woman suffragists, whose great Hyde-Park demonstration on Sunday next is rousing the attention of all London, yesterday made one of the most dramatic moves of their campaign—

With fine generalship the suffragists advanced on the Terrace at the best time of the day. Nearly 800 teas were served on this the record society afternoon of this session so far. The hot sun had gone off the Terrace. Several hundred M.P.s, Pan-Anglican clerics, constituents, and a host of delightfully dressed women friends sat in the cool shade, sipping tea, eating strawberries and cream, cress sandwiches, and other dainties, and enjoying the sunny river.

All at once a fast steam launch came towards the Terrace from the direction of Battersea. M.P.s set down their tea-cups and stared. The steam launch came nearer. A band played merrily on deck. Women stood in the stern waving—The suffragists' launch came close up. High over it was hoisted a large white banner with an announcement of Sunday's demonstration. Abaft was another banner with the inscription: 'Cabinet Ministers especially invited.'

As the launch drew alongside Mrs Drummond stood up on the cabin roof and, waving her arms, began to harangue the astounded M.P.s who had always fancied that on the Terrace they were safe from suffragist attacks.

Hyde Park Demonstration: 21 June 1908

Letter from Elizabeth Wolstenholme Elmy to a Friend

You probably know that Mrs Pankhurst and I headed the Euston Road procession – walking between the band and the great banner. We were the 'North Country' procession, Lancashire lasses mainly—The Bradford 600 women ought to have been with us; but their train was an hour late—I carried a lovely huge bouquet of ferns, huge purple lilies and lilies of the valley—I can never forget the wonderful beauty of the spectacle (*in the park*)—it was an hour of glorious life!!!

The Hyde Park demonstration was stunningly well organised. On a beautiful summer's day over 30,000 women marched in processions to the Park, and up to 500,000 people were estimated to have attended. As Louisa Garrett Anderson noted (below) the effect on Mr Asquith – Prime Minister since the recent resignation of Sir Henry Campbell-Bannerman on health grounds – was zero.

Letter to Millicent Fawcett from her Niece Dr Louisa Garrett Anderson

Harley St. W.
June 25.08

Dear Aunt Millie

Surely we must do *something*? These two great demonstrations have shown that the question is one that deserves Govt. attention. They have answered Mr A[squith]'s demand for proof that numbers of people cared & we have a right to expect change in his attitude. The S & P Union [WSPU] say that his reply to their letter shows that no constitutional measure can succeed in changing the attitude of the Govt. because our two have been tremendously successful & yet have apparently in no way altered the situation. Therefore they mean to protest at once & on a large scale & unless we can protest constitutionally & effectively I think it is the duty of everyone who is able to do it to join them—To do nothing at the present juncture is really too feeble—

Yrs always LGA

Unpublished Memoir

Joining the Militants

I joined the ranks and to the stirring music of the 'Marseillaise', mostly, marched along Oakley Street, Kings Road, Sloane Street and Knightsbridge into Hyde Park. I had thought it quite funny, like a pantomime Grand March, but when I listened to the speakers, I became serious. I heard my own ideas and ideals expressed much better than I could ever express them—The scales were falling from my eyes and I recognized the other 'mad women', the women who had actually been demanding changes in conditions of which I had practically only been 'talking in my dreams'—

As a member of the Actors' Association and the Variety Artists' Federation, I voted for the executive, then why should not women vote for members of Parliament? So I joined the militants—

One of the first things I learned was to sell the paper *Votes for Women* on the street. That was the 'acid' test. All new recruits who were anxious to 'do something' were told the *best* thing they could do was to take a bundle of papers and show the 'faith that was in them' by standing on the streets with it, even if they didn't sell any, as long as they held up *Votes for Women* to the public and advertized the cause.

What a lesson in self-denial, self-abnegation, self discipline! The first time I took my place on the 'Island' in Piccadilly Circus, near the flower sellers, I felt as if every eye that looked at me was a dagger piercing me through and I wished the ground would open up and swallow me. However, that feeling wore off and I developed into quite a champion paper-seller. I also carried sandwich boards in poster parades, advertising meetings and important events.

My friends all reacted differently to my interest in Votes for Women. Some always thought I was crazy, now they were sure. Some had always credited me with more sense, while others were converted, since it must be right if I, with all my common sense, believed in it—Mr Henri Gros, who had booked me several times, told me I need not ask him for any more work. He died soon after. A girl with whom I had played the leading part in a dramatic sketch told me how in course of conversation with her agent, he asked who had played the other part and when she mentioned my name, he said, 'Oh, that bloody Suffragette, she'd better not come here for anything.'

KITTY MARION

Press Cutting: June 1908

Suffragette Letters

On the strength of the new Post Office Regulations, which provides for the posting and delivery of human letters, two women were posted from the Strand to Downing Street on Tuesday morning. The officials at Downing Street, however, declined to receive them, or to sign the official form of receipt.

It was only by an ingenious interpretation of the new regulations that the suffragettes had themselves delivered.

Sanitary Towels in Holloway Prison

Moorgate Street, London E.C.

Aug 1st, 1908

The Right Hon Herbert J. Gladstone,

Sir,

I must first apologise for venturing to tackle you with regard to a statement made to my wife by one of the released suffragettes. I would begin by stating that, whilst heartily approving the giving of votes for women on the same conditions as to men, I am not in favour of many of the tactics adopted by the militant party.

The statement to which I refer is that in Holloway jail, certain at times indispensable clothing is not provided. [*By this Mr Wyatt meant sanitary towels but was too much an Edwardian gentleman to mention the words.*] The suffragettes have certainly committed no offence which should bring on them such filthy punishment but I would go much further and say that no offence should be punished in this way as it is an outrage on decency and health and a blot on our boasted civilisation. May I most respectfully ask you to either declare this statement to be a lie or to take immediate steps to see that such a reproach on our penal system be immediately removed. Hoping you will favour me with a reply,

I beg to remain,

Your obedient servant,

R.C. Wyatt

Sanitation in Holloway Prison

Letter from Lady Constance Lytton to her Sister Lady Betty Balfour

Whittinghame, Prestonkirk, N.B.

24 Aug 1908

The details of the prison life from the suffragists are some of them very exasperating. Such appalling bad hygiene when it would be such an opportunity for training ordinary prisoners. No air, only 1 and a half pints of cold water for both washing and drinking allowed in 24 hours. They are stripped & inspected in only a very short chemise – every detail noted. They were often given dirty clothes to wear, & combs with vermin in them to do their hair! Only one visit out of the cell allowed in the 24 hours at a fixed time. There is a pot in the room – but only emptied once in the 24 hours. One lady was given on arrival a pile of dirty mens socks to darn from which the smell was so overpowering that she was sick all night. But many of these horrors are now better and a woman inspector has been appointed for the first time. The food is apparently good & if you are a vegetarian you are given 3 pints of fresh milk a day instead of meat.

Herbert Gladstone Sent the Following Note to the Governor of Holloway

24 Sept 1908

The enclosed letter sent to me by Lady Betty Balfour is obviously untrustworthy. But I shd like specific answers in regard to (1) water supplied (2) the dirty combs (3) men's dirty socks.

The Governor's Response to the Home Secretary's Note

September 24, 1908

1) The statement that the hygienic condition for the prisoner is appalling is quite contrary to fact, and quite inconsistent with the health standard maintained amongst prisoners.

2) The water jugs, which are filled by prisoners themselves at the taps, contain 5 pints (good). They have been filled for suffragettes regularly three times a day, and at any other time at the request of the prisoners. There is no stinting of water for any prisoner.

3) Prisoners are never given dirty clothes to wear. It is quite untrue that combs with vermin in them were ever supplied to them. All combs and brushes issued to them were clean, and generally new— A few cases, I may add, have been found amongst former batches of suffragettes who had verminous heads on reception.

4) It is not correct that only one visit out of the cell is allowed in 24 hours at a fixed time. This has never been the case.

5) Neither is it correct that all chambers are emptied only once in 24 hours.

6) None of the batches of suffragettes have had socks or stockings to darn recently. The first on record batch a year or two ago may have had some given to them to repair, but socks and stockings are invariably washed before they are sent out for this purpose.

JAMES SCOTT

Studying in Holloway

Home Office Memo: 9 October 1908: re Irene Dallas

Mr H.A.V. Ransome asks permission to send books [Hall & Knight's *Algebra and Geometry* and Lock's *Trigonometry*] to this lady in connection with her studies for Cambridge. A lady who runs the risk of imprisonment has presumably calculated that her action is of more importance to her than her prospects of getting into Cambridge. No special privileges should be given but if there are useful mathematical books in the Prison Library, presumably the prisoner could use them, and it might be well to allow applicant to present the books to the library if they are not already there.

Home Office Response to Mr Ransome

Sir, In reply to your letter of the 2nd instant asking permission to send certain books to Miss Irene Dallas, I am directed by the Secretary of State to say the books mentioned may be sent to the prisoner on the usual condition that they shall belong to the prison library.

The influx of scores of well-educated, articulate middle- and upper-class women into prisons up and down the country was a nightmare for the governors. There were then different prison divisions and the suffragettes maintained that they were political prisoners entitled to the same First Division treatment as the Irish leader Charles Stewart Parnell, or Dr Jameson who had led the notorious pre-Boer War raid into the Transvaal, had received. In the early days a few women were transferred to the First Division but the Liberal Government refused to recognise any of them as political prisoners. The suffragettes were appalled by the conditions they found, not just for themselves, but for the predominantly working-class prisoners. Whilst in prison they complained constantly and once released wrote outraged letters to all and sundry. They had some success in improving dietary and sanitary conditions and in ameliorating the more draconian rules. By the end of the suffrage campaign prison libraries must have been filled with an amazing collection of books.

Daily Express: 29 October 1908

Suffragist Cavalry

The suffragist cavalry made their first appearance yesterday. London was startled to see fair horsewomen, from whose saddles hung posters announcing to-day's meeting in the Albert Hall.

Christabel Pankhurst had obtained her law degree from what became Manchester University, but as a woman was not allowed to practise. When she, together with her mother and 'General' Flora Drummond, were summonsed for issuing leaflets calling upon women 'to rush' the House of Commons, Christabel elected to defend herself as she was entitled to do. In effect she spoke for all three defendants and successfully issued subpoena for the attendance of Herbert Gladstone and Lloyd George – a brilliant publicity coup.

Daily Chronicle: 22 October 1908

The Suffragist Prosecution at Bow Street

After an exhausting day, marked by a brilliant display of persistence in the examination of two Cabinet Ministers by Miss Christabel Pankhurst, the suffragist case was again adjourned. Several appeals were made by the young lady for an adjournment and refused by the magistrate. When, however, at 7.30 Miss Pankhurst said she had another fifty witnesses, Mr Curtis Bennett [*the magistrate*] gave in. Both Mr Lloyd George and Mr Gladstone were called for the defence, and keenly question – irrelevantly the magistrate held – by Miss Pankhurst. All the witnesses were apparently called with the object of proving there was no obstruction and that the invitation to 'rush the House' did not necessarily mean violence.

The Evening News: October 1908

'Portia Breaks Down'

Miss Christabel Pankhurst, the 'Portia' of the Suffragettes, broke down at Bow-street this afternoon when the hearing of the charges against the three leaders for inciting the public to 'rush' the House of Commons was resumed. Sobs and tears interrupted her speech in defence, and at one time she was quite unable to proceed. For an hour she pleaded her cause—When she resumed her seat she sat quietly weeping—

Mrs Pankhurst and Mrs Drummond were each bound over in their own recognisances of £100 and two sureties of £50 each, or three months. Miss Pankhurst was bound over in her own recognisances of £50 and two sureties of £25 each, or ten weeks' imprisonment. In each case the defendants were bound over for twelve months—

Mrs Pankhurst said, 'We will go to prison.'

The crowd in the court burst into vociferous cheering which could not be subdued, and compelled the clearing of the court.

Actresses' Franchise League 1908

This League has been formed as a bond of union between all women in the Theatrical profession who are in sympathy with the Woman's Franchise Movement. The objects of the League are:

I.   To convince members of the Theatrical profession of the necessity of extending the franchise to women.

II. To work for women's enfranchisement by educational methods, such as, Propaganda Meetings, Sale of Literature, Lectures, etc. And in this way assist those women who may in the near future be called upon to exercise the franchise.

III. To help the cause by giving our professional services, acting as stewards for other societies, and helping to collect money.

This League consists of persons who qualify for membership by being, or having been, connected with the Theatrical profession in any of its branches, and by paying a minimum subscription of one shilling.

All subscriptions should be sent to the Honorary Treasurer, and cheques should be crossed London and Westminster Bank, Temple Bar Branch.

Daily Express: 29 October 1908

Chained to the Grille: Women Cause Uproar in the House of Commons

A scene without parallel in the history of the House of Commons occurred last night, when two suffragists chained themselves to the grille of the Ladies Gallery, and one addressed the House on 'Votes for Women'. The attendants were powerless to eject the women, and portions of the grille had to be taken out and the women removed with the ironwork still chained to their bodies. They were taken to a committee room, where a blacksmith filed off the fetters—The women – Miss Muriel Matters and Miss Helen Fox – were taken out of the precincts of the house and liberated, but Miss Matters was rearrested subsequently.

While Miss Matters and Miss Fox were chained to the grille in the House of Commons last night, Miss Maloney, heroine of the bell-ringing episode in Mr Churchill's Dundee campaign, was being chased round a statue by the police. She and four companions had ascended the equestrian figure of Richard Coeur de Lion in Old Palace-yard, and attempted to address the crowd from this elevation. They were dislodged after a struggle with the police.

This was part of a carefully arranged plan on the part of the Women's Freedom League to surprise the House from as many different parts as possible. As Big Ben struck half-past eight the cry of 'Votes for Women' rang through St Stephen's hall and the outer lobbies.

Campbell-Bannerman's Easter-time resignation as Prime Minister had obliged Cabinet Ministers, or any Minister changing posts, to seek re-election. Promoted to President of the Board of Trade, Churchill was defeated in his North West Manchester constituency, a defeat which Christabel Pankhurst claimed had been due to the WSPU's vigorous opposition and the voters' support for women's suffrage. By October 1908 Churchill was campaigning in Dundee, a safe Liberal seat in which suffrage interruptions such as bell-ringing did not produce a similar effect.

Daily Express: 17 February 1909

Suffragist in an Airship

The suffragists, not content with their infantry assaults, cavalry parades, motor and char-a-banc demonstrations, and steamboat trips, took to the air yesterday. At least, Miss Muriel Matters, one of their youngest but more determined warriors did. She sailed aloft from Hendon in the diminutive basket of a cigar-shaped dirigible balloon for the very latest thing in suffragist dashes to Westminster.

Miss Matters meant to teach the Government several lessons.

What the first lesson was it is hardly necessary to say. The second was the terror-laden lesson that there is still another way by which the suffragists might one day find their way into the House – a descent on the top of the Victoria Tower. The third had to do with dropping bills. The Government knows a good deal about dropping Bills already, but Miss Matters taught them still another way – how to drop them from an airship.

The leaflets – there were fifty-six pounds of them in the basket when Miss Matters started – had a secondary use in giving a clue to a party of suffragists who followed the swift airship in a kind of paper-chase throughout its long and sinuous course. The airship, after crossing London by way of Wormwood Scrubs, Kensington, Westminster, and Tooting, came down at Coulsdon near Croydon, helped to earth by a friendly though rather startled farmer. There was only one regret in Miss Matters' mind as she was lifted, cold, but cheerful, out of the basket. The latest phase of the suffragist movement had been rather over the heads of the people.

An American View

Office of Woman's Journal, Boston, Mass.

Feb 12 1909

My Dear Mrs Fawcett,

You are far better qualified to judge of the suffrage situation in England than any of us here in America can be; still, perspective sometimes enables one to get a different view of the thing, and to me it does seem as if the militant tactics were doing good. At all event, when so many thousand women are boiling hot on the subject (as is evidently now the case in all the English societies), it is only a question of time when they will carry their point, no matter what mistakes individuals may make. I only wish our American women were half as enthusiastic.

With best wishes and hearty congratulations,

Yours sincerely,

Alice Stone Blackwell

Recollections

'The movement made me believe I could do things for myself!'

I was born in 1895 in the Kings Cross area of London which was a pretty rough neighbourhood but we moved to Kentish Town which was a more 'respectable' working class district and that's where I grew up. Money was tight and I was the eldest of six but I did stay at school until I was fourteen, whereas lots of children in my position were 'half-timers' from the age of twelve, meaning they went to school half the day and worked the other half.

From school I went into service as a maid-of-all-work. That was in 1909 when the suffrage struggle was in the news. After I'd listened to a woman standing on a street corner somewhere in Camden Town, saying why we needed the vote, I became really interested. I went to several meetings and I bought myself a 'Votes for Women' badge. Tin it was, with a safety pin attached so you could fasten it on to your dress or coat.

When my mother saw the badge she said: 'What are you doing with that thing? Take it off this minute and throw it away!' Many of the older generation were like her. They saw life as a never-ending struggle, particularly for women, which wasn't ever going to change so you just had to put up with it the way they had. Well, I didn't throw my badge away but I have to admit I tucked it *under* the lapel of my coat because I didn't want to upset my mother and I couldn't afford to lose my job. Even if nobody else could see it I knew it was there! I wasn't a brave soldier in the women's army but what the movement did was to make me think and then to believe I could do things for myself. And I did! People like me didn't write books about their experiences so the effect on us gets forgotten. The suffragettes certainly helped to change my life.

ALICE KEDGE

The Women's National Anti-Suffrage League Manifesto

1.   It is time that the women who are opposed to the concession of the parliamentary franchise to women should make themselves fully and widely heard. The arguments on the other side have been put with great ability and earnestness, in season and out of season, and enforced by methods legitimate and illegitimate.

2.   An Anti-Suffrage League has therefore been formed, and all women who sympathise with its objects are earnestly requested to join it.

3.   The matter is urgent. Unless those who hold that the success of the women's suffrage movement would bring disaster upon England are prepared to take immediate and effective action, judgment may go by default, and our country drift towards a momentous revolution, both social and political, before it has realised the dangers involved.

4.   It is sometimes said that the concession of the franchise is 'inevitable' and that a claim of this kind once started and vehemently pressed must be granted. Let those who take this view consider the case of America. A vigorous campaign in favour of women's suffrage has been carried on in the States *for more than a generation*. After forty years it has been practically defeated. The

English agitation must be defeated in the same way by the steady work and argument of women themselves.

The Men's League for Opposing Woman Suffrage and the Women's National Anti-Suffrage League came into being as the militant movement gathered strength. By 1909 the Antis had become sufficiently alarmed by its impact that they founded the National League for Opposing Women's Suffrage, of which Lords Curzon, Cromer and Crewe, the popular novelist Mrs Humphry Ward, Mrs Frederic Harrison and Miss Violet Markham were the leading figures. The other popular novelist who registered her disapproval in purple prose, Marie Corelli, was not on the committee.

Woman or Suffragette?

Shall we make a holocaust of maidens, wives and mothers on the bronze altars of party? Shall we part with our birthright of simple womanliness for a political mess of pottage? With women alone rests the Home which is the foundation of Empire. Women are destined to make voters rather than be one of them. If it is true that Man is the master, woman has trained him to that position. Man is what woman makes of him. She bears and rears him. She is his sovereign and supreme ruler. From the first breath he draws she, and she alone, possesses him.

It cannot be denied that woman has suffered at the hands of man, but this is the result of women not having reared their sons properly. They must reap what they have sown—The clever woman sits at home and like a meadow spider spreads a pretty web of rose and gold spangled with diamond dew. Flies, or men, tumble in by the score and she holds them all prisoner at her pleasure with a golden strand as fine as a hair. Nature gave her at birth the right to do this, and if she does it well she will have her web full.

MARIE CORELLI

Suffragette Sing-Song

Little Jane Horner,
Sulks in a corner,
What is the reason why?
She says she'll be glum
Till she gets a thumb
And a finger in every pie.

Cabinet Pudding and How to Make It

Take a fresh young suffragette, add a large slice of her own importance, and as much young sauce as you like; allow to stand on a Cabinet Minister's doorstep until at a white heat; mix freely with one or two policemen, well roll in the mud, and while hot run into a Police Court; allow to simmer, garnish with a sauce of martyrdom. A popular dish always in season. Cost – a little self-respect.

PUBLISHED BY THE NATIONAL LEAGUE FOR OPPOSING WOMEN'S SUFFRAGE

The Danger of Woman Suffrage: Lord Cromer's View

I OBJECT TO THE GRANTING OF SUFFRAGE TO WOMEN:

BECAUSE I consider the measure fraught with DANGER TO THE BRITISH EMPIRE;

BECAUSE it would be subversive of peace in our homes;

BECAUSE it FLIES IN THE FACE OF NATURE, which has clearly indicated the spheres of action respectively assigned to the two sexes;

BECAUSE those who make the laws should have the Physical force to enforce them, and this women do not possess.

With the success of the WSPU's Votes for Women, *the NUWSS re-appreciated the value of a suffrage newspaper to propagate its views and engage its members. It therefore launched* Common Cause *with Helena Swanwick, one of the most cosmopolitan of suffragists and among the first students at Girton College Cambridge, as the editor.*

Common Cause: 15 April 1909

Vol 1: No. 1 Easter Week

This is a queer week to bring out the first number of a paper which is, in the main, intended as an organ of reform. For who cares about reform, when all the world is making holiday and winter has at last broken and the birds sing!—

Our Friends the Anti-Suffragists

Perhaps no one piece of agitation has done us quite so much good as the anti-suffrage agitation—Some of the speeches at the great Queen's Hall meeting were funnier than likely. Lord Cromer 'reminding women of their womanhood', was delicious.

Congress of the International Woman Suffrage Alliance

The Alliance is to open its fifth Congress in London on April 26. The growth of the organisation affords remarkable power of the world wide character of the Women's Suffrage Movement. The Alliance was created in 1902 at Washington, mainly through the efforts of a small group of American ladies. The veteran leader, Susan B. Anthony, was one of them. She was also present at the Congress in Berlin in 1904 and those who attended it will not easily forget her inspiring personality, carrying, as it did into extreme age, the fire and vigour of youth—At this Congress in Berlin in 1904 eight countries were represented. At the next Congress in Copenhagen in 1906 this number had increased to thirteen; the fourth Congress was held in Amsterdam in 1908 and then sixteen countries were represented; and now at the approaching Congress in London no fewer than twenty-one countries will be represented: Australia, Austria, Belgium, Bohemia, Bulgaria, Canada, Denmark, Finland, France, Germany, Great Britain, Holland, Hungary, Italy, Norway, New Zealand, Russia, Switzerland, South Africa, Sweden, the United States.

It is not only in Western lands that the women's movement shows signs of life. The East which so long remained dormant is beginning to awaken from the sleep of centuries. A year ago Mahommedan women from Southern Russia petitioned the Duma for their rights—In the recent revolution in Turkey also, all the papers recorded the notable part taken in it by Turkish women.

The British Society affiliated to the IWSA was the NUWSS. Millicent Fawcett was the International Alliance's first Vice-president.

Common Cause: 29 April 1909

Pageant of Women's Trades and Professions in Honour of the International Alliance

'The most wonderfully picturesque spectacle that London has seen for many a long day.' Thus a well-known London daily described the united effort of the London Society of the Artists' League, to do honour to the International Alliance. 'It had the best Lord Mayor's show that anyone can remember worn to the weariest frazzle.' The pageant was an artistic triumph, but it was more.

The Pit-Brow Women (emblem the winding machine at the pit brow, the pick, shovel and sieve)—and Weavers (emblem a golden spider and web for Arachne, the first weaver, shuttles, spools and threads) wrote that they had reached home 'very tired, but fully satisfied with all they had seen and heard.' An old, old Buckinghamshire lace maker carried her bobbins and pillows manfully with a young suffragist one either side to pull her along the weary way—

—Space forbids even an allusion to many of the beautiful groups, but the Glassworkers and Secretaries must not be left out— The former bore shields leaded up of stained glass, showing below the Rose of England, the tools of the glazier— the Secretaries exhibited secretary birds in red and silver, red tape, and sealed documents.

It was a black and stormy night. That was a pity, but if it had been lighter you would have been unable to see the procession gemmed and ablaze with countless old-fashioned watchmen's lanterns, swung aloft, winding its way along the skirt of Hyde-Park. The entry into the Albert Hall from the five approaches was effected amid a scene of warm enthusiasm, our foreign visitors and many of the general audience rising and waving their handkerchiefs.

from the WSPU Offices: 3 June 1909

Dear Friend,

I have arranged for the carriage in which Miss Patricia Woodlock is to ride in the procession on June 16th to be drawn by women dressed in white and wearing the colours. Would you let me know *by return* if you can be one of the 'horses'?

It would be necessary for you to be in the Clare market (close to Clement's Inn), at 6 o'clock sharp, where the carriage will be on the evening of the 16th. I expect we shall need to have a practice beforehand but all particulars would be sent to you later.

Yours truly,

Jessie Kenney.

Common Cause: 24 June 1909

Speakers Wanted in Cumberland

I wonder whether any of your readers are thinking of spending their summer holidays in Cumberland, and would be willing to help us in our work here? Cumberland is rather a difficult county to organise, owing to geographical conditions— The Egremont Division contains some of the best mountain climbing and the most beautiful scenary in England, and includes the lakes of Wastwater and Ennerdale. Seascale, on the coast, has excellent golf links and good bathing. Will not some keen Suffragette combine a pleasant holiday with a useful piece of work for the cause by holding one or two open-air meetings in the surrounding villages? A party of friends with bicycles could cover the whole of the Division, and could choose their audience from iron-workers and colliers in the north, from farmers in the agricultural and mountainous districts, or from the seaside visitors along the coast. I would advertise their meetings for them, and make good any reasonable expense incurred out of the Cumberland Organization Fund.

CATHERINE E. MARSHALL, HON. ORGANISING SEC. KESWICK W.S.A.

Beware! A Warning to Suffragists

This is a cosy little home
Whence no nice woman
Wants to roam.
She shuts the doors
And windows tight,
And never stirs.
From morn to night,—
With pots and pans
she spends her life—
Who would not be
A Happy wife?

Now turn your eyes
Another way,
A sadder picture
I'll display—
The female who
Is so depraved
She says she will not be
enslaved
Who thinks because
She earns her bread
By working with
Her hands or head,
She ought to have
Her little say
In making laws
She must obey

Now here are some
who want their rights

You see they all
Are perfect frights!
Their feet are huge,
Their stockings blue—
The Press says so:
It must be True—
Then bolder grown,
She waves her gamp
(and) Palace Yard
She gains at last—
Now in a cell
She sits and pines
And then off skilly
Daily dines:
But still repeats
As if by rote
'I want – I want
I want a vote.'

Take warning by
Her awful end.
And don't to poli
Tics attend.
Don't earn your living
If you can,
Have it earned for you
By a man.
Then sit at home
From morn till night
And cook and cook
With all your might

CICELY HAMILTON

Mid 1909–1911

I hear you want to know the exact
details of the tube feeding

LAURA AINSWORTH
WSPU ACTIVIST AMONG THE FIRST TO BE FORCIBLY FED

Of such stuff our mothers were!

ELIZABETH ROBINS
ACTRESS, AUTHOR, SUFFRAGETTE

By the early summer of 1909 the WSPU had made 'Votes for Women' a nationwide issue. The breakaway WFL was as militant as its parent body; the NUWSS had become much more pro-active; scores of new societies were being formed. When Asquith became Prime Minister he appointed David Lloyd George Chancellor of the Exchequer. The battle to get his controversial 'People's Budget' even through the Commons, where the Liberals had a large majority, was such that Parliament did not go into its usual summer recess.

It was against this background that the increasing frustration felt by many suffragettes erupted. The WSPU decided to make use of the 1689 Bill of Rights which had enshrined the subjects' right to petition the King. WSPU member Marion Wallace Dunlop and Victor Duval (from the Men's League) were the first to act. At the end of June Mrs Pankhurst led a widely publicised march on the House of Commons, claiming that as the King's representative Mr Asquith was bound to receive her deputation. The results were the now customary rugby scrummage with the police and individual initiatives that had far-reaching consequences.

Morning Post: 30 June 1909

Charge of Wilful Damage

At Bow-street; before Mr Curtis Bennett, Marion Wallace Dunlop, 44, described as an artist, was charged with wilfully damaging the stone work of St Stephen's Hall, House of Commons, by stamping on it with an indelible rubber stamp, doing damage to the value of 10s; and Victor Duval, 25, a clerk, was charged with aiding and abetting her.

On Tuesday last the female prisoner entered St Stephen's Hall accompanied by a man and stamped a notice on the wall by means of a wooden stamp (about 12in. by 10in.) covered with printer's ink. The notice read:- 'Women's Deputation. Bill of Rights. It is the Right of the subjects to petition the King, and all commitments and prosecutions for such petitioning are illegal.' After the stamp had been taken from the woman she was told that in future she would not be admitted to the precincts of the House, and was then allowed to go away. On Thursday the woman and the male prisoner presented themselves at the same entrance. The woman had changed her dress and method of doing her hair, and the police officer on duty, not recognizing her, allowed her to enter. The man said that he wished to see a member of Parliament. After sitting in St Stephen's Hall for a short time the female prisoner impressed on the wall with another stamp a notice similar to the one she had stamped on Tuesday. The male prisoner was found to be in possession of a portion of the instrument which was used to deface the wall.

Daily Telegraph: 1 July 1909

120 Women Arrested: Extraordinary Scenes

The much-advertised suffragist raid on the House of Commons was duly carried out last evening, and resulted in the arrest of between 120 and 130 women, among whom were the Hon. Mrs Haverfield, daughter of Lord Abinger; Miss Joachim, niece of the famous violinist; Mrs Mansell, wife of Colonel Mansell; Mrs Solomon, wife of a former Cape Premier; Mrs Pankhurst, who smacked a police inspector's face, and several other well-known women.

from Votes for Women: 16 July 1909

'We had decided that the time for political arguments was thoroughly exhausted, and we made up our minds that the time for militant action had arrived. We decided to wait till nine o'clock, when we could be sure that the peaceful deputation headed by Mrs Pankhurst had been arrested, then we determined to show by our action what we thought of the Prime Minister in refusing these ladies admission to the House of Commons. That was our motive for throwing the stones at the windows' [*of the Home Office, the Privy Council and Treasury buildings*].

STATEMENT BY A MRS BOUVIER, ONE OF THE ARRESTED STONE-THROWERS

Up to this time, although they had been militant, the suffragettes had not been violent. The first stone-throwers said they had acted of their own initiative which is probably correct. The Pankhursts later tended to claim that all tactics of which they approved had been sanctioned by Clement's Inn. For defacing the wall in St Stephen's Hall Marion Wallace Dunlop was sentenced to one month's imprisonment. Refused the First Division treatment she demanded as a political prisoner, she went on hunger strike. After going without food for 91 hours she was released. As hunger-striking became so important it must again be emphasised that Marion Wallace Dunlop took the step of her own initiative. Nobody knew of her decision, though at the time the militants believed she had found the weapon to defeat the Government. They reckoned without Edward VII and the pressure he, and others, brought to bear on the Home Secretary, Herbert Gladstone.

Edward VII's Private Secretary to Herbert Gladstone

Marienbad, 13 August 1909

His Majesty would be glad to know why the existing methods [*i.e. forcible feeding*] which must obviously exist for dealing with prisoners who refuse nourishment, should not be adopted.

Birmingham: The First Forcible Feeding: September 1909

One of my most exciting experiences that resulted in my second imprisonment was when I was with Mary Leigh in Birmingham. We climbed on to the roof. We got on the roof through working our way round through someone's wood-yard where he was working, and we climbed various walls and eventually got on a sloping roof and there we stayed until the police tried all sorts of things, throwing stones and trying to get us down, and eventually they got the fire hose and put that on us, and we were in the end brought down by the fire escape ladder. And Asquith was speaking in the Bingley Hall across the way, and there were a lot of hansom cabs in

94

a row, and the detectives brought us down and put us each in a hansom cab, Mary Leigh with two detectives and I following, also with two detectives, in another cab. They took us to New Street, to the police station.

As a result of that I got three months' imprisonment and the Stipendiary Magistrate insisted that Mary was the ringleader, although I told him firmly that she was nothing of the sort, that I scouted out and found this way the day before. However, he insisted that she was, and she got four months, and I got three. And that was the occasion when nine of us were arrested and for the first time in the history of this country, when we went on hunger strike, forcible feeding was resorted to, and we, that little group in Winson Green, Birmingham, were the first group of forcibly fed prisoners.

CHARLOTTE (CHARLIE) MARSH

Details of the First Forcible Feeding 1909

London S.W.

Dear Miss Wallace Dunlop,

I hear you want to know the exact details of the Tube feeding. The doctors wear their ordinary clothes but one has a towel round his neck. There were always four wardresses & two doctors. Two wardresses (one each side) hold you up in bed (ex-ordinary prison cell bed) propped up by pillows, and hold your arms and legs. You have a towel wrapped round you. One doctor (with a towel round his neck) kneels at the back of your right shoulder, & forces your head back, there is a wardress at the back to help him, he forces your mouth & the other doctor (who faces you) pushes the tube down you mouth about 18 inches; while this is being done you first have a very great tickling sensation, then a choking feeling, & then you feel quite stunned; when the tube has gone down the required distance the gag (a cork one) is forced down between your teeth. (Before the gag is put in, your mouth is held open by the doctor.) At the other end of the tube is a china funnel into which the food is poured, this is held up fairly high by the other doctor. About a pint of Bengers is poured in. While the food is poured in, one of the doctors holds and feels your pulse.

A basin of hot water is then put in front, the tube withdrawn from your mouth & put into this basin. A great deal of mucous & phlegm comes up with the tube. You are then laid back again in bed by the wardresses. I was always kept in blankets. You feel quite stunned & dizzy & do a great deal of spitting for some time after the tube is withdrawn. You also have an ache in your chest, & feel very sick.

When I was fed by the teaspoon the doctor used to put it in drops between a gap in my teeth & then he held my nose & stretched the muscles of my throat until I choked. I know I must have looked as if I was being hurt because of the wardresses' faces. And while I was being fed by the tube, they used to implore me to take it through the feeding cup. I hope you will understand my description.

Sincerely Yours
Laura Ainsworth

It was a significant fact that when I was fed by the tube my heart was tested always before and after.

Memorial Signed by Medical Practitioners and Sent to the Prime Minister: 4 October 1909

We the undersigned, being medical practitioners, do most urgently protest against the treatment by artificial feeding of the Suffragist prisoners now in Birmingham Gaol.

We submit to you, that this method of feeding when the patient resists is attended with the gravest risks, that unforeseen accidents are liable to occur, and that the subsequent health of the person may be seriously injured. In our opinion this action is unwise and inhumane.

We therefore earnestly beg that you will interfere to prevent the continuance of this practice.

We are, Sir

Yours faithfully,

VICTOR HORSLEY, F.R.C.S.

W. HUGH FENTON, M.B., M.A.

C. MANSELL MOULLIN, M.D., F.R.C.S.

FORBES WINSLOW, M.D.

ALEXANDER HAIG, M.D., F.R.C.P.

GUSTAVUS HARTRIDGE, F.R.C.S.

HELEN WEBB, M.D.

CAROLINE STURGE, M.D.

VICTOR MUNRO, M.B., C.M.

E. VIPONT BROWN, M.D. ....116 SIGNATURES IN ALL

While the struggle for Lloyd George's Budget continued – after an unprecedented 42 days and almost as many nights in the committee stages the Finance Bill finally passed its third reading in the House of Commons on 4 November 1909 – Millicent Fawcett and the NUWSS persevered with their constitutional efforts. Appalled by the horrors of forcible feeding – if that wasn't violence, what was? – the militants responded in kind, arguing that by slamming the door on peaceful protest the Liberals had left them no option. The suffragette violence, though shocking to many, remained comparatively mild and the perpetrators waited, or demanded, to be arrested.

Mr Asquith to Mrs Fawcett

Downing St, Whitehall, SW.
27 September 1909

Dear Madam,

I am desired by the Prime Minister to say that he has carefully considered your request for a further interview by way of deputation, and regrets that he is at present unable to accede to it. He quite recognises that such a request, proceeding from the organisation with which you are connected, stands on a totally different footing from similar demands put forward by those who have for the last three years been discrediting your movement by methods of petty annoyance and open violence.

But your organisation is only one of several which are aiming at Woman Suffrage by constitutional means, and which differ widely among themselves as to the practical solution to the problem. If Mr Asquith were to receive your deputation he would be obliged in fairness to do the same to those other Associations, and he could not refuse the request, which would almost certainly follow, to listen to the views of the large body of women who have organised themselves to oppose any grant of the political franchise to their sex.

Mr Asquith's time is at present fully occupied with urgent public concerns, and, while he will now, as always, be glad to receive any written statement of new facts or arguments that have come to light since he received you in the early part of 1908, he is unable at this season of the year, and under existing political conditions, to engage to receive any deputations.

Newcastle Daily Chronicle: 11 October 1909

Militant Suffragists in Newcastle

On Friday night twelve women, most of them young, and none of them very strong, met together to concert their plans—Every one of the twelve did exactly what she had undertaken to do, precisely at the moment when she had promised to do it, and in the way in which she had meant to do it—A woman apparently engaged in selling 'Votes for Women', quietly takes a stone from her pocket, and without a word drops it through a pane of glass. She then strolls quietly along the pavement until the Liberal stewards can sufficiently recover from their astonishment to give her in charge to the policeman towards whom she is walking. Another woman with a hatchet concealed behind a big bunch of chrysanthemums stands for twenty minutes facing five policemen, and when the moment arrives, flings away the flowers, and brings the hatchet down upon the barricade. A third, just before seven o'clock, ascertains that no one is standing in danger of injury behind the post office window, and then, on the stroke of the hour, sends her stone through the pane. The police run up, well-mannered but excited, and the woman coldly remarks as they seize her arm, 'Don't be so hysterical.' The hysteria was all on the Government's side – above all that hysteria of panic which refused the prisoners bail over Sunday.

I have seen brave things done by men on the battle-field, among comrades, hot-blooded, flushed and excited. This was the rarer courage which does its deeds coldly and alone—What they were facing was the certainty of starvation, which may be followed by the torture of forcible feeding—a steel instrument between their teeth, the insertion of a gag, and outrage of the stomach-pump—

P.S. Lest it should be thought unbecoming on my part to speak when my wife is in danger, I should like to state here that I resigned my position as leader-writer on a Government organ ten days ago as a protest against the torture of the Birmingham prisoners, who are all strangers to me.

H.N. BRAILSFORD

Letter to Mrs Fawcett: The Newcastle Arrests

October 1909

The ineptitude of the Government is beyond all words. They prosecute the unknown and friendless and release Lady C. Lytton and Mrs Brailsford because their relations are influential people.

HELEN DOWSON
NOTTINGHAM NUWSS BRANCH

Letter to the Editor 'Votes for Women': Forcible Feeding

November 1st, 1909

Will you allow me, as one who has gone through the experience of being fed by force, in Newcastle, to state my experience with regard to one or two specific points that have been under discussion, as to the manner in which this treatment is carried out.

First, with regard to the feeding tube – the glass funnel at the end of the nasal tube was always clouded and dirty. Two of my Suffragist fellow prisoners were trained nurses and they also testify to this. The tube itself was not kept in a boracic solution, as stated in the House of Commons. On the morning before my release I had occasion to go into the reception-room. It is this room that in-coming prisoners change their clothes and don the prison uniform. Imagine my horror then, when near the window, in an open basket-tray (which had often been brought into my cell) I saw the tube lying open and exposed and the jug by the side from which the liquid was poured. We were still being forcibly fed – there was only one tube used, and this is where it was kept apparently, in the intervals of use.

Carelessness and callousness to a marked degree, characterized the treatment of the prison Doctors. It was not until within four days of my release, and when the nasal passages were very much swollen and inflamed, that the tube was dipped in glycerine to facilitate its passage and relieve the agonizing pain. Furthermore, unnecessary violence was used. I complained of this to the Government medical Inspector, who visited me on the day previous to my release—in the presence of the doctor (whose) reply was: 'Of course one was not in the best of tempers. Miss Pethick was not the first I had to deal with!'

Yours faithfully, Dorothy Pethick

The Times: 29 October 1909

Bermondsey By-Election: Outrages by Women.

In the forenoon a woman was permitted, upon some pretence or other, to enter the polling booth in the Grange-road. She at once threw a bottle upon one of the ballot boxes, and, the bottle breaking, the liquid which it contained splashed into the eyes of the presiding officer, Mr George Thorley, a school teacher. A doctor who happened to be present declared the liquid to be corrosive, and Mr Thorley was taken to Guy's Hospital, where a grave view is taken of the injury to his right eye. At the Laxton-street Schools, another polling station, a similar incident occurred, although fortunately in this case no personal injury was done.

The woman at Grange-road was arrested, but the other was allowed to walk away.

Letter to the Editor

Sir, I must state emphatically that a corrosive acid was not used. The fluid was an alkaline solution of pyrogallol and its use was decided upon only after many experiments had been made with it.

Yours faithfully, Edith How Martyn, Women's Freedom League

The Times: 5 November 1909

Bermondsey Outrages

The defendant (Alice Chapin) then gave evidence. She said she broke the glass tube upon the ballot box as a protest against the exclusion of women from the franchise. She had been told the fluid was absolutely harmless and she honestly believed it could not hurt anyone. She intended to obliterate the ballot papers. Mr Hemmerde (appearing for Mrs Chapin) said she was exceedingly sorry that in making her protest she had injured Mr Thorley.

The defendant was committed for trial at the Central Criminal Court, bail being accepted in £100.

The following incident was the first of Emily Wilding Davison's dramatic, headline-grabbing acts. She was never part of the inner circle at Clement's Inn and until her death – see June 1913 – the Pankhursts regarded her as a very loose cannon.

Sunday Dispatch: 31 October 1909

How I Defied the Fire-Hose: Suffragette's Story of her Experiences in Strangeways Gaol, Manchester

—Saturday was only varied by two of the torture processes (*i.e. forcible feeding*). On Sunday I had the joy of hearing our comrades outside cheering. Otherwise I spent my time planning how to barricade my cell. About two o'clock that afternoon my wardress came and removed me from my cell to the empty one next door, while a pane of glass I had broken was being mended.

As the wardress shut the cell door of H.43, I saw to my joy that there were two plank beds in the cell—Quick as lightning came the realisation that my chance had come. Down went the two beds as quietly as possible, lengthwise exactly between the door and the window. About a foot's space remained, which I filled with the stout stool, face down, strong legs up. There was still a tiny crack to be filled, into which I stuffed my leather shoes, and a hairbrush. My blockade was complete.

—The matron came, different people came, begged me to get off the planks, and threatened me with punishment. To each and all I turned a deaf ear—Then warders were brought to burst open the door. After a time they got their iron crowbars through the top, but seemed to give up the task. A voice said, 'Davison, if you do not get off the plank and open the door we shall have the hose-pipe turned on you.'—

A ladder appeared at the window. Then I heard a crash of glass. I looked round and saw the nozzle of a fire hose thrust through the window. After a long time this was trained on me, and they began. The first jet of water went over my head, but the next came full on me, so that I had to hold on like grim death. The force of the water was terrific, and it seemed as cold as ice. On it came whilst I gasped for breath, and for an age it seemed – but perhaps it was only fifteen minutes – my gasps getting worse and worse. A voice outside called, 'Stop! No more, no more!'

Then they resumed operations on the door. I could see the crowbars working. They called out, 'If you don't move off that plank you will be badly hurt.' I could see that if the door fell it would crush me. At last it gave! It gave further! A male warder climbed in, rushed at me, lifted me up, and then the planks. I was rushed out through the now open door. The water, which was about six inches deep in the cell, rushed out into the hall below.

I was hurried into my own cell by the matron and wardress. My clothes were literally torn off, and I was wrapped in blankets, put in a carrying chair and rushed through the building to the hospital. There they had a hot bath ready for me. After a few moments I was lifted out, rubbed hard all over my body, and then put straight into a bed between blankets with a hot bottle.

I was then forcibly fed through the nose.

Memo to Official Statement of Friday, October 29th, 1909

I think it is necessary to state that after the hose-pipe incident the menstruation process began. No enquiries had been made before the turning on of the hose to ascertain my condition. The risks were taken.

EMILY WILDING DAVISON B.A.

To the Chairman of the Visiting Committee
Manchester Prison

Home Office, Whitehall
30th October 1909

Sir,

I am directed by the Secretary of State to acknowledge the receipt of your letter of the 28th instant with regard to the action of the Visiting Committee in authorising the use of the fire hose in the case of Emily Davison, a prisoner who had barricaded herself in her cell—

The Secretary of State recognises that in this matter the Visiting Committee acted from a desire to uphold the authority of the officers of the Prison in dealing with a recalcitrant prisoner and he accepts their statement that they were also anxious to secure the opening of the prisoner's cell in a manner which they thought least likely to involve risk of her being injured; but in his opinion they were guilty of a grave error of judgement in authorising the use of the hose pipe in such circumstances. It was not an emergency in which it was necessary to gain admission to the cell without a moment's delay, and had a little patience been exercised it would clearly have been possible to break open the door without exposing the prisoner to any risk of injury, as was in fact actually done; while the use of the fire hose, especially in the case of a prisoner of poor physique and enfeebled by her own attempts to starve herself, was an act nearly approaching to cruelty and might well have involved risk to health or even to life.

Further, the Secretary of State would point out that in giving the order to use the fire hose, the Visiting Committee were going entirely outside their proper jurisdiction. The Visiting Committee have vested in them certain judicial and advisory powers which are clearly stated in the Prison Act, 1877, and in the Prison Rules, but they have no authority to give orders to the Governor or the Deputy Governor of the Prison or to interfere with authorities in

dealing with disobedient or recalcitrant prisoners. The order of
the Visiting Committee was in fact entirely *ultra vires*, and ought
not to have been accepted by the Deputy Governor. But for the
fact that he is a recently appointed Officer with little experience
of Prison administration, he would have incurred the very gravest
censure and possible dismissal from the Service.

Press Cutting 1910

The Treatment of Women Prisoners

Judge Parry yesterday delivered his considered judgement in the
action brought in Manchester County Court by Miss Emily
Wilding Davison, B.A. against certain visiting Justices of
Strangeways Prison, Manchester—She claimed £100 damages for
what was alleged to have been an unjustifiable and violent
assault.

Mr Justice Parry said there was no doubt that the defendants
were parties to an assault upon the plaintiff and, indeed, it was
not denied. Their contention, however, was that they were justified in what they did—and that the assault was reasonable and
necessary under the circumstances of the case—What the Justices
did was done in good faith—but they had no right, duty, or power
to deal with the matter and therefore they could not justify their
assault—

The hose-pipe was used for two minutes, and had no evil result
on the plaintiff's health. On the contrary, it appeared to have had
the result of releasing her from prison—The plaintiff had had
the satisfaction of spurring the Visiting Justices to a momentary
indiscretion, of providing herself with copy for a vivacious and
entertaining account of the affair for the Press, and advertising a
cause in which she and many others were greatly interested. In

these circumstances the damages should be nominal, and be assessed at 40s, with costs on C. scale.

The militants were not averse to using legal channels when it suited them. The Hon. Evelina Haverfield had transferred her allegiance from the NUWSS to the WSPU. A brilliant horsewoman, she perfected a technique of making police horses sit down during demonstrations! Mary Leigh, who took her action backed by the WSPU, was one of its more ferociously militant members.

Votes for Women: 3 December 1909

The Right to Petition: Judgement Against Mrs Pankhurst and Mrs Haverfield

In the Lord Chief Justice's Court on Wednesday last the special case involving the Right to Petition was heard before the Lord Chief Justice and Justices Chamnell and Coleridge. Lord Robert Cecil, appearing on behalf of the Hon. Mrs Haverfield, urged three main points – first, that women had a political right to petition the Prime Minister; second, that this right would be naturally exercised by personal presentation; and, thirdly, that they were behaving reasonably in persisting in their attempt to enter the House because his blank refusal provided no other alternative except that of abandoning altogether their hope of presenting it to him. The Lord Chief Justice told Mr Horrocks, who appeared for the Commissioner of Police, that it was not necessary to hear him, and proceeded to deliver judgement. He said that he recognised the right to petition the Prime Minister, but he did not recognise the right of deputation to him. There was no inherent right to enter the House of Commons, and in the present instance the women ought to have desisted when they received word from

Mr Asquith that he was not willing to receive them. He therefore gave judgement against the appeal with costs.

Daily Express: 10 December 1909

Home Secretary Victorious: Suffragist Fails in her Action

The Home Secretary and the governor and medical officer of Winson Green Prison, Birmingham, successfully defended an action which was brought against them in the King's Bench Division yesterday by Mrs (Mary) Leigh, a suffragist, whose hunger strike was brought to an abrupt end by forcible feeding—

[*There followed a catalogue of Mrs Leigh's crimes, statements about her condition after hunger striking and legal arguments about the definition of assault.*] The Lord Chief Justice said he should rule that it was the duty of the governor and medical officer of the prison to take all reasonable steps to keep the prisoner in health. The only question he would leave to the jury was whether the steps taken were reasonable, having regard to the condition in which the woman was.

The jury returned their verdict without leaving the box, that Mrs Leigh was not entitled to damages for assault.

From the WSPU Offices: 7 December 1909

Welsh Speakers Wanted

Dear Member,

In view of one or two meetings at which Mr Lloyd George is to speak in a week or so, we are especially anxious that our militant women should learn appropriate sentences in Welsh. In order to do this Mrs Davies, of 57, Racton Road, Fulham, (who is a Welsh woman) has kindly consented to teach those willing to learn, and has asked me to call a class at her house next Sunday night, December 12th at 7.30. I am enclosing your copy of words and syllables which you can be thinking over. Let me have a postcard saying if you can attend Mrs Davies' class on Sunday night, so that I can inform her how many are going. Please keep this *strictly private* as it is to be used on many future occasions.

Yours sincerely,

Jessie Kenney

The Vote: 23 December 1909

Women Writers' Suffrage League: Interview with Miss Bessie Hatton

Miss Hatton's account of the formation of the Women Writers' Suffrage League is very interesting. It was thought that a society headed by the names of some of the cleverest women writers of the day might form another good reason for the granting of the Suffrage to women. One night Miss Hatton was at the Dramatic Debates, where she heard Miss Cicely Hamilton speak on the Suffrage. She was immensely struck with her earnestness, and the power she exercised over the small audience, which was composed largely of 'Indifferents'. The next day she wrote to Miss Hamilton and said how much she had enjoyed her speech. She received a prompt reply in which was expressed the desire to found a Women Writers' Suffrage League 'if only someone would undertake the secretaryship'. The wish was immediately fulfilled by Miss Hatton—

She maintains that many who would not have belonged to any

other league have joined them – the fact that it is a neutral League appealed to them. It was founded on a generous basis – to help other Suffrage Leagues to the best of its ability, whether militant or constitutional. It proposes to hold frequent receptions, where many well known literary men and women will speak. It publishes and sells literature by famous writers on the cause—Miss Hatton hopes that branches will be founded in some of the important provincial towns—

The Vote *was the title of the WFL's newspaper.*

By December 1909 the country was in the throes of a General Election. The House of Lords then had the power to veto any Bill sent up from the Commons, though it had become accepted practice that they did not reject Finance Bills. On 30 November, with their massive in-built Tory majority, their lordships 'denied their assent' to Lloyd George's Budget. The Liberals dissolved Parliament and went to the country on the issue of the Lords' veto or, more simply, 'The People v the Peers'. During a gruelling eight-week General Election campaign the militants did their utmost to harass the Liberals, as the unsung Violet Bryant. The saga of Lady Constance Lytton was triggered by what happened to Selina Martin and Leslie Hall in Liverpool but it had its roots, as she explained, in her own release from Newcastle Gaol and the Government's claim that class played no part in the treatment of imprisoned suffragettes.

Confidential Report from the Governor, H. M. Prison, Preston

Re: 748 No. Violet Bryant
Haslingdon Petty Sessions,
6th December 1909
Wilful Damage to Windows and a Lamp.
1 month 111 Division – or pay £6.15.8.

15th December 1909

Gentlemen,

I have the honour to report with reference to the above named Suffragette prisoner that she still persists in refusing her food, is insolent and violent. I visited her at about 9.0 a.m. today, and she asked for a library book. I told her the rules did not admit of her having one, as her sentence was only a month, but she might have a set of devotional books, if she would tell me what her religion was, to which she replied my only religion is 'Votes for Women', and she turned to one of the female Officers and said 'It is a damned shame she could not have a library book'. Shortly afterwards the matron reported at my Office that the prisoner had smashed 4 panes of glass in her cell window and was violent. I ordered her to be restrained with figure and handcuffs fastened behind her back, at 9.30 a.m. and removal to special cell, pending the arrival of, and instructions of, the Medical Officer. The handcuffs were removed when the Medical Officer fed the prisoner through a tube, assisted by Dr Pumblett at 10 a.m., and were not again placed on her, but she was put in the Special Cell on the recommendation of the Medical Officer.

Lancashire Daily Post: 5 January 1910

This morning, shortly before half-past seven, the remaining suffragist in Preston gaol was liberated after having served practically a month's term of imprisonment. This was Miss Violet Bryant, a hospital nurse—Miss Bryant was too weak and ill to submit to an interview, but from what our representative was able to ascertain the prison officials are probably not in the least sorry that Miss Bryant is off their hands, for it is understood that during the whole period of incarceration she had maintained her 'protest' with unusual vigour and determination. For seventeen days, attired in a canvas dress, she was placed in a punishment cell, and even then she managed to secure a piece of glass with which she severed the straps which formed part of her punishment costume—

Food was refused throughout, and it is stated that for the first week Miss Bryant had absolutely nothing, but the second week she was compelled to submit to forcible feeding, and from then to her release she was fed in this way.

Liverpool Echo: 21 December 1909

Suffragists Arrested Disguised as Orange Sellers
Ginger Beer Bottle Used as a Missile

Just as the motor car was moving away from the entrance to the Reform Club, after the Prime Minister had gone in, a suffragette, who was dressed as a basket women, suddenly raised her right arm and deliberately threw something with great violence at the body of the motor-car. The missile, which turned out to be an empty ginger-beer bottle, went through the open window of the car, and landed on the cushions without doing any damage worth speaking about—The suffragette was immediately arrested, as was also another suffragist, who was taken in charge just as she was in the act of following the tactics of her companion. They were both taken to the main Bridewell, where they were booked as Selina Martin and Leslie Hall.

Votes for Women: 3 January 1910

Atrocities in English Prison

On December 20th Miss Selina Martin and Miss Leslie Hall were arrested in Liverpool, and were remanded for one week, bail being refused.

Accordingly, while still unconvicted prisoners, they were sent to Walton Gaol, Liverpool. There, contrary to regulations, intercourse with their friends was denied to them. As unconvicted prisoners they refused to submit to the prison discipline or to take the prison food. Forcible feeding was threatened and Miss Martin therefore barricaded her cell. The officials, however, effected an entrance, fell upon her and handcuffed her, dragged her to a punishment cell and flung her on the floor, with her hands tightly fastened together behind her back.

All that night she was kept in irons. Next day her cell was entered, she was seized, thrown down, rolled over with face upon the floor. In this position, face downwards, her arms were dragged up behind her till she was lifted from the ground. Her hair was seized by another wardress. In this way she was 'frog-marched' up the steps to the doctor's room, her head bumping on the stone stairs. In the doctor's room the operation of forcible feeding was performed – causing intense suffering – and then this tortured girl, in a terrible state of physical and mental distress, was handcuffed again, flung down the steps and pushed and dragged back into her cell. Her companion,

Leslie Hall, was kept in irons for two and a half consecutive days and nights—

If such deeds were done in Russia there would be an outcry in this country. Are they to be tolerated here?

(Prison) Visiting Committee Report on Martin & Hall

Walton Gaol: Liverpool

8/1/1910

As a result of this inquiry we are satisfied:-

(a) That on the 23rd December, 1909, the prisoner walked upstairs from her cell to the Doctor's room with the assistance of the officer.
(b) That by reason of her violent struggling, it was necessary for the officers to carry her down stairs when going from the Doctor's room back to her cell.
(c) She was carried down stairs *face* downwards because she herself chose that Position. (The prisoner admitted to us that this was so.)
(d) That if her head was bumped at any time, which we are not satisfied was the case, it was done during the struggle.
(e) In the struggle going downstairs, the prisoner managed to put her feet round one of the posts and force had to be used to release her from that position.
(f) None of the officers seized the prisoner by the hair.
(g) No intentional injury was caused to the prisoner by kicking or otherwise by any of the officers.
(h) It was necessary for Dr Morton to use a certain amount of force in connection with the gag by reason of the prisoner's resistance, but no undue force was used by him.
(i) All the officers specifically denied having at any time taunted the prisoner by saying 'Votes for women' or remarks of that description.

(j) The prisoner made no complaint to the Medical Officer about any injury to her head, or other parts of her body from kicks or otherwise.

Doctor's Report on Rose E.N. Howey

Liverpool
Jan 29 1910

The Prison Commissioners,
Gentlemen,

I have the honour to report that today I saw and examined Rose E.N. Howey at H.M. Prison, Walton, in consultation with Dr Price. I also took part in the artificial feeding by the oesophageal tube. Rose E.N. Howey is about 25 years of age, a spare, fair complexioned woman but highly neurotic.

She was sentenced on January 15th to six weeks imprisonment. From the records I find that on committal she weighed 114 lbs, and today she weighs 108½lb. Her height is 5ft 5½". Her lungs and heart are quite healthy; respiration quiet; pulse 72 regular, fair volume, medium tension, capillary circulation active. Tongue clean, teeth good, no distension of stomach or abdomen; bowels regular; menses regular; knee jerks excessive. Her throat is rather small and slightly granular but not inflamed. She evidently had in childhood post-natal adenoids, but her nostrils are now quite free.

On passing the oesophageal tube there was slight spasm at the upper end of the oesophagus 5 to 6 inches from the teeth; this no doubt increases the discomfort of the passage of the tube, but it can be easily got over by using a fine moderately stiff tube with only one side opening near the end of the tube and in the stiff part. Personally I would be inclined to leave her without food for two or three days and by that time the spasm will have passed off. Any ordinary individual can survive with only water for a couple of weeks, and there is no damage to life in a healthy individual from any loss of body weight up to 25 per cent, or say 20 per cent, including the weight of the clothing. This woman can therefore afford to lose 23lb without any risk.

I have the honour to be, Gentlemen,

Your obedient servant,

James Barr

Daily Telegraph: 25 January 1910

Lady Constance Lytton
Release from Gaol: Disguised as Sempstress

Her ladyship said her object in courting arrest at Liverpool was to test the accuracy of Mr Gladstone's statement that no distinction was made among Suffragist prisoners based on class difference. She disguised herself as a working sempstress, and took part on Friday, Jan 14, in a demonstration outside the gaol at Liverpool in protest at the treatment of Selina Martin. She was arrested while calling upon the crowd to follow her into the prison yard, and was brought up the following morning at the police-court, and charged with obstruction and insulting behaviour.

She gave the name of Jane Wharton (sic), and so complete was her disguise that neither police nor magistrates suspected her identity. She was fined 10s and costs, with the alternative of fourteen days' imprisonment, and elected to go to prison. Immediately on entering the gaol 'Jane Wharton' commenced the 'hunger strike' as a protest at being treated as a common criminal, instead of as a political offender. She also refused to perform the work given her, and on Monday, Jan 17, she was accordingly put in the punishment cell. For four days she refused to take any food, and on Tuesday, Jan 18, at 5.30 p.m. the first attempt was made to feed her by force.

Lady Constance Lytton, who had previously been released from

Newcastle Gaol, on the ground that she suffered from a weak heart and that forcible feeding might have grave consequences, stated that on this occasion no effort was made to test her heart—

'Jane Wharton' was brought before the magistrates and severely reprimanded for writing upon the walls of her cell. She had written the quotation from Thoreau, 'Under a Government that imprisons any unjustly, the true place for a just man or woman is also in prison.' She also wrote the Bible injunction, 'Only be ye strong, very courageous.' The magistrates, she says, read her a long lecture upon the enormity of her offence.

Up to Saturday the Liverpool Gaol authorities had no idea that 'Jane Wharton' was other than the poor sempstress she had 'got up' to resemble—Lady Constance Lytton was released on grounds of health. She alleges, however, that this decision was not arrived at until her identity had become known. She further states that the prison doctor, who saw her on the Wednesday evening during the forcible feeding, said, 'heart famous; pulse steady; go along; it's all right.'

Lady Constance Lytton: Prison Commissioners' Report to the Home Office

The Commissioners adhere to the opinion that no case exists for a special or formal inquiry. Such allegations, if made by an ordinary prisoner on discharge, and when disposed of by such inquiry as has been made in this case, would not be deemed to call for any further action by the Secretary of State, and any exceptional action would not, in the opinion of the Commissioners, be justified by the mere fact that in this case the discharged prisoner is a woman of gentle birth, highly educated, and thus enabled to make public her alleged grievances through the medium of the Press and of her influential friends.

Besides being a militant Suffragette, Lady Constance Lytton is also an active member of the Penal Reform League, and the Commissioners are of the opinion that there is reason to think that her object in disguising herself in this way, and submitting herself to this experience, was not so much that she desired to be a martyr in the Cause for 'Votes for Women', as to furnish sensational matter for the monthly bulletin of this disingenuous League, who, as the Secretary of State is aware, is a persistent, and I may say, malicious critic of the Prison administration, and does not hesitate to make use of any weapon that comes to hand to injure its reputation, and to create the impression that prisoners in H.M. Prisons are grossly maltreated.

Letter to the Times: 30 March 1910

From the Earl of Lytton

Sir, On February 10 a letter was sent to the Press by Sir Edward Troup [*Permanent Under-Secretary at the Home Office*] relative to a statement made by my sister, Lady Constance Lytton, regarding her treatment in Liverpool Prison, in which he declared on behalf of the Home Secretary that there was no foundation for any of the charges which she had made. I am anxious to explain why this official imputation of untruthfulness has hitherto remained unanswered.

Lady Constance was seriously ill at the time as the result of her prison experiences, and unable to defend herself. I therefore undertook the task of vindicating her veracity—I have had several communications with the Home Office on the subject, and owing to the retirement of Mr Gladstone and the appointment of a new Home Secretary [*Winston Churchill*], they have necessarily been protracted over a considerable period—the only claim which I have made was that in the interests of justice, charges of this nature should be submitted to a full and impartial inquiry—This claim has been refused by the Home Office on the grounds that the Prison officials have been closely interrogated, and that as they deny entirely every one of the charges made, 'no useful purpose' would be served by granting my request.

In the absence of such an inquiry as I asked for, the matter must be left to the opinion of unbiased minds. I desire, however, to say that nothing which I have been able to learn has in any way shaken my belief in the substantial accuracy of my sister's account. The idea that her charges can be disposed of by the bare denial of the persons against whom they are made, is not likely to commend itself to anyone outside the Home Office, and no amount of denial can get over the following facts:

1. Lady Constance Lytton, when imprisoned in Newcastle, after refusing to answer the medical questions put to her and adopting the hunger-strike, received a careful and thorough medical examination, which disclosed symptoms of 'serious heart disease', and on these grounds she was released as unfit to submit to forcible feeding.
2. Three months later 'Jane Warton', when imprisoned at Liverpool, also refused to answer medical questions or take prison food. On this occasion she was entered in the prison books as having refused medical examination, and was forcibly fed eight times. Such medical examination as took place during the forcible feeding failed, according to the medical officer's report, to disclose any symptoms of heart disease, and she was eventually released on the grounds of loss of weight and general physical weakness.

These facts are incontrovertible, and though the Home Office is quite satisfied that in both cases the prison officials performed their duty in the most exemplary fashion, your readers will form their own opinions of the justice of a Government Department which brings accusations of untruthfulness against an individual whilst refusing the only means by which the truth can be established.

I am, your obedient servant,

Lytton

Polling for the General Election took place towards the end of January 1910. The Liberals lost nearly 100 seats to the Tories and emerged with no overall majority, dependent on the votes of the 82 Irish Nationalists whose overwhelming interest lay in Home Rule for Ireland and the Labour Party whose 40 MPs mostly supported women's suffrage but in a period of great industrial unrest did not regard it as their prime concern.

As noted in Lord Lytton's letter to The Times *the re-elected Government saw a change of Home Secretary with Winston Churchill replacing the less than successful Herbert Gladstone who was despatched to South Africa as Governor-General.*

It was the journalist and staunch suffragist Henry Brailsford who recognised that the new facts of political life demanded a new approach to the women's suffrage question.

Letter from Henry Brailsford to Millicent Fawcett

18 January 1910

I have some thought of attempting to found a Conciliation Committee for Woman's Suffrage. My idea is that it should undertake the necessary diplomatic work of promoting an early settlement. It should not be large, and should consist of both men & women – the women in touch with the existing societies but not their more prominent leaders, the men also as far as possible not identified officially with either party.

By the end of January the WSPU had been persuaded to accept the idea of a Conciliation Committee. Mrs Pankhurst announced that for the foreseeable future militancy was at an end, constitutional methods the order of the day. By the spring the Conciliation Committee was in being. It consisted of 54 suffragist MPs from all parties, including Tories, with Lord Lytton, himself a Tory but drawn into the struggle by his sister Constance's treatment in Liverpool, as Chairman. The committee members drafted a Bill which would have enfranchised only a million women but which would, they hoped, gain the support of all but the most dedicated Antis.

Conciliation Committee for Woman Suffrage
Chairman – The Rt. Hon. the Earl of Lytton
Hon. Sec. – H.N. Brailsford

Text of the Bill

A Bill to confer the Parliamentary Franchise on Women, Be it Enacted etc.

1. Every woman possessed of a household qualification within the meaning of the Representation of the People Act (1884), shall be entitled to be registered as a voter, and when registered to vote in the County or Borough in which the qualifying premises are situate
2. For the purposes of this Act, a woman shall not be disqualified by marriage, for being registered as a voter, provided that a husband and wife shall not both be registered as voters in the same Parliamentary Borough or County Division
3. This Act may be cited as The Representation of the People Act, 1911

Non-militancy or what became known as 'the Truce' lasted nearly two years, from January 1910 until November 1911, with the exception of the few days surrounding 'Black Friday' – see November

1910. In May Edward VII died and George V became King. Mid-1910 was the high water mark of the women's hopes of an early breakthrough. In July the Conciliation Bill in fact passed its second reading in the House of Commons, but Lloyd George and Churchill voted against it, believing that the million possible women voters would be mainly Tories. And political events were once more conspiring against the women. The 'People's Budget' had eventually passed through the Lords, but an even greater storm was about to break over the Parliament Bill designed to curtail the powers of the House of Lords. It was temporarily postponed when Parliament went into recess until November.

Common Cause: 13 October 1910

How to Deal with Awkward Questions

A meeting was held by the local branch of the Anti-Suffrage League in Whitby on October 3rd. Members of the Whitby and District Women's Suffrage Society attended the meeting to ask questions, and Suffragists staying in the town were also present— It required some self-control to listen quietly to the misrepresentations of fact made by the second speaker (Mr Newman). In response to his assertion that women were a privileged class under the law, Miss Pringle asked if he could give any idea of the percentage of men who suffered through the legal privileges enjoyed by women compared with the percentage of women who suffered through the inequality of the divorce laws and the laws concerning the relations of the sexes—

The Chairman, in reply, said such questions could not be discussed before a mixed audience with young girls present. (There were, so far as the writer of this report could see, three girls present aged about 17 years.) Miss Pringle replied that no woman in the audience ought to be left in ignorance of the laws under which she lived; but the meeting was cut short at this point by the playing of the National Anthem.

And How Not to Vote

Overheard in a Leeds tramcar, returning home from a debate: Man (to friend) 'No, I dined at the club, spent a quiet evening, and then I strolled to the Woman Suffrage Debate. Didn't hear any of the speeches, but arrived just in time to vote against the women.'

Clifton (Bristol) Chronicle & Directory: 9 November 1910

Pageant of Women

The matinee at the Princes Theatre, organised by the Women's Social and Political Union on Saturday afternoon, was a huge success. The theatre was filled from floor to ceiling, so that the result from a pecuniary point of view must have been very satisfactory, and to judge by the applause, a very large majority of those present were sympathisers and enthusiastic supporters.

There were three parts to the programme, of which the first was undoubtedly the prettiest and most popular. This was a series of country and Morris songs and dances—The scene was set on a village green on the edges of a wood. There were gathered the villagers, represented by about fifty children [*all their names listed*]—Then following the more serious part of the programme, a one-act play by Cicely Hamilton and Christopher St John, called 'How the Vote was Won'. According to this play, this was achieved by a general strike of all unmarried women—

For the pageant the stage was set as a large hall with a raised empty dais on each side. In the centre was a lofty golden throne, and on it was seated Justice. To the steps of the throne comes Woman who demands justice and freedom. She is opposed by Prejudice who sets out his case that woman is the plaything of man and not capable of acting independently. Woman opposes this, and calls forth a number of characters representing learned women, graduates, artists, saintly women, heroic women, rulers and warriors. Prejudice, convinced and silenced against his will, retires, and Justice decides in woman's favour—

Common Cause: 17 November 1910

Joint Mass Meeting in the Albert Hall

No less than fifteen Suffrage Societies united to make that brave show on the 12th. I use the word 'brave' deliberately. It was the last gathering of a long week entirely devoted to Suffrage. The average woman must have become a little tired of turning out night after night in the wet – it seemed always to be wet – to attend meetings in distant parts of London—Therefore to see the Albert Hall so well filled on Saturday night was encouraging, and may well be described as 'brave'. Once more women poured through the long tunnel from South Kensington to the Albert Hall. The railway official on duty in that dim place took a fatherly interest in us all—The Artists' Franchise League had concentrated its efforts upon the platform, and the effect was very good. Chrysanthemums, white and gold and brown, with arum lilies and autumn green, made a charming front screen—Most effective was the long line, stretching away on either side of the organ, made up of dull red banners, bearing on them big white letters the number of voters who had signed the women's petition: '3,000 men of Crewe', '2,444 men of Carlisle' and so on; and at the end the grand total – 290,000—

Mr Brailsford, who was received with immense enthusiasm, said that for one brief happy moment, when he opened the morning paper, he had thought he would have to congratulate this meeting on victory already achieved. Seeing the name of Mr Lloyd George under the words, 'A ringing appeal to the democracy and the rights of the people', he thought for one moment that the resolution of the Welsh women had had its effect—'But I forgot, you are not people; you are not citizens; your birthright as Englishwomen, as Scotchwomen, as Irishwomen is denied. You are helots—But your time is at hand.'

Parliament reassembled on 18 November 1910. Mrs Pankhurst had earlier declared that unless Mr Asquith agreed to give parliamentary facilities to the Conciliation Bill she would lead a deputation to the House of Commons. On the 18th Asquith informed the Commons that negotiations with the Lords about the Parliament Bill had broken down and Parliament would be dissolved. Unsurprisingly he made no mention of the Conciliation Bill. On hearing the news Mrs Pankhurst led 300 women from a pre-arranged meeting at the Caxton Hall to the House of Commons. The result went into suffrage history as 'Black Friday'.

Black Friday: 18 November 1910

I, MARY FRANCES EARL, of 39 RAGLAN ROAD, IN THE COUNTY OF DUBLIN, Wife of HENRY CECIL EARL, make Oath and say as follows:

That on Friday, November 18th, many small contingents of the deputation of the Women's Social and Political Union left Caxton Hall on a peaceful errand to present a Memorial to the Prime Minister at the House of Commons. The Memorial was as follows:

125

This meeting of women, gathered together in the Caxton Hall, protests against the policy of shuffling and delay with which the agitation for women's enfranchisement has been met by the Government, and calls on the Government at once to withdraw the veto which they have placed upon the Conciliation Bill for Women's Suffrage, a measure which has been endorsed by the representatives of the people in the House of Commons.

That in each contingent there were not more than 12 women. The Irish Contingent, of the Irish Women's Franchise League, of which I was a member, was the fourth to start, and, though the police tried to stop us, all of us succeeded in reaching the steps of the House of Commons— When we arrived we found there Mrs Pankhurst, Mrs Garrett Anderson and others—

(Later) I went out as one of the party of eight women who were to try and reach the House by an underground passage. The scene down there was terrible, but the most terrible part to me was the disgusting language used to us by the police, who were, I understand, brought specially from Whitechapel. In the struggle here the police were most brutal and indecent. They deliberately tore my undergarments, using the most foul language – such language as I could not repeat. The seized me by the hair and forced me up the steps on my knees, refusing to allow me to regain my footing. I was then flung into the crowd outside—We made our way back to Caxton Hall—

SWORN this 15th day of December, 1910, at 116 Grafton Street, in the City of Dublin, before me, and I know the Deponent, John J. McDonald, a Commissioner to Administer Oaths in the Supreme Court of Judicature in Ireland.

Further Statements

'For hours one was beaten about the body, thrown backwards and forwards from one to another, until one felt dazed with the horror of it—One policeman picked me up in his arms and threw me into the crowd saying 'You come again, you B—B—, and I will show you what I will do to you.'—a favourite trick was pinching the upper part of one's arms, which were black and blue afterwards—What I complain of on behalf of us all is the long-drawn-out agony of the delayed arrest.'

'Several times constables and plain-clothes men who were in the crowd passed their arms round me from the back and clutched hold of my breasts in as public a manner as possible, and men in the crowd followed their example. I was also pummelled on the chest, and my breast was clutched by one constable from the front. As a consequence, three days later, I had to receive medical attention from Dr Ede as my breasts were discoloured and very painful. On the Friday I was also very badly treated. My skirt was lifted up as high as possible, and the constable attempted to lift me off the ground by raising his knee. This he could not do, so he threw me into the crowd and incited the men to treat me as they wished. Consequently several men who, I believe, were policemen in plain clothes, also endeavoured to lift my dress.'

'Later I found myself near Westminster Bridge, where Mrs Saul Solomon was valiantly struggling against the crowd, for although there were many constables near her, and an inspector, it seemed to me that instead of protecting her from the mob – a position one would have thought her age merited, if nothing else – they offered her no assistance, but rather aided than prevented the rough element in the crowd in pushing and knocking her—these men, one felt convinced, were more than merely onlookers.'

These statements were incorporated – with others – into a Memorandum entitled TREATMENT OF THE WOMEN'S DEPU-TATIONS BY THE POLICE Evidence collected by Dr Jessie Murray and Mr Brailsford forwarded to the Home Office. *It dealt with Unnecessary Violence: Methods of Torture: Acts of Indecency: After Effects: State of Mind of the Police: Plain Clothes Men. It concluded:*

CONCLUSION We claim that the evidence here collected suffices to justify our demand for a public inquiry into the behaviour of the Metropolitan Police on November 18, 22 and 23 [*there were further demonstrations on these days*]. The object of such an inquiry should be to ascertain, not merely whether the charges of aggressive violence, torture, and indecency here made can be substantiated, but also to ascertain under what orders the police were acting. The order to make no arrests goes some way to explain their conduct, and must in itself have led to much unnecessary and dangerous violence. But it would not explain the frequency of torture and indecency, nor the more obvious unprovoked acts of violence which many of the men committed. A man acting under this order might feel that he was justified in flinging a woman back with some violence when she attempted to pass the cordon. But this order alone would not suggest to him that he should run forward and fell her with a blow on the mouth, or twist her arms, or bend her thumb, or manipulate her breasts. The impression conveyed by this evidence is from first to last that the police believed themselves to be acting under an almost unlimited licence to treat the women as they pleased, and to inflict upon them a degree of humiliation and pain which would deter them or intimidate them. We suggest that the inquiry should seek to determine whether such an impression prevailed among the police, and if so, whether any verbal orders (which may or may not have been correctly understood) were given by any of the men's superiors by way of supplement to the general order—

H.N. BRAILSFORD

HON. SECRETARY FOR THE CONCILIATION COMMITTEE

Draft Memorandum by Edward Henry, Commissioner of the MetropolitanPolice, on Allegations Contained in Mr Brailsford's Memorial

There must (*amended to may*) be grounds for the belief so widely held by those who took part in these demonstrations that many of their number were indecently handled but there is no foundation for the suggestion that this was done by members of the Police Force dressed in ordinary clothes and forming part of the crowd and this can be proved. Amongst this crowd were many undesirable and reckless persons quite capable of indulging in gross conduct – but for their presence the organisers are responsible as they specially invited the public by messages chalked on the footways and by leaflets to be present—but there are 5 allegations that Constables behaved improperly—No particulars are given to enable one to identify the Constables alleged to have committed these acts—I need hardly say that any such conduct on the part of Constable would be universally reprobated by the Police Service, and when the police were told on parade of this charge they were naturally very indignant—

For weeks past the official organ of the W.S. and P.U. has published a notice inviting persons who could make statements as to police misconduct on the 18th November and subsequent dates to place themselves in communication with Mr Brailsford and this probably accounts for the number received. There can be no doubt that these various accusations are brought forward with the object of embarrassing the authorities and of fettering police action in future.—

The Police are even accused of using their heavy helmets to batter the women. I have had a helmet with all its trappings weighed and find that it is only 3½ ounces heavier than an ordinary silk hat. What may have happened is that when a Constable's helmet was knocked off by a woman he, in his convulsive effort

129

to secure it, may have struck some one with it, but not necessarily intentionally, and certainly a helmet that weighs only 11 ounces cannot be considered heavy—

Lastly I would point out that although over 200 women were brought to the Police Station and charged there not a single complaint was made at the time of undue violence or of misconduct on the part of the Police, and no medical attention was needed by any of the women.—It is difficult to understand why if they had been treated as they now allege they did not complain at the time.

The Times: 11 March 1911

The Woman Suffragists: Mr Churchill's Response
'A copious fountain of mendacity'

No fresh instructions, verbal or written, were issued to the police on or before November 18—It was my intention from the beginning of my tenure of the Home Office—to have these women removed from the scene of disorder as soon as was lawfully possible, and then to press the prosecution only of those who had committed personal assaults on the police or other serious offences. The directions which I gave were not fully understood or carried out on November 18—I have given explicit instructions that in the future, with a view to avoiding disagreeable scenes, for which no one is responsible but the disorderly women themselves, police officers should be told to make arrests as soon as there is lawful occasion—

I cannot but conclude without reaffirming my conviction that the Metropolitan Police behaved on November 18 with the forbearance and humanity for which they have always been distinguished, and again repudiating the unsupported allegations which have issued from that copious fountain of mendacity the Women's Social and Political Union.

Needless to say no public enquiry ensued. The men from 'A' Division which covered the Houses of Parliament were by then accustomed to dealing with suffragettes and Churchill made a grave mistake – which he did not repeat – in allowing policemen from Whitechapel and other East End districts to be brought in. The declared aim of avoiding arrests was in any case spectacularly unsuccessful. There is little doubt that on 18 November 1910 some policemen considered they had been given unlimited licence. Hugh Franklin took his own revenge. 'The special regulation' to which Evelyn Sharp referred was Rule 243a introduced by Churchill. Its aim was to make life easier for suffragette prisoners, though the attempt to cure them with kindness met with as little success as his strategy on Black Friday.

Horse-whipping Mr Churchill

Statement by Hugh Franklin

On the evening of 22nd I was near Downing Street by the Park Step with Miss Vera Wentworth. Mrs Cobden Sanderson came down the steps and informed me that she was in Downing Street feeling faint when Mr Churchill appeared and said to an Inspector 'Turn that woman away, allow no one to loiter hereby.' Then I said 'I am protesting at his Meeting to-night I'll give him a whipping.' Thereupon I bought a dog whip—(it) was bought by me entirely on my account and without suggestion from anyone or any of my political friends and consequent on the incident above referred to.

After this I heard Mr Churchill was to speak at Bradford and I went up there taking Hull on the way. This was on the following Friday. I took the whip with me. I was ejected from the Hull Meeting and also from the Bradford one on the Saturday after.

I had intended returning to town with Miss Ainsworth by the 5:10 p.m. from Bradford the same evening. I did not know before hand whether Mr Churchill would travel by the same train. I only knew it when I saw the police at the platform entrance. I got into the same carriage as his and sat down near the corridor. A few minutes before Mr Churchill came Sergeant Sandercock asked Miss Ainsworth to move her bag that he might sit next her in spite of the fact that there was only one other occupant of the compartment. By this we guessed that Mr Churchill would be coming through the carriage. As soon as Churchill entered the carriage I jumped and struck at him with my whip saying 'Take this you cur for the treatment of the Suffragists'. I did not say 'dirty'. Sandercock pushed me down and with Parker's help and some other passengers overpowered me and took away my whip. I then sat in my seat until we reached Kings Cross being told I was under arrest.

I consider that the only way in which Mr Churchill could be made to understand his behaviour and treatment of the women was by the action which I took. There are occasions in this World when the ordinary process of the law does not avail one and one is driven to use means which in ordinary circumstances one would not employ.

from Unfinished Adventure

Reflections on Imprisonment

My first imprisonment was shared by over three hundred suffragettes, and the tax on Government was so great as to necessitate short sentences, which could be served while the rest were remanded from day to day at Bow Street. But fourteen days was quite long enough for me. The hardships feared by my mother had momentarily ceased to exist, for, in addition to the prison reforms instituted after the suffragettes had exposed the worst abuses, a special regulation [Rule 243a] had been invented for us by the Home Office in a vain attempt to cure us with kindness. Our friends were therefore able to send us in food and home comforts, and also needlework materials as an occupation; but I was not allowed my writing materials, in spite of endless arguments with the Governor—

I asked the chaplain to find me something more serious to read than the bound volumes of *Little Folks* and similar works in the prison library, but when he suggested quaintly that I should give my brain a rest and read the Bible, I am sure his irony was as unconscious as that of the authorities, who placed, not only a Bible, but also a copy of a book called 'The Home Beautiful' (I think that was the ironic title) in all our cells. The Governor, too, would probably have been quite willing, had the Home Office allowed him, to give me writing materials for some other purpose than that of writing my will, a privilege that is open to all prisoners and is only difficult of accomplishment because the prison pen, like the curious tin instrument provided for eating the prison egg, is useless for the purpose intended, though no doubt suicide-proof.

I soon came to the conclusion that of all my journeys this one demonstrated most clearly my defects as a traveller. I am not a good prisoner. I moped apart when we all met in the prison yard for exercise, while my fellow Suffragettes, allowed to talk under the new regulation bravely cracked jokes, made absurd plots to escape or to smuggle notes out to friends, or to get them smuggled in (baked in cakes and buried in jam), and generally made the best of things. I never made the best of anything—

At night, a thousand impressions of unhappy lost souls seemed to crowd in upon me; and when an occupant of a distant cell, some ordinary prisoner who would have to face disgrace instead of applause on her discharge, lost control and began to scream and batter her cell door in the midst of the ghostly silence, I, with all my education and acquired self-control to help me, had a hard matter not to follow her example. My sense of humour seems to have failed me utterly at this crisis. Yet, afterwards, I could see the humorous side of prison life, the absurdity of being expected to keep rules without being told what they were, of being allowed to ring one's bell with scarcely a chance of its being answered, or of sending up petitions to the Home Office that would not be granted, with a hundred other administrative follies arising from the fixed idea of officialism that every woman prisoner is in a state of arrested development.

EVELYN SHARP

Actresses' Franchise League

Secretary's Annual Report 1910

Monthly At Homes: We are glad to be able to report that success and popularity continue to attend our At Homes at the Criterion each month.—we find they attract the most obstinate of Antis and, more important still, members of that class most difficult of all to get at 'the women who take no interest at all in Votes for Women' and have never been to a Meeting before. Our patrons Book bears witness to the fact that this is no longer true when they leave!

The second General Election within a year was fought on the constitutional issue of curtailing the powers of the House of Lords. By the start of 1911 the Liberals had been re-elected without further loss of seats. Despite the violence of Black Friday the WSPU decided not to renew militancy but to wait and see what the new Parliament would bring. To the delight of all suffragists one of the MP supporters, Sir

George Kemp, secured first place in the ballot for a Private Member's Bill and announced that he would sponsor a slightly revised Conciliation Bill. In May the Bill passed its second reading in the House of Commons with a massive majority – 255 to 88 votes. Although contradictory noises came from various members of the Government, by the summer of 1911 hopes were high that Sir George's Bill would be successful. Much of the year was devoted to organising meetings and peaceful but effective protests – such as avoiding the national census and refusing to pay taxes – culminating in the Women's Coronation Procession in July, the first and last time militants and non-militants thus collaborated.

from Female Pipings in Eden

'March of the Women'

In those early days of my association with the W.S.P.U. occurred an event which, in her pride, the writer must recount ere the pace becomes such that a personal reference would be unthinkable, namely the formal introduction to the Suffragettes of 'The March of the Women,' to which Cicely Hamilton fitted words after the tune had been written – not an easy undertaking. A Suffragette choir had been sternly drilled, and I remember Edith Craig plaintively commenting on the difficulty of hitting a certain E flat. But it was maintained that the interval is a peculiarly English one (which is true) and must be coped with. We had the organ, and I think a cornet to blast forth the tune (a system much to be recommended on such occasions), and it was wonderful processing up the centre aisle of the Albert Hall in Mus.Doc. robes at Mrs Pankhurst's side, and being presented with a beautiful *bâton*, encircled by a golden collar with the date, 23rd March 1911.

ETHEL SMYTH

135

'The March of the Women'

Shout, shout, up with your song!
Cry with the wind for the dawn is breaking.
March, march, swing you along,
Wide blows our banner and hope is waking.
Song with its story, dreams with their glory,
Lo! they call and glad is their word.
Forward! hark how it swells
Thunder of freedom, the voice of the Lord.

MUSIC BY ETHEL SMYTH: WORDS BY CICELY HAMILTON

from We Were Amused

For those who have forgotten or never knew, the W.S.P.U. colours were chosen as symbols: purple for loyalty 'to cause and King', white for purity, and green for hope, a piece of information incorporated into one of the verses of a composition by Dame Ethel Smyth. She was a keen suffragette, and wrote 'The March of the Women' for the W.S.P.U. band. Mother, Roma and I found it embarrassingly awful, especially as regards the lyric, composed by I don't know whom, though it might have been Dame Ethel. It began;

March, march, up with your song
[Something or other] for the dawn is breaking! March, march,
swing you along . . .

and this conjured up an unappetizing vision of eager women, barging forward with overmuch action from the rump. The type that describes itself as Awf'ly fit.

RACHEL FERGUSON

136

No Vote No Census! Night
Evening Standard & St James's Gazette: 3 April 1911

Aldwych Skating Rink London

I have had the unusual experience of being counted out in the company of hundreds of militant suffragists of the WSPU who have stayed in the Aldwych Skating Rink all night—They started to skate at five o'clock, and the interminable circling has made me think and blink in circles. I am glad it is all over. It has been a long and a cold vigil – nine and a half hours. The meeting went with a swing from the start. Dr Ethel Smyth led the audience in the chorus, 'The March of the Women', and members of the Actresses' Franchise League, headed by Miss Decima Moore, in a gorgeous evening gown of gold and black, thrust home the Suffragist arguments by recitals of Suffragist poems and other pieces—and a Spanish lady trilled a melodious Spanish song.

Morning Post: 4 April 1911

Evaders in the Provinces

Cardiff Suffragists to the number of about a hundred spent the night in an untenanted shop in the suburbs—At Bristol one party spent the night in a caravan—The 'No vote No census' revolt appears to have been loyally supported by the Liverpool and Birkenhead contingent. They spent the night at an house in Birkenhead, 'packed like sardines', according to Miss Davies, the organising secretary, who added that for breathing purposes it was necessary to keep the windows open—A census paper had been delivered to the house, and Miss Davies took charge of it, filling in the name of a manservant on the premises, and then writing, 'No other persons, but many women.'

Daily Sketch: 4 April 1911

Midnight Supper Party on Wimbledon Common

If you take enough to eat and drink, a midnight caravan picnic to Wimbledon Common is not a bad way of dodging the census. Stealthily through the West End of London on Sunday night, there crept three handsome travelling caravans—Not a soul was about when Wimbledon Common was reached at half-past one, and in the privacy of a carefully selected pitch, the census-slinkers got busy on a spread of roast fowl, boiled ham, pasties, sweetmeats, coffee, and especially tea. Everyone had brought something; one lady brought two maids and a dog.

In Victoria Park, Manchester

A large number of Manchester suffragists spent the night in Denison House, Victoria Park, which was lent to them by a prominent supporter of the movement. A *Daily Sketch* photographer, properly primed with pass-words, was admitted after a parley through the letter-box. Some of the suffragists stayed up all night: but others, quite tired out, nailed their colours 'No vote, no census!' to the wall, and went to sleep.

Daily Express: 4 April 1911

Guy Fawkes in Petticoats

It has often been hinted by rude little boys that some suffragists, when on the warpath, look like the celebrated Guy Fawkes. But it has been left to Miss Emily Wilding Davison to accomplish all that Guido Fawkes did – that is to conceal herself under the Houses of Parliament for forty-six hours—

'I just went round with a party,' she told an 'Express' representative last night, 'and at a quarter to four, when they all went up the crypt stairs, I stayed behind the door. It was pitch dark, and I did not know what might be in the room so I dared not make a noise. There was a dramatic moment later in the afternoon when an M.P. – I do not know who he was but he had such a nice voice – brought down two women—One of the women shuddered as she peered into the darkness, and said 'I wonder if there are any ghosts hers?' If she had come one inch further forward she would have seen my hat behind the door. I held my breath, but nobody saw me. I found, however, after they had left, that the outer door was locked.

'So then I tried to move about in the darkness to make myself comfortable—I had some food with me. This was my menu:- Meat lozenges, Biscuits, Lime juice and water—I found there were some boxes near, so I dragged them together behind the door, as quietly as I could and made a bed. So I passed all Sunday. You have no idea how monotonous it seemed—I slept a little on Sunday night, but woke at five, because I wanted, as soon as the door opened, to rush in the House if I could and hide myself until I could stand up and say, "Mr Asquith, withdraw your veto from the Women's Bill and women will withdraw their veto from the census."

'I climbed some rails and found I was in St Stephen's Chapel; I also found that there was an electric light, and now and then I turned it on for a moment. Then, to my horror, a cleaner came in. He cleaned the chapel through, creeping inch by inch nearer my little dark room. At last he opened the door and it banged against my box bed. He peered cautiously – very cautiously – round and saw me.

Then he leapt back and said, 'You'd better come out.'

'So I came. I pleaded with him not to say anything about me— But he said, "I must do my duty," and locked me in and fetched a policeman—'

Miss Davison's escapade was mentioned in the House of Commons yesterday. Mr Dudley Ward said he had just been informed that a lady was found in the crypt that morning. Presumably she was there in order to avoid the census. The only step he proposed to take at present was to inform the president of the local Government Board, so that she might be enumerated with the rest of the population.

The Times: 1 May 1911

The Anti-Suffrage League and the Women's Bill

Inquiries have already been addressed to 94,181 women municipal voters in 76 districts, and of these only 14,008, or less than 15 percent, have replied that they are in favour of the vote. On the other hand, 345,879, or over 38 per cent, have declared that they are opposed to woman suffrage and 37,071, or over 39 per cent, have sent no replies. These figures, it is urged, show that any M.P. who votes for Sir George Kemp's Bill will most probably be endeavouring to inflict a burden upon women which would be keenly resented by the majority of women in his constituency.

Letter to Millicent Fawcett

Stockholm, May 16, 1911

My Dear Mrs Fawcett,

Having heard through Mrs Catt [*President of the IWSA*] that your intention is to stay away from the Stockholm Convention next month, I take the liberty of writing to urge you in the name of the Swedish N.W.S.A. to give us the honour of your presence.

Your presence at the Stockholm convention would be of quite exceptional value to Sweden just now. No doubt you have heard of all the trouble we had had on account of the suffragette movement in England and especially after the raids last autumn. [*Public buildings had been denied them and subscriptions had fallen*]. We have done our best to explain to the Swedish public the difference between the National Union and the militants and also the difference of your methods. We have always quoted you, so that at present you are the best known of English suffragists in this country. Your words would have a higher authority to set right before the Swedish public all the misrepresentations that have taken place as regards the English women's suffrage movement. We need you, the convention needs you, Sweden needs you.

I am, dear Mrs Fawcett,

Yours very sincerely, Signe Bergman

A prominent Swedish suffragist, Signe Bergman was also one of IWSA's Secretaries.

Daily Telegraph: 19 June 1911

Immense International Procession:
The Oldest Militant Suffragette

The Great Procession of Women Suffragists on Saturday was a triumph. Forming up the Embankment, with about 100 bands, marching seven abreast at about two and a half miles per hour, it occupied two and a half hours in passing Hyde Park Corner—As the procession went along St James's-Street to Piccadilly, quite a royal salute was given to an old lady who occupied a seat on a balcony decorated with the Suffragist colours. Bannerettes were dipped in military fashion as the cavalcade marched past. Along the railing was the following inscription: 'The Oldest Militant Suffragette Greets You.' It was Mrs Wolstenholme Elmy, who, for nearly half a century, has been championing the cause with fine persistence and intelligence. She looked bright and hale, and seemed immensely gratified as she surveyed the vast column of women who now share her views and her still alert enthusiasm.

from Fire of Life

The Mare's Tale

On the occasion of the general procession of all the Suffrage Societies to the Albert Hall on June 17, 1911, I was asked to ride at the head of our Men's Political Unions bearing our standard, an enormous flag attached to a large and heavy pole. Happily, I was mounted on a wide and beautiful mare, who, though disturbed in mind by the shouts and cheering all the way from the Embankment, through St James's and along the length of Piccadilly, entered into the spirit of the occasion and marched with decorum; except that every now and then she turned round to wonder at the banner, and once while we were halted outside the Ritz Hotel, seeing within reach a little girl's straw hat surrounded with life-like daisies, festooned about the brim, she proceeded to bite at it for hay, costing me half-a-crown in compensation.

HENRY NEVINSON

from Memories of a Militant

Processional Secrets

During one of the big processions the idea was to have a white horse for a special feature. The day of the great event arrived. Only those behind the scenes saw the anxious looks on the faces of Miss Hambling, and my sister Jessie, one of the hardest workers at these times. She and Mr Lawrence seemed to me to have the greatest responsibility on these occasions. The news was whispered to me, the white horse had not appeared, and we were to start in fifteen minutes. We were noted for promptness. This reputation we were proud of, as few processionists ever get a good name in this respect. What was to be done? Miss Dunlop rushed off to our friend, and asked for the reason for the appearance of a brown horse instead of a white one. Profuse apologies from our friend, and a definite promise that a white horse should be round in a few minutes. Five minutes passed. Another taxi was hailed. Miss Dunlop, very angry at the mistake, rushed into the stables, and there was the brown horse practically finished. He was being whitewashed!

A<small>NNIE</small> K<small>ENNEY</small>

Votes For Women: 30 June 1911

Speech to the Writers' League:
Of Such Stuff Our Mothers Were!

I stood the other day before a boy's bookcase—all those stirring stories, those high adventures—rows on rows. Which among all these has anything to say about a girl's resourcefulness, a girl's endurance, a girl's courage? Have these qualities been lacking in our sex? We know the answer to that. These qualities were all there, but they had to wait for women themselves to celebrate them. I do not complain of men in this connection. We all write best about what we know best. And in a way, the untilled field is a great piece of good fortune for the women writers of the future—

Fellow-members of the league, you have such a field as never writers have known before. You are – in respect of life described fearlessly from the woman's standpoint – you are in that position for which Chaucer has been so envied by his brother poets, when they say he found the English language with the dew upon it. You find woman at the dawn. The Great Adventure is before her. Your Great Adventure is to report her worthily, so that her children's children, reading her story, shall be lifted up, proud and full of hope. Of such stuff our mothers were!

ELIZABETH ROBINS

from Myself a Player

An Iron Curtain

It is impossible to realise now the scorn which women who thought that they should be recognised as citizens drew on themselves from otherwise quite polite and sensible people. Managers, authors, pressmen became quite passionate in their resentment and, wise in their generation, did not associate themselves with this unpopular movement. Once when I went to see [Sir Beerbohm] Tree I had in my hand a book called 'The Soul of a Suffragette,' by W.L. Courtney. Tree picked it up and with a magnificent gesture of contempt flung it into the far corner of the room.

Despite the unpopularity of the cause, we had an Actresses'

Franchise League, and when the Women's Suffrage Deputation was received in Downing Street, as the only woman then in management, I was asked to represent our society. The whole affair was irresistibly comic because it was so tragic. We were just a very ordinary little group of women, received by the flunkeys as if we had a strange odour and had been temporarily released from the Zoo. We were ushered into a room where rows of chairs faced a door at the end. As we sat patiently waiting a head was thrust round the edge of the door and stared contemptuously at us; then the door was shut, but presently the other door, by which we had entered, was opened and again this hostile person surveyed us – Mrs Asquith, the wife of the Prime Minister!

I had a place in the front row of the deputation and was not only able to hear all the speeches made by the different leaders of the movement but to watch the effect on the Ministers. The speech that Mrs Despard made seemed to move Mr Lloyd George the most, though all were listened to with attention and each was admirable. But Mr Asquith was not interested for he had made up his mind. His expression made me think of that iron curtain which descends in the theatre to ensure that the stage is completely shut off from the auditorium. When the speeches were ended, after a few polite phrases he said that so long as he was Prime Minister he would give no facilities for the discussion of the Bill. A clear voice from the back of the room called: 'Then you must be moved.' With his thumbs in the armholes of his waistcoat and a spreading movement of his chest and abdomen, his head well thrown back, he said firmly, I will not say defiantly, 'Move me.' And, like a gentle refrain of the Litany, the deputation replied, 'We will.'

LENA ASHWELL

145

Actresses' Franchise League

Secretary's Annual Report 1911–12

Membership There are now about 700 names on our books i.e. nearly doubled in the last two years.

Provincial Branches Edinburgh continues to be the most energetic. It would be helpful towards the expansion of our provincial work, if members would before leaving London, send their touring lists to the office, in order that they might be put in touch with the Provincial Secretary, when there is one in any town they may visit.

Political Work During this year the A.F.L. has taken part in two deputations: (1) The Deputation to the Prime Minister of all the chief Suffrage Societies, which took place on November 17th and (2) a Deputation of Professional and Self-supporting women to Mr Ramsay MacDonald [*recently elected leader of the Labour Party*] on May 10th.

Annual Matinee A Grand Matinee organised by the A.F.L. on October 27th of which the special features were a new play by Laurence Housman 'Alice in Ganderland' and the pageant of the Leagues, resulted in a very delightful afternoon and a substantial addition to the funds.

An Assessment of the Present Situation

London, 10 Oct 1911

Dear Mrs Arncliffe Sennett,

I thank you for your kind letter. The present 'situation' is one full of hope & full of danger. Merely blackguarding the government won't advance us an inch. We have to recognize that the great mass of our 'supporters' in the House won't lose so much as a penny piece on a vote at an election for our fair sakes. We have suffered immensely from the lack of leadership within the House & Government & if anything we can do to engage Lloyd George so deeply that he can't get out – why I want to do it. To bang at him & break up his meetings seems to me the height (?) of folly & we shall do nothing to associate ourselves with those who take this line. This would prevent our action at the present juncture with the W.S.P.U.

I see no following for a 'desperate' course & I see no necessity either—I believe we shall succeed in getting women in the Reform Bill before it leaves the Commons & with the knowledge that once in they stay in. The only thing that may wreck such a result is the unwise recourse to violence in language & action. But I still hope we are strong enough to live it down. You say I am a fighter? In a sense that is true. But I never fight for the sake of fighting. I want the vote for women & I will go the best way I can see to get it.

Yours truly

H.M. Swanwick

This is a curious letter. Unless is was mis-dated, both Maud Arncliffe Sennett and Helena Swanwick appear to have had prior knowledge of the 'Reform Bill' which came as a bombshell to the majority of activists, including the WSPU leaders. It was not until 7 November 1911 that Mr Asquith announced that in the next session of Parliament the Government would introduce a Manhood Suffrage Bill which would replace the proliferation of voting qualifications with a single residential qualification. The Bill would apply to adult males but would be drafted so as to admit amendments to include women, should Parliament so desire. On 17 November Asquith received the deputation from nine suffrage societies including the Actresses' Franchise League. While making it clear that women's suffrage would not become a government measure while he was Prime Minister, he insisted that the Manhood Suffrage Reform Bill would not affect the chances of the Private Member's Conciliation Bill. Few believed him, even fewer after Lloyd George's performance at Bath.

from I Have Been Young

He [Lloyd George] was to speak at a great Liberal rally at Bath on November 24, and he asked me to come round and let him run over his speech with me. I did so, and it was one of the queerest experiences. The little man walked up and down spouting passages of the speech he intended to make.

'We have torpedoed the Conciliation Bill!' he cried

I protested, 'No, no. You mustn't say that!'

He cocked an eye. 'Why not? I rather like the phrase.'

'Well, don't you see that if you boast of having torpedoed the bill for which all the suffragists have been working for two years, it will not exactly endear you to them?'

'Perhaps not. But it's true.'

'Well, our people won't stand it.'

'Very well,' he replied sadly. 'I won't say it.'

I saw young [Victor] Duval and tried to get from him an undertaking not to interrupt that meeting. (Women were being rigorously excluded from Liberal meetings, and a body of men had taken on the work of interruption.) I failed. Mr Lloyd George was interrupted a good deal at Bath and he made the censored statement, 'We have torpedoed the Conciliation Bill.'

It is worth while comparing the above records, made at the time, in private letters sent daily to my husband, with Mr Lloyd George's own account of things. In the private papers of Mr C.P.

Scott [*editor of the Manchester Guardian*] there is an entry dated December 2, 1911, in which he describes a talk about women's suffrage with Mr Lloyd George:

> Incidentally he (Ll.G) mentioned that the unlucky phrase about 'torpedoing' the Conciliation Bill was an impromptu – 'It wasn't even in my notes – the speech was almost unprepared.'

It may not have been 'in his notes', because I had done what I could to expunge it, but unprepared? Well, few of us can have such a full dress-rehearsal for our speeches as Mr. Lloyd George had on that occasion.

HELENA SWANWICK

Suffragette Sing-Song

The Conciliation Bill

Taffy is a minister: aided by his chief
Taffy has betrayed us, brought our cause to grief.
We backed up Taffy's bill, helped him tax the rich,
Taffy sneered at our bill, queered our little pitch.
Taffy's got a new bill, sure to cause a split.
What's become of our bill? Why he's torpedoed it.

PUBLISHED BY THE NATIONAL LEAGUE FOR OPPOSING WOMEN'S SUFFRAGE

The WSPU did not wait for Lloyd (Taffy) George's speech. On 21 November while Emmeline Pethick-Lawrence led a march from Caxton Hall to the House of Commons, other WSPU members

smashed windows, this time not only of Government offices but of hostile newspapers, men's clubs, and department stores. 220 were arrested, plus 3 male activists. Emily Wilding Davison's arson activities were not sanctioned by Clement's Inn and did not initially meet with approval.

from The Suffragette Movement

On December 15th (1911) occurred a militant incident of a new type. Emily Wilding Davison was arrested in the act of thrusting into a pillar-box a piece of linen, alight and saturated with paraffin. She had already set fire to several other boxes, even calling a constable to arrest her, and had previously announced her intention to the Press. She was committed for trial and sentenced to six months' imprisonment.

SYLVIA PANKHURST

A Letter to Comrades

Longhorsley, Northumberland,
Dec 23 1911

My Dear comrades, Miss Carwin & Miss Nelligan

Many many thanks for the beautiful flowers which gave me your welcome at my diggings. They gave me much pleasure! You have read what has happened to me! Fancy my being worth £1000! I am amazed! It is a grand advertisement for the cause, isn't it? I came away last night to my mother, who is delighted to have me, & now quite resigned to the after-results. You know it is the Old Bailey at which I have to appear! That is rather fine, isn't it? I wonder if either of you can be there. One thing, it has given them a good fright. I wish you both a right merry time!

With love and thanks,

Yours in the Cause,

Emily Wilding Davison

from The Militant Suffrage Movement

I believed in it, worked in it, suffered in it, and rejoiced in it, and I have been disillusioned. I do not believe in votes for women as a panacea of all evils. I do not believe that any and every interest and consideration and principle should be sacrificed to the immediate getting of any measure of suffrage legislation—I do not believe that woman is the superior of man any more than I believe that she is his inferior. Pretensions of sex-superiority are like bad coins, they are just as bad whichever face is turned up—

I am setting out to condemn the militant suffrage movement, but not to condemn militancy, for I shall be a militant rebel to the end of my days. I am setting out to expose the tone and tactics of the Women's Social and Political Union and the suicidal weakness of the Women's Freedom League. I have served in both these societies, have shared the burdens of the early days in both, have had my part in their successes and in their failures, and now I find both inadequate, fallen from a high estate full of promise to narrowness and incapacity—What I condemn in militant tactics is the small pettiness, the crooked course, the double shuffle between revolution and injured innocence, the playing for effects and not for results—These are the things by which militancy has been degraded from revolution into political chicanery; these are the means by which it has been led to perjure its soul—I am not at all concerned that the militant movement has outraged convention, that it has shocked self-satisfied and blind benevolence;

it is not for convention that I plead. The crime of the militant suffrage movement in my eyes is that it is not real, that it is itself dangerously and determinedly conventional—Other movements have failed in rebellion, but it has been left to this woman's movement to ape rebellion while belittling and abusing it. Other rebellions have failed; this movement has failed rebellion.

The Freedom League Failure

We had broken up the original militant body (the WSPU) because such action was forced upon us—We started out with eyes open, stronger in some ways because of our disillusionment, to make the militant movement what it ought to be—I have to admit frankly that we have failed. There are some half a hundred good reasons that can be urged in excuse of this fact, but none in denial of it—At first brave efforts were made to grapple with the almost insuperable difficulties, and some sturdy fighting has been kept up to this time, but the original hope of the seceders has long vanished, and the Freedom League has dropped steadily to a position of mediocrity—I have been called the first traitor—but I am not the first to leave the movement discouraged. I am but the last of a long line of women who have had to do the same—The Freedom League had its opportunity, and lost it. It tied its own hands and committed political suicide—

There was little to be expected from a society that commenced its separate existence by making a free gift of the funds, name, prestige, and achievements, which had been acquired by the efforts of all combined, to the section from which it had to secede on a matter of principle—The movement next committed itself to a course that meant general impotence—its speakers and writers were debarred from any utterance that might be construed as a reflection upon Mrs Pankhurst's organisation. Under such restraint the League lost its distinctive character almost before it acquired it, and became a mere echo of the larger group. One example of the conditions which prevail will suffice.

The Tax-Resistance Campaign was organised first by the Freedom League, was regarded with scant respect by its members, and in the course of over three years only about one hundred women took this line of protest against disenfranchisement. But when some months ago the Social and Political Union declared that 'the time has now come for women to refuse to pay taxes' the policy was hailed with acclamation as a new and brilliant stroke of genius. A few words of gentle reminder that the policy had been applied for three years by the Freedom League, while individual women had resisted taxation since the early seventies, and that a special Tax-Resistance League formed with Freedom League assistance now existed, was commented upon as ungenerous by our own members—

We were committed to submit to all criticism and to utter none—we could only appear as bad seconds in the game. It is astonishing to me now that we managed to make any militant changes at all.

TERESA BILLINGTON-GREIG

153

1912–1914

The argument of the broken pane of glass is the most valuable argument in modern politics

Emmeline Pankhurst

If it had been the Prime Minister's intention to enrage every woman suffragist to the point of frenzy, he could not have acted with greater perspicacity

Millicent Garrett Fawcett

The 'torpedoing' of the Conciliation Bill was for the Pankhursts the final, if not at all unexpected, betrayal. In February 1912 Mrs Pankhurst made her famous pronouncement about 'the argument of the broken pane of glass', which her disciples proceeded to implement. Millicent Fawcett and the NUWSS were less than pleased with the torpedoing, but for them all was not yet lost. Mr Asquith had said the Reform Bill could be amended to include women and a Conciliation Bill remained in the pipeline. But at the end of March the latter Bill's second reading – virtually the same as had passed with a large majority the previous year – was defeated by fourteen votes. MPs' reaction against WSPU violence came top of the list of the reasons why. There were others. An Irish Home Rule Bill bitterly opposed by Ulster and Tory Unionists had just been introduced. Fearing that Asquith might be pushed into resignation over the suffrage issue which would be a disaster for them, the Irish Nationalists voted against the Bill. And more than half the Labour MPs were engaged with the miners' strike up north.

What Line Should We Take Now?

London, Jan 22–1912

My Dear Mrs Fawcett,

I have just had a long conversation on the telephone with Mr Brailsford. He was fresh from an encounter with Mrs Pankhurst whom he found even more intransigent than the others. He says any idea of a conference is absolutely out of the question. Mrs P. accuses him of being a traitor, regrets ever having touched the Conciliation Bill & refuses to look at anything except an equal suffrage bill for men and women introduced by the Govt.— Brailsford telephoned in despair—He says his mind is in utter confusion, he can't think what line to take & he is coming into the office (probably) at 4 pm tomorrow. Could you possibly come down then?

Yours v. sincerely,

K.D. Courtney

Kathleen Courtney had just been elected the NUWSS Hon. Sec. after a successful stint with the North of England Society in Manchester.

Daily Mirror: 15 January 1912

'No Obey Wedding'

Is a woman at liberty to refrain from pledging herself to 'obey' her husband during the marriage service, as performed according to the rites of the Church of England? Miss Una Stratford Dugdale, daughter of Commander Dugdale, and niece of Viscount Peel, did not repeat after the clergyman the word 'obey' at the ceremony of marriage between her and Mr Victor Duval, at the Chapel Royal, Savoy, on Saturday—

It had been announced on Friday that the Chaplain of the Chapel Royal, the Rev. High Chapman, would himself omit the words 'and to obey', in deference to the wishes of the bride and bridegroom—Miss Dugdale is a member of the Women's Social and Political Union. Mr Duval is secretary of the Men's Political Union for Women's Enfranchisement. But a dramatic surprise awaited the congregation on Saturday when Mr Chapman advanced to the communion steps and said:

> Before the commencement of the service I wish to state that, owing to the publicity given to it by the Press, I have been contacted at the last moment to take advice as to the legality of a wedding with the omission of certain words which may not commend themselves to those concerned. Having been informed that the omission of those words is sufficient to render its validity at least doubtful, more especially in a royal chapel which belongs exclusively to the King, we have agreed among ourselves to read the service throughout as an act of loyalty to His Majesty, while we sincerely hope that before long there may be an amended form of service which shall render it possible for Christian people to receive the blessings of the Church without hurt to their susceptibilities—

It was at once apparent from their demeanour that the bride and bridegroom had at the last moment acquiesced in the chaplain's decision. Mr Chapman made no pause at the critical moment longer than was necessary for the bride to say the words: 'And to obey', which she did not utter.

Una Dugdale's refusal provided an alternative topic of outraged condemnation. Its revolutionary nature may be difficult for the young to comprehend.

The Standard: 14 February 1912

The Case of Mr Ball: Removal from Colney Hatch

It will be remembered that Mr Ball was sentenced on December 22 last to two months' imprisonment for breaking with a stone two windows at the Home Office. In prison he demanded treatment accorded to suffrage prisoners under Mr Winston Churchill's regulations, and was refused. He accordingly adopted the hunger strike. The authorities proceeded to feed him by force, the operation being performed twice a day. This was continued for five and a half weeks. He was also on two occasions sent to the punishment cell.

Meanwhile, Mrs Ball, at the suggestion of a friend, endeavoured to send in a doctor connected with an insurance society in order that her husband's life might be insured. Permission for the doctor to come in was refused, and Mrs Ball was informed that she would not be permitted to see him, or write to him, or have a letter from him during the whole of his imprisonment.

Subsequently, in reply to a further letter, Mrs Ball was informed that he was 'in his usual health'. That was about a fortnight ago. The first intimation she had of his present condition was on Monday morning, when she received a curt letter from the governor to the effect that her husband was to be certified insane that very day.

Though Mrs Ball lost no time in taking steps to obtain admission to her husband, she was too late, and found that the certificate had already been granted and Mr Ball had been removed to Colney Hatch. She at once proceeded to the asylum, where she gained access to her husband, who told of the treatment to which he had been subjected in Holloway.

Yesterday Mrs Ball succeeded by persevering efforts in securing the transference of her husband from the pauper side of the institution to the paying side, and subsequently on visiting the asylum she was able to obtain the custody of her husband herself. Mr Ball is in a very emaciated condition, but it is hoped that with care and attention his state of health will improve.

Anti-Suffrage Rally

Albert Hall, London: 28 February 1912

Lord Curzon

—Now, it is always good to turn to other countries, even small countries, and see what they are doing there. Well, now, in Norway, a very democratic country, the women obtained the vote in 1906 (some cheers and laughter)—They also obtained the right to sit in parliament—Were they content with this? Not a bit. They at once commenced an agitation, and so successful has it been that already every office in Norway is open to them, with certain notable exceptions. They are not yet allowed to be Cabinet Ministers, but it is generally recognised that this is the first barrier that will go, because you can hardly have a Parliament open to women and the Cabinet reserved to men (cheers).

Secondly, female clergymen are not yet allowed in Norway (laughter) but already an agitation is springing up. The third category is that of consuls and diplomatists and this for the reason that each of us will understand very well, that the Norwegian Government is rather afraid that female Consuls and Ministers might somewhat diminish their respect in foreign lands. And the last category from which women are at present excluded is that of military commanders (laughter).

Yet, strange as it may seem, there is a party in Norway which is arguing the analogy of Joan of Arc (laughter)—Well now, you may think this is a joke, but I assure you it is solemn fact. What has happened, is happening, in Norway would ultimately happen here (applause).

Miss Violet Markham

—Until you repeal Nature's salic law the average political experience of the average women is bound to be less than that of the average man—If the work of the Imperial Parliament belongs more naturally to men, the work of local government, with its splendid opportunities for civic betterment and the uplifting of the race, belongs more naturally to women (applause)—Yet, while suffragists tramp the streets and smash windows, what do we find? This great field of equal rights and opportunities with men is practically neglected (hear, hear).

Think of it, in the length and breadth of the United Kingdom, there are only 21 women elected to town councils, only three on county councils, and you have no fewer than 232 boards of guardians without a woman on them (applause). These figures are the most ironical commentary, the most crushing condemnation of the whole suffrage agitation (cheers)—

The ugly scramble for place and power for the loaves and fishes of preferment and offices – that is all part and parcel of these public functions of men some women are anxious to assume. We say this is a bad game when played by men; it would be an abominable game if played by women.—We hold that it is through the faithful fulfilment of duty that woman will arrive at a true conception of her place in the body politic (loud cheers).

The Antis

Mrs Frederic Harrison to Lord Curzon 1912

'Our society must in the main depend on women: women have to destroy a women's movement.'

Lord Cromer to Lord Curzon 1912

'I suffer tortures from dyspepsia and I really have not the health, strength, youth, or may I add the temper to go on dealing with these infernal women.'

Mrs Humphry Ward to Frederic Harrison 1913

'I don't believe there is a fear of Woman Suffrage as practical politics for some years to come – though no doubt the horrid fight will have to be kept up.'

Janet Courtney

'It was our fate, as antis, to attract all the ultra-feminine and the ladylike incompetents.'

Militant Memories

Window Smashing 1912: 'As though I was playing hockey'

From the Town Mall Square in Portsmouth I jumped on a bike and went with a friend to the beach at Southsea and sat on the beach and filled my pockets with pebbles, great big stones you could call them, the idea being that I should take those in my pockets to London and if whatever we had to use in London ran out, I would always have something to fall back on.

I was given the top of Villiers Street. To fill in time I went over and bought a bunch of violets, then I bought an evening paper, and then I looked at the clock and it was a quarter to six, and that was my moment.

In my right hand I had a hammer, my pockets of my raincoat

were bulging with pebbles, and I went over to the corner shop. There were two people looking at rings, a young boy and girl. I waited, they moved and then – bang went my hammer, and it was a great moment for me because I was so afraid that the hammer would hook, and hook me into the glass and stop me doing any more. But I found, by taking my hammer broadside, that that didn't happen at all; it came back with me, and so on I went. And I walked down the Strand as though I was playing hockey, and I just boldly went on like that, and I did at least nine windows.

CHARLOTTE (CHARLIE) MARSH

Daily News: 9 March 1912

Broken Windows – And after

There has been an undoubted crisis in the Suffrage movement since last Friday, caused by the intense indignation naturally aroused by the window-smashing of a small group of so-called Suffragettes on that day and subsequently—The errors of the Suffragists are the meat and drink of the anti-suffragists—Their joy is so hysterical that they have given rein to their fancy and are circulating many inventions. For instance, I read in the evening paper: 'Mrs Fawcett is in despair.'—I knew I was not in despair, and had never uttered syllable to justify anyone saying I was—

Some suffragists, not a very numerous group, have temporarily lost faith in all human honour, and are attempting to grasp by violence what should be yielded to the growing conviction that our demand is based on justice and common sense—We [the NUWSS] have made immense progress. The number of our societies which was 211 a year ago is now 365. The number of our subscribing members has run up in the same interval from 21,000 to 30,000. There is no cause for despair; there is every cause for confidence and hope—

Mrs Henry Fawcett LL.D.

from The Suffragette Movement

On March 5th the police appeared at Clement's Inn and arrested the Pethick-Lawrences on warrants charging them with conspiracy 'to incite certain persons to commit malicious damage to property'; Mrs Pankhurst and Mrs Tuke [*Mabel Tuke, the WSPU's Hon. Sec.*], who were already in prison, were also named in the charge. There was a warrant too, for the arrest of Christabel, but she was absent from the Inn. When, late that night, she learnt what had occurred, she determined to escape. Making no other attempt at disguise than to substitute a close-fitting pink straw hat for the large floppy one she habitually wore she crossed to Paris next day and took rooms there, styling herself 'Miss Amy Richards'.

Sylvia Pankhurst

The Standard: 8 March 1912

Miss Pankhurst Still at Large

For two days now Miss Christabel Pankhurst has played hide-and-seek with a hundred detectives. It has been tiring work – for the detectives. All through Wednesday night they crouched in obscure corners at Clement's Inn waiting, hoping, conspiring against this lady 'wanted' for alleged conspiracy. They hobnobbed with night watchmen near an hotel in Holborn, shivered on the quay at Dover and Newhaven, lounged about the railway stations—No will-o'-the-wisp ever flitted over a wider area with such swiftness as did their 'wanted' organiser. She was seen in Dover at precisely the same moment as she was recognised in Dieppe; was observed walking down The Strand yesterday morning hiding her eyes behind blue spectacles, just as she was expected to be in a flat at Chelsea. From Hampstead came the news at midday that she was in a house in Gainsborough-gardens, and detectives were then watching another house in Notting Hill.

The jingle from Baroness Orczy's popular novel The Scarlet Pimpernel *(1905) was amended to: 'They seek her here, They seek her there, That d—d elusive Christabel'.*

Pinner Gazette: 4 May 1912

Mrs Terrero: The Hunger Strike

Our representative has received the following letter from Mr Terrero, which is of local interest, and speaks for itself:

'When Mrs Terrero was sentenced on March 27th to four months imprisonment for some cracked glass, having in addition been 25 days in Holloway, I was informed officially I was not to see her, to write or receive a letter, for two months, and no food to be sent in. This seemed a needlessly cruel and vindictive, not to say mean, deprivation of the privileges accorded under the Churchill regulations, and for which the women fought so hard and suffered so severely a few years ago. As a natural consequence, after vainly petitioning for some weeks, the hunger strike was started both at Aylesbury and Holloway, with the prompt result that substantial concessions were granted. Our authorities, though deaf to justice and fair play, are thus shown to be squeezable when threatened with the public indignation likely to made manifest if any of these splendid women die in prison—

I may now visit Mrs Terrero once a month, write and receive a letter once a fortnight, and send food in weekly. I saw her last Friday, and grieve to say she was weak and ailing after four days' fast and forcible feeding, but proud of her victory won, and full of quiet courage and determination as regards the future. If the Home Secretary thinks that the spirit of such women is to be broken by severity and brutality he is lamentably ignorant of the material with which he has to deal and Mrs Terrero is but one of hundreds prepared to suffer likewise for the cause, which to them is what their religion was to the Christian martyrs.'

from The Suffragette Movement

Mrs Pankhurst and the Pethick-Lawrences at the Old Bailey

On May 15th began the conspiracy trial—The defendants made no denial of the changes; the burden of their argument was that the Government had dealt falsely with the Votes for Women Cause. Accepting the charges as they did, the hostile speech of Justice Coleridge was not necessary to secure a conviction. Party feeling in a Judge is unbecoming. The jury displayed a more generous spirit. While finding the defendants guilty, they added:

> We desire unanimously to express the hope that taking
> into consideration the undoubtedly pure motive that
> underlie the agitation which has led to this trial, you will
> be pleased to exercise the utmost leniency in dealing with
> the case.

The Judge pronounced sentence of nine months' imprisonment, and refused, in harsh terms, the application of the prisoners to be treated as First Class misdemeanants.

SYLVIA PANKHURST

Aware of the Pethick-Lawrences' wealth, the judge also ordered that they pay the costs of the prosecution. The WSPU then announced that unless Mrs Pankhurst and the Pethick-Lawrences, and the window-smashers already on hunger strike and being forcibly fed, were transferred to the First Division the leaders would join them. On 19 June they did, though forcible feeding was one horror to which Mrs Pankhurst was never subjected. After a huge protest by 100+ British MPs and such persons as Marie Curie (who had just been awarded the Nobel Prize for Chemistry), the French socialist Jean Jaurès, authors Romain Rolland and Upton Sinclair, the leaders were transferred to the First Division and by early July the suffragette prisoners had been released. Emily Wilding Davison's attempted martyrdom was part of the uproar.

Daily Herald: 4 July 1912

Desperate Leap: One Big Tragedy to Save Others

As a desperate protest against the indignities suffered by herself and others while in prison, Miss Emily Wilding Davison threw herself down the staircase. What actually happened is given below in Miss Davison's own words:

'We decided that most of us would barricade our cells after they had been cleaned out. At ten o'clock on Saturday a regular siege took place in Holloway. On all sides one heard crowbars, blocks and wedges being used; men battering on doors with all their might—My turn came, and my door was forced open with crowbars. I protested loudly that I would not be fed by the junior doctor, and tried to dart into the passage. Then I was seized by about five wardresses, bound into a chair, still protesting, and they accomplished their purpose.

'In my mind was the thought that some desperate protest must be made to put a stop to the hideous torture. As soon as I could get out I climbed on to the railing and threw myself on to the wire-netting, a distance of between 20ft to 30ft. The idea in my mind was that one big tragedy might save many others; but the netting prevented any severe injury. Quite deliberately I walked upstairs, and threw myself from the top on to the iron staircase. If I had been successful I should undoubtedly have been killed—but I caught once more on the netting.

'I realised that there was only one chance left, and that was to haul myself with the greatest force I could summon from the netting on to the staircase. I heard someone saying, 'No surrender!' and threw myself forward on my head with all my might. I knew nothing more except a fearful thud on my head. When I recovered consciousness it was to a sense of acute agony.

'That first night was one of misery—I was left alone until about two o'clock, when a specialist came in with the prison doctors. He thoroughly examined me. To my amazement, the doctors came to forcibly feed me that afternoon, in spite of the torture it caused me.'

Daily Mirror: 20 July 1912

Fire and Petrol in Irish Theatre

Extraordinary revelations of an alleged gunpowder plot by suffragettes to mark the visit of the Prime Minister were made at Dublin Police Court yesterday. Enormous public interest was taken in the case when four women appeared before Mr Macinerney viz:-

Gladys Evans, Muswell Hill, London N
Mary Leigh (thirty-three) address refused
Lizzie Baker, 66, Chatham-street, Stockport
Mabel Capper (twenty-three), 21 Oxford-street, Manchester

—The police looked upon this case as the most dastardly out-rage—Sergeant Cooper, of the 2nd Connaught Rangers, said that, as he was leaving the theatre, he saw fire in front of the cine-matograph box. There was petrol on the carpet, and a woman was striking matches and throwing them down—A woman opened the door of the cinematograph box and threw matches into the interior. He closed with her, and in the struggle they fell down-stairs together. The woman said: 'This is only just the start of it. There will be more explosions in the second house.' Afterwards a canister, which smelt of gunpowder, was found near the scene of the explosion—

John O'Brien, the chief marshal of the procession on Thursday night, then gave evidence of the throwing of the hatchet at the carriage containing the Premier, Mrs Asquith, Mr John Redmond [*the Irish Nationlist leader*] and the Lord Mayor. As the carriage passed along O'Connell-street Mary Leigh rushed towards the carriage and fired something, he could not say what. She clung to the carriage, and when the witness tried to remove her she bit him on the face for all she was worth (Laughter)—Mr O'Brien took her away from the carriage after a struggle, during which she tore both the epaulettes from his coat (Renewed laughter). He then handed her over to two men. The thing she threw struck Mr Redmond on the ear. Afterwards he found it was a hatchet—

Crowds Set Upon Women

Some suffragettes who attempted to parade in the thronged streets were set upon by the populace. Ultimately they took refuge in tramway-cars and the General Post Office, the windows of which were smashed a few weeks ago. An attempt was made to throw the women in the Liffey, but this was prevented by a police official's appeal to the crowd to be 'Irishmen'.

Daily Mirror: 8 August 1912

Dublin Theatre Fire: Five Years for Two Suffragettes

For the first time in the history of the English suffragette movement two militant women were sentenced yesterday to penal servitude – five years each. They were Miss Gladys Evans of Muswell Hill, London, and Mrs Mary Leigh, and they had been found guilty by a Dublin jury of setting fire to the Theatre Royal during Mr Asquith's visit—A defiant speech from the dock was made by Mrs Leigh, who asserted that she would fight: 'I will put my back against the wall and nothing will bring me to submission.'

In the case of the two other suffragettes who were also indicted in connection with the Dublin outrages, Miss Lizzie Baker, of Stockport, pleaded guilty to damaging property and was sentenced to seven months' imprisonment, while the case against Miss Mabel Capper, of Manchester, was withdrawn and she was discharged.

After hunger strikes and forcible feeding Evans and Leigh were released on licences and never served the rest of their sentences.

Press Cutting: 6 September 1912

Battle with Women at Eisteddfod

WREXHAM, Sept 5 – There were wild scenes at the Welsh National Eisteddfod this afternoon, when suffragettes and male supporters continually interrupted Mr Lloyd George in his address to the meeting. When the Chancellor rose to make his speech there must have been fully 15,000 people in the pavilion and nearly as many outside. Hardly had he opened his mouth ere a woman jumped up, and shouted out: 'Why don't you give women their rights?'

She was removed, but not easily, for it took the united efforts of twelve police-constables to get her to a small room at the back of the hall. When Mr Lloyd George attempted to resume another woman shouted out: 'Votes for women.' She was also removed, and in the process was roughly handled by the audience— After a male supporter, with one eye closed and mouth cut, had been taken out Mr Lloyd George made another attempt to speak, only to be interrupted by a woman, who called out: 'How dare you forcibly feed women!'

To quieten the meeting, on the suggestion of the Bishop of St Asaph, the Welsh National Anthem was then played by the band, the huge audience joining in. No sooner, however, had the Chancellor resumed than a man, and directly afterwards a woman, had to be removed. With each removal the work of the police grew more difficult, for by this time the crowd had become thoroughly incensed. The climax was reached when the police and stewards had brought down yet another woman from the platform. As she was being led towards the exit two men managed to reach her. They tore off her hat and dragged handfuls of hair from her head.—

The trouble of those who interrupted, however, did not end with their ejection, for as they were pushed through the doors they came in for some very rough handling by a large crowd outside. Particularly unfortunate was the plight of one of the men ejected— He was stripped almost naked, bruised from head to foot, and seemed to have been kicked and struck on almost every part of his body.

The scenes at Llanystymdwy a week later, when Lloyd George was interrupted on his home ground, were even worse.

Frederick Pethick-Lawrence's account of his and his wife Emmeline's ousting from the WSPU covers the period from their release from prison in July 1912, their summer visit to Canada, and their return to England in the autumn, by which time Christabel Pankhurst's presence in Paris had been made public, a move which informed the membership that their exiled leader remained in control.

from Fate Has Been Kind

After our release from prison and the hunger-strike, Emmeline and I rested for a short time at our country house and then set out to spend a fortnight with a Swiss friend—We broke the journey in Boulogne to have a talk with Mrs Pankhurst and Christabel, who came from Paris to join us.—

I had always had a very high opinion of Christabel's political genius. She had had in my view an almost uncanny instinct for diagnosing public opinion and for choosing a line of action that would make the greatest appeal to it. But I did not feel the same about her present attitude. It seemed to me that her impressions, obtained for the most part second-hand, did not fully accord with the facts—I had always been in the habit of telling Christabel what I thought even when I differed from her, and I did not hesitate to do so now—

I took the view that the window-smashing raid had aroused a new popular opposition, because it was for the first time an attack on private property; and that therefore before it was repeated, still more before graver acts of violence were committed, there was need for a sustained educational campaign to make the public understand the reasons for such extreme courses. I took it for granted that she herself would return to London and resume her leadership of the campaign. This would place the Government in the awkward predicament of having to choose between repeating the conspiracy trial in her case, or of declining the challenge to do so. Whichever course they adopted would enhance her position and that of the W.S.P.U.

Christabel took the view that such popular opposition as there might be was not essentially different from that which had over and over again manifested itself when other new forms of militancy had been inaugurated, and that the right method of overcoming it was to repeat and intensify the attack in the early autumn. The suffragette motto that 'deeds speak louder than words' would thus be once more exemplified—it was necessary that she herself should remain outside the reach of the Government, so that whatever happened she might be in a position to continue to direct it.

Our discussion became somewhat heated, and attracted the attention of Mrs Pankhurst—(who) as a born rebel, was even more emphatic than Christabel that the time had come to take sterner measures. She appeared to resent the fact that I had even ventured to question the wisdom of her daughter's policy—We did not pursue the matter further. Next morning, after a friendly talk with Christabel, we departed for Switzerland.

When we returned to England it was the political dead season. We therefore decided to prolong our holiday by paying a visit to Emmeline's brother, who was an engineer in Victoria, British Columbia—It will be remembered that, in passing sentence upon us at the Old Bailey, Lord Coleridge had further ordered us to pay the costs of the prosecution. This I had not done, and while we were still on the American continent we learnt that the Government—had placed bailiffs in my house at Holmwood. [*The Pethick-Lawrences were brought close to bankruptcy, though friends brought treasured possessions at the enforced sale.*] We also received a letter from Mrs Pankhurst, suggesting to us that we remain in Canada—That would set her free to carry out her revolutionary programme without giving the Government the opportunity of attacking my private fortune. Emmeline, after consulting with me, wrote immediately declining this proposal, and we continued our journey to England.

It was a strange homecoming. Though our flat in Clement's Inn remained to us, the landlords had resumed possession of all the offices there which I had taken for the suffragettes. When we went across to the new headquarters of the Union at Lincoln House in Kingsway, we found that no rooms had been definitely allotted to my wife or myself. When we traversed the passages, conversations abruptly terminated as we approached. Next day Mrs Pankhurst invited us to her room. She then told us that she had decided to sever our connection with the W.S.P.U.

This announcement was shattering—Even now we found it difficult to believe that Christabel was a party to it. But Mrs Pankhurst was resolute. In order to settle the matter once and for all, she invited us to meet her a few evenings later at a house in the west of London, and when we arrived at the appointed rendezvous we found Christabel there in person! She had risked detection in crossing to England in order to convince us that she and her mother were absolutely united in this matter.

We saw, then, that the breach between ourselves and the Pankhursts was complete and irrevocable. There was, further, no appeal against our exclusion from the W.S.P.U. Mrs Pankhurst was the acknowledged autocrat of the Union. We had ourselves supported her in acquiring this position several years previously; we could not dispute it now. It was, of course, open to us to drag the issue into public controversy—We refused to pull down, in this, way, stone by stone, the edifice which we had with such care and at such cost assisted to build up.

The last scene of this drama, like the first, was enacted in Boulogne. There, in a little hotel facing the quay, the four of us drew up the terms of our separation. The newspaper 'Votes for Women' reverted to my wife and myself. The whole of the rest of the organisation, including the Woman's Press, remained under the control of the Pankhursts—

FREDERICK PETHICK-LAWRENCE

from My Part in a Changing World

There was something quite ruthless about Mrs Pankhurst and Christabel where human relationship was concerned. This ruthlessness was shown not only to us but to many others—Men and women of destiny are like that—Thus in October, 1912, my direct participation in the militant movement came to an end. The cleavage was final and complete. From that time forward I never saw or heard from Mrs Pankhurst again, and Christabel, who had shared our family life, became a complete stranger. The Pankhursts did nothing by halves!

EMMELINE PETHICK-LAWRENCE

Albert Hall London: 17 October 1912
Speech By Emmeline Pankhurst

When I began this militant campaign I was a Poor Law Guardian, and it was my duty to go through a workhouse infirmary, and never shall I forget seeing a little girl of thirteen lying in bed

176

playing with a doll—I was told she was on the eve of becoming a mother, and she was infected with a loathsome disease, and on the point of bringing, no doubt, a diseased child into the world. Was not that enough to make me a Militant Suffragette?—We women Suffragists have a great mission – the greatest mission the world has ever known. It is to free half the human race, and through that freedom to save the rest—And my last word to the Government: I incite this meeting to rebellion. I say to the Government: You have not dared to take the leaders of Ulster for their incitement to rebellion, take me if you dare.

Ulster Protestants were already threatening armed rebellion should Irish Home Rule be implemented. The contrast between the Government's ambivalent treatment of the gun-running Ulstermen and the Pankhurst militants became a favourite theme.

Petition for the Pethick-Lawrences

Feb. 1st 1913

Dear Madam,

We should be much obliged if those of your members will sign this Petition who feel that the retirement of Mr & Mrs Pethick-Lawrence is an irreparable loss to the Union, and that one pair of shoulders should not and cannot bear the great weight of responsibility resting on them in this crisis of the Women's Movement.

We wish to present the Petition to Mrs Pankhurst at the earliest possible date, by an influential Deputation. The Deputation will also point out that not one valid reason for the dismissal of Mr & Mrs Pethick-Lawrence has been given to the members of the Union. The Petition is an effort after unity and in no sense to cause trouble or annoyance to Mrs Pankhurst. The Union is terribly weakened by this heartbreaking split, at a time when all its strength is needed; therefore we feel on every account that this step is imperative. We shall be glad to receive the Petition back within ten days at latest.

Truly yours,

Anna K. MacLeod

The unknown Anna MacLeod's petition with its accurate résumé of the situation had no effect on Mrs Pankhurst. Scores of the more questioning, independent-minded women simply resigned from the WSPU. Many of the remaining members increasingly regarded Mrs Pankhurst and Christabel as infallible leaders of a holy war – against whom was not always clear. While the WSPU shed members and ratched up the violence, the Reform Bill continued on its way through the House of Commons and the NUWSS had considerable success with its latest campaign. In January 1912 the Labour Party had become the first political party to commit itself to women's suffrage. Henry Brailsford suggested a NUWSS/Labour alliance to put pressure on the Government. Herself a lifelong Liberal, Millicent Fawcett did not object to what she saw as a sensible, if temporary measure. As the NUWSS Hon. Sec. Kathleen Courtney entered into formal negotiations with the Labour Party and in May 1912 a special council meeting ratified an Election Fighting Fund (EFF). The Resolutions show the extent of the support for the EFF, though in a supposedly non-party political organisation all were initially careful not to mention the word 'Labour'. During 1912 the NUWSS campaigned in four by-elections. In three previously Liberal seats the Labour vote doubled and the Tory was returned, which made the Government a little more dependent on Labour backing. What happened to George Lansbury when backed by the post-split WSPU, rather than the revitalised NUWSS, is instructive.

from The Suffragette Movement

George Lansbury and the Bromley and Bow By-election

Lansbury spoke at the usual W.S.P.U. 'At Home' in the London
Pavilion, and there announced his intention to resign his seat in
support of what he then deemed '*the* movement in the world'
and 'the biggest fight socially that is going on in our country.'
Only after making this public declaration, which was immediately
reported in the Press, did he consult his sponsors, the Poplar
Labour Party, a fact which caused great dissatisfaction amongst its
members, and especially its officials—

The election having been called it was important for Suffragists
of all schools that it should be won. Lansbury was in close accord
with the W.S.P.U.—The proper course for the W.S.P.U. was to
place itself in contact with and work under the local Labour Party
which was responsible for Lansbury's candidature. The proper
course for the Labour Party was to assume control of the campaign, putting the W.S.P.U. workers to the best possible use.
Unfortunately both organisations were possessed of wholly
incompetent officials, who immediately took up an attitude of
acute hostility towards each other—

The most ridiculous episodes took place on Polling Day. The
Labour Party had very few vehicles at its disposal, whilst the
W.S.P.U. had many cars sent by its prosperous supporters. These
stood idle outside its committee rooms in Bow Road throughout
the breakfast hour, whilst Conservative cars were rushing voters
to the poll. Banks [*the Labour agent*] refused to send the lists of
voters to the W.S.P.U., demanding the cars be sent to him; their
organiser replied: 'Mrs Pankhurst would never allow the Union
to work under men!' When Mrs Pankhurst arrived late in the
morning she dispatched the cars to the Labour Party.—In the
evening Lansbury sent to me, begging me to get a party of
women together, to assist in persuading electors drenched by

the torrential rains, to turn out to vote. The need for such efforts was quite genuinely unknown to the organiser of the W.S.P.U.

When the news came that Lansbury's majority of 863 had become a minority of 731, the [WSPU] representatives were astonished—The organiser exclaimed, 'What will Christabel say?', then opened her mouth and cried noisily like a child.

SYLVIA PANKHURST

NUWSS Council Resolutions

Half Yearly Council Meeting, Midland Theatre, Midland Hotel, Manchester

Thursday, 10th October, 1912

That no Candidate who does not personally pledge himself to vote against the Third Reading of the Reform Bill unless women are included, be supported by the National Union. **Proposed by Glasgow and West of Scotland W.S.S.**

That this Council is of opinion that the National Union should adopt a policy of opposition to all Government Candidates at by-elections, until the Government consent to the inclusion of women in the Franchise Bill. **Proposed by Macclesfield W.S.S.**

That members as well as officers and Committees of Women's Suffrage Societies in the National Union be pledged not to work for any Anti-Suffragist Candidate for Parliament. **Proposed by Exeter W.S.S.**

Labour Leader: 5 December 1912

The passing of the Reform Bill with the inclusion of women will be the outward and visible sign of a profound psychological change in the attitude of men towards women and of women towards society – it marks the growth of ideas—

The need for a fresh and vivid discussion is very urgent at this particular time. The Anti-Suffragist is always with us. The 'anti'-press is glorying in the tactical mistakes of our friends, and asserting that 'the Suffrage cause is dead – killed by the Peths and the Panks'.

So, my comrades, I would urge you to gird up your loins, trot out your arguments, and do some practical work in your branch club-room, or workshops. You *know* that the women must march side by side with you, that anything which shackles them equally shackles you, that no New Jerusalem can be built, no Socialist State achieved by men alone—

All sorts of wild rumours are floating about. Pay no heed to them. Let your demand be insistent, simple, and direct, and apply your influence to your local M.P.— Mr Asquith, in leaving the question of the inclusion of women to the House of Commons, issued a challenge to the rank and file; he is gambling on your indifference. Take up the challenge. Prove that you are ready for and mean to take this next great step in the progress of the human race.

MARGARET BONDFIELD

At the end of January 1913 the Speaker of the House of Commons delivered the coup de grâce to any realistic hope of any women obtaining the vote in the foreseeable future, when he ruled that the amendments to include women would so alter the Reform Bill that it would have to be reintroduced in a new form. It was, to say the least, a curious ruling for a Bill which had been kicked around for a year. However, Asquith's various biographers deny/doubt that he connived with the Speaker. At the time, unsurprisingly given the Prime Minister's track record, both militants and non-militants believed he had. Mrs Fawcett expressed the NUWSS anger, while Mrs Pankhurst declared a war in which her 'guerillists' would hit and run and if caught hunger strike. In war people get killed and the WSPU was hamstrung, albeit to its credit, by declaring human life sacrosanct. Its choice of targets – empty mansions owned by the rich, golf courses, summer houses and cricket pavilions – while expensive for insurance companies, was not calculated greatly to upset the majority of the population. Attacks on the property and person of members of the Government, both pro and anti suffrage, were regarded by many as counter-productive.

Daily Telegraph: 26 February 1913

Suffragist Outrages

Sir,

Everyone seems to agree upon the necessity of putting a stop to Suffragist outrages; but no one seems certain how to do so. There are two, and only two, ways in which this can be done. Both will be effectual:

1. Kill every woman in the United Kingdom
2. Give women the vote.

Yours truly,

Bertha Brewster

Metropolitan Police Report

Criminal Investigation Department,
New Scotland Yard,
7th day of March, 1913

Referring to the recent outrages by Suffragettes in the Metropolitan Police District and at Walton-on-the Hill, I beg to report that at 3.25 p.m. on the 19th. ultimo a telephone message was received from Superintendent Coleman, Surrey Constabulary, stationed at Dorking, stating that at 6.10 a.m. that day an explosion had occurred at Sir George Riddell's house at Walton-on-the-Hill, and that a tin of unexploded black gunpowder had been found in the house—

The explosion is supposed to have been caused by a 5 lb. tin of coarse-grained gunpowder which had been placed in a bedroom on the first floor in the north wing of the house. The gunpowder had been fired by means of a piece of cloth which had been soaked in wet gunpowder thus converting it into tinder. One end of the tinder was placed in the aperture of the tin of gunpowder while the other end connected it with a tin bowl containing shavings saturated with paraffin, surrounding a candle in a candle-stick. The candle had been lighted and when the flame reached the shavings they became ignited, also the tinder, and the explosion followed.

The room in which the explosion took place was wrecked in the interior; the western wall was bulging about four inches, and the eastern about one inch, while cracks were visible on the outside of the walls. The whole of the north wing showed signs of having been severely injured. The amount of damage is estimated at about £400—Inquiries have been made regarding the outrage (and) the movements of car LF-4587 on the 18th and 19th ultimo—

These are detailed at length and though 'grave suspicion' attached to the car's registered owner, Miss Norah Veronica Lyle Smith, and to Miss Olive Hocken, an 'artist painter', the police were unable to prove their complicity. Mrs Pankhurst's responsibility was a different matter.

In consequence of Mrs Pankhurst's public utterances regarding this and other outrages, the Director of Public Prosecutions decided to take proceedings against her under section 10 of the Malicious Damage Act, 1861—and a warrant was granted for her arrest on the 24th ultimo. This was effected at 2.15 p.m. the same day at her address, No. 159 Knightsbridge. She was subsequently conveyed to Leatherhead Police Station by motor car, and formally charged with 'Having feloniously, unlawfully, and maliciously, counselled and procured certain persons, whose names are unknown, to feloniously, unlawfully, and maliciously place in a certain building, situate at Walton Heath, in the county of Surrey, certain gunpowder and explosive substances, with intent thereby to damage the said building, contrary to the previsions of the Malicious Damage to Property Act. 1861.'

The Times: 18 March 1913

The Case of Miss Lenton

To the Editor,

Sir,

The Home Secretary recently issued a formal statement in regard to the sudden release of Miss Lenton that she 'was reported by the medical officer at Holloway prison on Sunday, February 23, in a state of collapse and in imminent danger of death consequent upon her refusal to take food. Three courses were open:-

1. To leave her to die. 2. To attempt to feed her forcibly which the medical officer advised would probably entail death in her exhausted condition. 3. To release her on her undertaking to surrender herself for the further hearing of her case. The Home Secretary adopted the last course.'

From these expressions employed in this letter the public were completely misled as to the true facts of the case. She was certainly in 'imminent danger of death' on that Sunday afternoon, but this was not due to her two days' fast, but to the fact that during forcible feeding executed by the prison doctors on the Sunday morning food was poured into her lungs. The statement issued from the Home Office quoted above was constructively misleading in that it made no mention whatever of the prisoner having been forcibly fed—

The plain facts of Miss Lenton's case prove clearly that the food which was forcibly injected into her lung set up a pleuro-pneumonic condition which, but for her youth and good healthy physique, could have ended more seriously. That the prison doctor and the governor recognised immediately what they had done is also obvious. They hurriedly and at the further risk of injury to the patient immediately removed her from the prison, so that at least she should not die there and thus compromise the Home Office, and our horrible prison administration of which they were the instruments.

Yours faithfully,

AGNES SAVILL, M.D., CHAS. MANSELL MOULLIN, F.R.C.S.,

VICTOR HORSLEY, F.R.S.

Recollections

Petitioning His Majesty

A few days before the opening of Parliament (March 1913) by King George V Mrs Ayrton Gould sent for me & asked if I would present a petition to King George V as he drove to Parliament along the Mall. After some hesitation I agreed to do this & paired with Dorothy Smith to lead off in a group of women stationed in pairs along the route between Buckingham Palace & the Houses of Parliament.

On March 14th we arrived in the Mall about 9 a.m. & took up our stand on the left side of the road (facing the Palace opposite Marlborough House). I felt terribly frightened & downcast and felt quite sure I would never be able to get through two rows of soldiers almost shoulder to shoulder & one line of police. Presently a murmur went through the crowd 'Here they come'. As the cheering grew nearer & feeling more dead than alive & shaking from head to foot I watched the stately procession coming nearer, when suddenly a thought flashed through my horrified mind 'At the salute' & hope revived within me. I whispered to Dorothy Smith as the royal equipage came almost opposite us – Our only chance is 'At the Salute'. Almost immediately the soldiers were grabbing their muskets & like lightning I ducked under the arms of the soldiers in front of me & ran swiftly up to the Royal carriage, raising my written Petition in my right hand and calling out in a loud voice, 'Will your Majesty mention Votes for Women in your opening speech & put an end to the torturing of women in your prisons.' By this time I was among the flunkeys grouped round the coach and quite close to the steps. It was my intention if I could to throw my Petition into the Coach, but unfortunately the windows were closed. Never shall I forget the faces of the flunkeys – they were more flabbergastedly astonished than any I had ever seen.

By this time I was gripped by both arms by police & conveyed up across St James's Park to Cannon Row Police Station. Before long all the other women had been brought in too in couples. Miss Maud Joachim fainted & was in consequence unable to present her petition. We based our action on a clause in the Bill of Rights which reads 'A subject has a right to petition the king, & any attempt to prevent this is illegal' which Statute still holds good.

MARIE BRACKENBURY

Winston Churchill and Reginald McKenna had by now exchanged posts. Churchill had become First Lord of the Admiralty, McKenna the Home Secretary. It was the latter who rushed the notorious Prisoners (Temporary Release for Ill-Health) Act through Parliament. Lord Robert Cecil, among the more illustrious Tory supporters, is usually credited with the vivid description 'Cat-and-Mouse Act', though Frederick Pethick-Lawrence also claimed it as his brainchild. When Mrs Pankhurst was sentenced for the second time at the Old Bailey the Act was about to become operative.

Daily Herald: 2 April 1913

McKenna's Cat-and-Mouse Bill

To-day the Government – in pursuance of its perverse and wrongheaded methods against the only political opponents it needs to take seriously – will ask the House to give a second reading to the measure which we have already styled the 'Cat-and-Mouse Bill'.

This measure proposes to deal with Suffragist hunger-strikers by letting them go until they have recovered from the effects of their fast, then suddenly re-arresting them and throwing them into goal once again, and so continuing until every day of the sentence has been served in prison.

In order that they may be at call when wanted, the prisoners will be watched and beset day and night by detectives and police-spies, their correspondence intercepted, telephone communication tapped, servants, where possible bribed—the Liberal Home Secretary is to be empowered by Parliament to extend, at his pleasure, the often grossly unfair sentences which magistrates or judges have already passed on disenfranchised women.—

The House of Commons has fallen pretty low of late, but it is difficult to believe that it can fall so low as to support the Government in a proposal which while it discredits its authors does not even promise to effect in the slightest degree the suppression of the Militant movement.

The Times: 4 April 1913

Mrs Pankhurst Sentenced

The trial of Mrs Pankhurst on the charge of inciting certain persons unknown to place an explosive in a building at Walton, Surrey, with intent to destroy or damage it, was concluded at the Central Criminal Court yesterday. Mrs Pankhurst, who conducted her own defence, was found *Guilty*, with a strong recommendation to mercy, and Mr Justice Lush sentenced her to three years' penal servitude. She had previously declared her intention to resist strenuously the prison treatment until she was released.

A scene of uproar followed the passing of the sentence. A number of women repeatedly shouted 'Shame', and in the excitement which followed the voice of male sympathisers joined in the demonstration. There were ironical cheers, and a woman's voice struck up, 'For he's a jolly good fellow'. Mr Justice Lush uttered an indignant protest against such behaviour and warned the demonstrators that, unless the disorder ceased, he would have the court cleared. This rebuke, however, fell on deaf ears, and the police, amid continued uproar and the singing of the 'Marseillaise', removed those responsible for the disorder.

Daily News: 29 April 1919

Sir A. Conan Doyle's View

A meeting last night at Tunbridge Wells, where recently a cricket pavilion was burnt down, passed a resolution condemning the outrages of the militants.

Sir A. Conan Doyle referred to the militants as female hooligans, and said that those who supplied them with money, but did not do anything, were, if possible, a more contemptible kind of people. They had one act to add to their malicious monkey tricks, and that was to blow up a blind man and his dog.

The Jewish Chronicle: 9 May 1913

Is England Russia?

Mr Israel Zangwill was one of the speakers at a meeting of some 2000 persons at the Kingsway Hall, held last week, called under the auspices of the Men's Political Union for Women's Enfranchisement—Mr Zangwill said:-

This meeting was originally called to demand the immediate release of Mr Franklin. The Government getting wind of our proposed resolution, hastened to liberate Mr Franklin yesterday, lest they might seem to be yielding, even superficially, to reason and justice. (Laughter and applause). Mr Franklin, has, however, been released under the 'Cat-and-Mouse' Bill, by which, after having been fed forcibly one hundred and fourteen times, he is expected to take up his bed and walk back into prison on May 12th, there to be tortured again. (Shame.)—Could one have imagined such proceedings under a Liberal Government? The 'Cat-and-Mouse' Bill could only have been carried by rats. (Great laughter and applause) I feel that I must drop into poetry, and ask:

> Is England Russia? Must we raise Gehenna,
> To save, the face of Asquith and McKenna?
> (Renewed laughter)

I am glad that Mr Franklin is of my race. (Loud cheers.)—Jews have been accused of crucifying Christ. As a Jew I have always been uneasy under that accusation. I have told myself that crucifixion was a Roman and not a Jewish punishment, but, nevertheless, I could not shake off some suspicion that the accusation was true. Now, however, my experience of the Suffragist movement, and the treatment of people like Mrs Pankhurst and Mr Hugh Franklin, have set my mind at rest. They have convinced me that there is no Christian people that would not crucify Christ if he came to them. (Loud and prolonged applause)

Hugh Franklin was the first suffragist prisoner to be released under the Cat-and-Mouse Act.

Letter To H.A. Franklin (Lunatic)

We are writing young man to inform you what 18 Tradesmen of the City of London would do with you and other LUNATICS and Arson-Mongers that burn Railway Carriages and Destroys the

190

Correspondence of the General Public. We would give you and old Mother Pankhurst (the fossil-worm) 5, Years Penal Servitude and then burn you both together. YOU ARE A DIRTY TYKE AND A DANGEROUS MADMAN From W. Crosbey

The Standard: 1913

No Vote, No Tax

Tax-resistance is coming more and more into fashion among suffragists as a means of haranguing the Government and making a strong public protest the anomaly of women being taxed just as men are and yet being refused the vote—

To-day the goods belonging to Miss Beatrice Harraden, ('Ships that Pass in the Night') are to be sold at Gill's Auction Rooms, Kilburn, following her refusal to pay Income-tax—At the same time Dr Hardie and Miss Gibbs will also have goods sold— Tomorrow there will be a sale of goods for tax resistance at Romford. On Wednesday there will be another at Islington. Friday, again, will see the sale of possessions belonging to two ladies in Battersea.

The other day, too, the first tax-resistance sale took place in the Lake District, the resister being Mrs Henry Holiday, wife of the well-known artist, who has a house at Hawkshead.

Seventh IWSA Congress: Budapest
15-21 June 1913

Sunday June 15: 10.30 a.m. Religious service at Protestant Church in Buda, Rev. Anna Shaw preaching.

Morning Session Monday June 16th: Mrs Catt announced that records of suffrage speakers were to be taken in a gramophone at the back of the hall. The President reported that the Board of officers wished to announce that many requests had been received that this Congress should express condemnation of 'Militant Methods', and as others had been received asking that it should express approval of them, the Board deemed it necessary, in order to avoid misunderstanding, to recommend the following resolution:

Resolved: That as the International Woman Suffrage Alliance stands pledged by its constitution to strict neutrality on all questions concerning national policy or tactics, its rules forbid any expression favouring or condemning militant methods. Be it further resolved: that since riot, revolution, and disorder have never been construed into an argument against man suffrage, we protest against the practice of the opponents of woman suffrage to interpret militancy employed by the minority of women in one country as an excuse for withholding the vote from the women of the world. The resolution was carried without dissent.

The President reported that while she and Dr Jacobs were in China, the Chinese Woman Suffrage Society had applied for affiliation to the International Alliance. She had not been able to read their constitution which was in Chinese, but the ladies had assured her that it was in accordance with the conditions of regular Auxiliaries.

Morning session Tuesday June 17th: The Chair announced that a cable had been received from the women of Persia, namely: 'Greetings from Persia. What hath God wrought?'

In the early summer of 1913 the English Federations of the NUWSS organised a Pilgrimage 'in response to Mr Asquith's statement that there was no demand for women's suffrage in the country' – partly because there had already been a march from Edinburgh to London, the Scots decided not to participate. The first English contingents set off from Newcastle, Carlisle and Land's End on 18 June. Together with those walking the old Pilgrim's Way through Kent and other less distant routes they reached London on 25 July, held their demonstration in Hyde Park on the 26th, a rally in Trafalgar Square and a service in St Paul's Cathedral on the 27th. Despite the tone of the American Alice Park's comments, the Pilgrimage was generally agreed to have been a well organised success. It was also important to keep holding public meetings as the WSPU had by now been banned from London parks and denied access to the Albert and other Halls. One concrete result was Asquith's agreeing to meet a deputation headed by Mrs Fawcett.

Labor Clarion, San Francisco: Labor Day Issue 1914

Three Signs of the Times

Three of the many phases of the woman's rebellion in England can be illustrated by three stories of my own experience. On my way home from the International Woman Suffrage Congress in Budapest in June, 1913, I spent a month in England. The first three days of the month I was a pilgrim, one of the thousands of woman suffragists who made a pilgrimage from every corner of England into London. The next day I marched three miles in London with the working people from the east end. The day after, I attended a militant meeting and heard Mrs Pankhurst address her followers—

The Saturday pilgrimage was non-militant. It represented 500 branch societies. All the way from village to village, the banners and speakers proclaimed the pilgrims law abiding—It had taken six weeks for the pilgrims from the Scotland border to reach London. From day to day meetings were held in town squares

193

and on village greens, literature was distributed, and a gay appearance presented with ribbons, and regalia in 'the colors.' On every hat was a straw cockade in imitation of the shells of the medieval crusaders. It was expected that the pilgrimage would prove that the non-militant women outnumber the militants, and that this fact would impress the nation.

'One-day pilgrims' joined when the women marched thru their own towns. But even with this temporary increase, the groups were only of medium size—The final day inside the London boundaries, the number increased suddenly, and the entrance into Hyde Park was a creditable showing. But in 1910, the militants had led the greatest parade London had ever seen. The pilgrimage of the non-militants fell far short of that epoch-making demonstration—

Sunday afternoon I joined the working people in White Chapel. We marched through London streets to the famous Trafalgar Square to make a protest in favor of free speech. We were not dressed in white, nor did we have special hats and decorations to make a gay showing. Everybody wore working clothes—It was a spirited procession—On both sides of the procession marched policemen in single file, so close together that they seemed a barricade—The presence of large numbers of police is not conducive to peace. Crowds gather out of curiosity, and the police and crowds together create disorder, followed by arrests of those who by chance are within reach—The word had been whispered that Sylvia Pankhurst, who was then in hiding, would appear at the square and make an address. This she did, although the monument was surrounded by 'bobbies'. At the end of the meeting a resolution was offered. It passed with shouts of approbation and hands held high in air. It is the working people of London whose threats are heard by the prime minister and parliament, and their share in militancy is a notable one—

ALICE PARK

Mrs Pankhurst scored higher than the non-militants but lower than the East Enders. When not in hiding on a Cat-and-Mouse licence Sylvia Pankhurst was busy running the East London Federation of the WSPU on a semi-autonomous basis.

from NUWSS Annual Report 1913

Deputation to Mr Asquith

Mrs Fawcett said: I readily admit that the maintenance of law and order is one of the first duties of Government. Another is to redress the grievances from which disorder has sprung.

Mr Asquith said that Parliament would yield to the opinion of the country. When asked how he expected the judgement of the country to express itself, Mr Asquith replied: 'I think in the long run, there is only one way of finding out what people think and that is by an election.'

It would be hard to find a more conclusive justification for women's claim to have a voice in Elections than Mr Asquith's own words!

The Death Of Emily Wilding Davison
from Laugh A Defiance

Derby Day 1913

It was not until the end of the third race that I saw Emily Davison. We had met several times and from the talks we had had I had formed the opinion that she was a very serious minded person. That was why I felt so surprised to see her. She was not the sort of woman to spend an afternoon at the races. I smiled to her; and from the distance she seemed to be smiling faintly back at me. She stood alone there, close to the white-painted rails where the course bends round at Tattenham Corner; she looked absorbed and yet far away from everybody else and seemed to have no interest in what was going on round her—I shall always remember how beautifully calm her face was—

I was unable to keep my eyes off her as I stood holding *The Suffragette* up in my clenched hand. A minute before the race started she raised a paper of her own or some kind of card before her eyes. I was watching her hand. It did not shake. Even when I heard the pounding of the horses' hooves moving closer I saw she was still smiling. And suddenly she slipped under the rail and ran out into the middle of the racecourse. It was all over so quickly. Emily was under the hooves of one of the horses and seemed to be hurled for some distance across the grass. The horse stumbled sideways and its jockey was thrown from its back. She lay very still.

There was an awful silence that seemed to go on for minutes, then, suddenly, angry shouts and cries arose and people swarmed out on to the racecourse. I was rooted to the earth with horror until a man snatched the paper I was still holding in my hand and beat it across my face. That warned me of my own danger. I pushed a way through the crowd and my assailant came pushing his way after me and shouted out to others to stop me. But I managed to reach the roadway and run across it just in front of the King's carriage as he and the Queen were hurriedly leaving from the back of the grandstand. Their Majesties' carriage and the carriages of their party which followed baulked my pursuers and gave me just the few minutes head start I badly needed. Mercifully, I was able to run faster than I had ever run before. I reached the Downs Station not a moment too soon. My pursuers, who now seemed legion, were pelting across the Downs after me and shouting and howling like maniacs.

'Quick! Hide me somewhere,' I gasped to an astonished porter.

He pointed towards the lavatory. 'Get in there,' he said. 'And bolt the door behind you.'

Next minute the tiny station seemed to be seething with the angry mob. The porter was trying to quieten them. I could hear him say, 'What's all the fuss about?' He seemed admirably cool about it.

'A Suffragette! Where's she gone?' a man gasped. He was so breathless, so angry he could scarcely get the words out.

'Oh her?' the porter's voice said. 'You're too late, pal. She nipped on to the train that just left. What's been going on, anyway?'

'A Suffragette.' The voices were raised again. 'Brought down the King's horse.'

The porter kept silent. Then a train came in. Most of the people seemed to get on it. It was growing dark, hours later, when the porter tapped on the lavatory door. 'Train for Waterloo's due, Miss,' I heard him say. 'Now's your chance to hop it.'

I unbolted the door and came out, glad to find my return ticket to Waterloo was still in an inside pocket.—The train, with its lights on, came in. I thanked him and boarded it. It was quite dark when I reached Bloosmbury. I felt I could not go and deliver my report. Instead I went straight to bed, exhausted and stunned—

The vision I had of Emily as she darted under the rail at Tattenham Corner and then lay in the grass horribly stretched out recurred. Over and over again I saw it. And now, after nearly forty years, it remains as vivid.

MARY RICHARDSON

The Times: 9 June 1913

The Suffragist Outrage at Epsom
Death of Miss E.W. Davison

Miss Emily Wilding Davison, the suffragist who interfered with the King's horse during the race for the Derby, died in hospital at Epsom at 4.50 yesterday afternoon. She underwent an operation on Friday and had remained in a grave condition ever since.

A number of lady friends called at the Epsom Cottage Hospital on Saturday afternoon to inquire as to the condition of Miss Davison. Two visitors draped the screen round the bed with the W.S.P.U. colours and tied the W.S.P.U. colours to the head of the bed. A sister of Miss Davison and a lady friend of her mother stayed at the hospital for many hours, and on Saturday night Captain Davison, a brother of the patient, arrived. Only members of the staff, however, were present when the end actually came.

from My Commonplace Book

We took the tube to Holborn in the fond hope of seeing Miss Davison's funeral; but when we got near the church we found the densest crowd I have ever seen – right along Holborn and all down those little streets that lead off to the British Museum. We tried to get up to a window but they were all full and we only succeeded in seeing the tops of moving banners; so we again set out, to cut it off at its goal (King's Cross Station); and after struggling through more dense crowds all along Euston Road, finally secured a position of vantage on the steps of St Pancras Railway Depot – overlooking the whole of Kings Cross and the entrance to the station. There we saw a most remarkable sight; for the whole space was dense with crowd except for the little winding passage which the police with great difficulty kept clear for the procession. They evidently hadn't expected anything like half the crowd – nor had I, when I abused the W.S.P.U. for making a public funeral. On the whole it was the most beautifully arranged thing they have done – and it really succeeded in being very impressive. I was much interested to watch the attitude of the crowd – and most of them I think were thoroughly taken by surprise. But what a strange thing the London Public is! It breaks up meetings and throws clods of earth at unoffending law-abiding National Unionists, and it turns out in its thousands, with its hat in its hand and tears in its eyes, to watch the funeral of the most destructive militant who ever milled. Truly there is some excuse for the people who throw reason to the wind and address it in its own language!

Mary Stocks

Votes For Women: 20 June 1913

The Funeral on Sunday

No less impressive, though in a different way, was the simple ceremony in Miss Davison's Northumberland home with which she was laid to rest last Sunday morning. Suffragists kept vigil over the coffin throughout the long train journey, and dense crowds again lined the route when it was conveyed from the station to the church at Morpeth. A procession of Suffragists dressed in white accompanied it, and it was followed by five coaches containing relatives and other mourners. The service at the church was private; and the coffin was buried in the family burial ground; it was covered with purple cloth from Mrs Davison, bearing the words, 'Welcome the Northumbrian Hunger-striker.'

from We Were Amused

The star turn on the programme was that Miss Emily Wilding Davidson (sic) who later pulled the King's horse in the Derby and died of her injuries—It was about the bravest thing I ever knew. Afterwards, I saw it on a newsreel, and it was horrible. How she grasped the bridle – or even the right bridle – of a horse flashing and thundering by I cannot imagine. But she got it, all right – and turned a complete *upright* somersault—As a speaker she was interminable. But I shall respect her all my life.

RACHEL FERGUSON

The Times; 20 June 1913

In the debate on the Dickinson Bill Mr Asquith for the first time opposed the franchise for women on the ground that woman is not the female of the human species, but a distinct and inferior species, naturally disqualified from voting as a rabbit is disqualified from voting—A man may object to the proposed extension of the suffrage for many reasons. He may hold that the whole business of popular election is a delusion, and that votes for women is its reduction to absurdity. He may object to it as upsetting convenient divisions of labour between the sexes. He may object to it because he dislikes change, or is interested in businesses, or practices which women would use political power to suppress. But it is one thing to follow a Prime Minister who advances all, or some, or any of these reasons for standing in the way of votes for women. It is quite another to follow a Prime Minister who places one's mother on the footing of a rabbit.

GEORGE BERNARD SHAW

Mr Dickinson was an MP supporter. The reference is to yet another Bill which everybody agreed was now futile. To succeed, women's suffrage had to be a Government measure.

from The Life of Ada Nield Chew

To most thinking women, especially those who, like my mother, were concerned with social justice, the securing of the vote was only a first but a necessary step towards the removal of the social and economic burdens placed upon women, which she believed retarded the progress of the human race. It might appear that her forthright opposition to injustice and oppression would have made her a natural militant, but she was a convinced opponent of the use of physical force in any context (including international relations), and therefore opposed to the methods of the Women's Social and Political Union—Any organisation she chose to join would have to be run democratically. Because of this belief, she had become a member of the National Union of Women's Suffrage Societies—

In everything she said and did it was the working woman she was concerned for, and as a working woman she spoke. It was, of course, her origins and experience that made her so valuable to the NUWSS, most of whose members were middle-class. On the whole, my mother liked and certainly admired those middle-class women with and for whom she worked. In (an) article she emphasised the fact that neither trade unionism among women nor the suffrage movement could exist but for men and middle-class women giving freely of their time and experience. They in turn fully acknowledged their debt both to her and to the other working class women among them.—

On 5 September 1913 a letter signed A.N.C. appeared in the *Common Cause* urging that paper to give advice on dress to its readers, because many well meaning but stupid suffragists did not know how to dress. To illustrate this, she quoted a comment from a nameless gentlemen to the effect that 'You can always tell Suffragists by the way they are dressed. There's Mrs Chew, for instance – her hat's never on straight!' How much easier it would have been today when she would not have needed to wear a hat!

Doris Nield Chew

from Myself and Friends

The Prime Minister's Blotter

We were all suffragettes in those days, and need I say that Ann Whitefield [*the role she created in Bernard Shaw's* Man and Superman] would have made me become one if I hadn't been a suffragette already! I had walked processions. I had carried banners for Mrs Pankhurst and the Cause. I had made a mess of the accounts as treasurer of the 'Actresses' Franchise League,' and was only prevented from leading the Society to insolvency by the financial ability of Mr Pethick-Lawrence, whose kindness and corrections enabled me at last to give a good account of my stewardship. I had made a yet greater mess of public speaking for, without the footlights to protect me, I was lost. Imagine my elation, therefore, when one day I found myself alone in the Cabinet Room at No. 10. There were the baskets of papers and there was the blotting pad with its large sheet of immaculate white blotting paper, the austere, solid ornaments of the Prime Minister's desk. Fervour for the cause took hold of me. I felt like a Joan of Arc of the ballot-box. Martyrdom or not, the occasion must be seized. I opened my box of grease paints, took out the reddest stick I could find, and wrote across the blotting paper 'Votes for Women.' I went out of the room exultant.

Lillah McCarthy

The Suffragette: 23 September 1913

Women's War Continues: Gigantic Fire at Liverpool

The biggest fire which has as yet been attributed to Suffragettes occurred last Tuesday, when Seafield House, Liverpool, a magnificent structure leased by the West Derby Board of Guardians, was practically destroyed. The northern portion of the building was completely gutted, and the whole of it suffered enormous damage.

Two other very serious fires, one at a mansion at Waltham Cross and the other at the Municipal Buildings at Withernsea, Yorkshire, have been attributed in the Press to Suffragettes, while lesser fires have been reported from various parts of the country. In several places golf links and bowling greens have been cut up, and attacks still continue to be made on pillar-boxes.

Speeches: David Lloyd George

Oxford, 22 November 1913: To the Men's Suffrage Union

It has been suggested that I can on occasion push through Bills which have not the support of the majority of the people. I will admit, for instance, that if you had had a plebiscite on the Insurance Act while it was going through it it would probably have been thrown out—There are two ways you can carry Bills—One is by having a great wave of feeling behind the Bill, the other is by the use of party machinery. You have not got the party machinery—Therefore the only alternative is to secure a majority of the country, and you have not got it.

Same day to NUWSS Members

The dominant fact of the situation now is the irritation of public opinion caused by the militants. The Pilgrimage undertaken in the summer by your Society I regard as the most helpful thing that has been done in support of the suffrage for some years. It was extremely effective.

Middlesborough, 7 November 1913 to NUWSS and WFL Deputations

The mere fact that an insignificant handful of women have chosen to adopt tactics which are in my judgement very fatuous is no reason why the vast majority of women should be regarded as incapable of exercising the elementary duties of citizenship.

Militant Memories

Arson and Bombs 1913-14

Well, I was at the Suffragette Headquarters and announced that I didn't want to break any more windows but I did want to burn some buildings, and I was told that a girl named Olive Walley had just been in saying the same thing, so we two met, and the real serious fires in this country started and thereafter I was in and out of prison – six times I think it was – and whenever I was out of prison my object was to burn two buildings a week.

At one of the times when I was being tried – as a matter of fact I wasn't being tried, actually, I was in the witness box – the police had arrested somebody else in mistake for me, and the only way to get her free was for me to announce that I was the person who had been guilty of whatever it was they were accusing us of that night. I said that I went to that house with the idea of burning it, and the magistrate said, 'But had you any grievance against the owner of the house?', and I said, 'No, but whenever I see an empty house I burn it'; which caused a considerable amount of consternation in court, according to the papers next day.

Well, the object was to create an absolutely impossible condition of affairs in the country, to prove that it was impossible to govern without the consent of the governed. A few young men were very anxious to help us. But these young men only seemed to have one idea, and that was bombs. Now I don't like bombs. After all, the rule was that we must risk no-one's lives but our own, and if you take a bomb somewhere, however great the precautions, you can't be one hundred percent sure. But a young man landed two on me. Well, I went to stay with some people near Edinburgh and when the lady there knew I had two bombs in a little attaché case she was very frightened, and she insisted that I took them away to some friend of hers who had a big estate with a lake in the garden, and that I dropped them in the lake.

Well, at that time I was wanted by the police under what was called the Cat and Mouse Act and any policeman who spotted you could arrest you and charge you if you hadn't been tried, but that didn't make any difference; I used to walk about quite openly. Well, I got into Edinburgh and walked up to a policeman and I asked him the way to somewhere so that I could get to this house, and he began to tell me and the he said:

'Well, as a matter of fact, I am just going off duty myself; I'll take you.' Well, naturally I jumped to the conclusion he had recognised me. But there was nothing to be done about it, so I said, 'That's very kind of you, thanks very much.'

So then he said, 'Let me carry your case for you.' He was a very polite man. It struck me as a joke to let the policeman carry the bombs, so I said, 'Thanks very much, it is rather heavy.'

So he took it from me and he said, 'My, it *is* heavy.'

He took me round various streets in Edinburgh and handed me on to the right tram and told me where to get off, and all was well, but when I got off the tram I left the bombs behind me. However, the conductor noticed and picked up the case and said, 'You've left your case!', so of course I had to go to get the case.

Well, that's just one little instance of the sort of things that happened in those days. We burned buildings. We got arrested now and then. We went to prison. We went on hunger strike. We were released under the Cat and Mouse Act, and then were taken to a house which was surrounded by police, and the game was to get out of the house without the police knowing. On one occasion I was told that the car with me in it, followed by the car with the police in it, passed certain men's clubs where betting was going on as to whether or not I should succeed in getting away from the police. Well, I had a bit of a reputation by then, and I understand the betting *started* at a hundred to one!

LILIAN LENTON

No 'Mice' Allowed

London, November 1913

Dear Friend,

It has been decided that no mice shall be present at the big [WSPU] meeting on December 8th. It is very disappointing to those who have looked forward to this event. The police will be on the alert for mice and are determined to arrest any or all if possible. I am sure you will understand perfectly that it would be disastrous to have the attention taken away from the speakers and attracted to possible arrests of various mice. Miss Pankhurst is very strong about this. I am very sorry to have to ask you to keep away. I myself am tremendously disappointed that I cannot go. Will you take care not to be near Earl's Court that night?

Yours sincerely,
Marie Roberts
Prisoners' Secretary

Edinburgh Evening News: 21 November 1913

Glasgow Suffragists Escape

Mrs Dorothea Smith and Miss Margaret Morrison, the militant suffragists who were released from Duke Street Prison under the 'cat and mouse' Act, are still at liberty, neither having yet fulfilled her obligation to return to prison. The house of Mrs Smith in Dennistoun was strictly watched night and day by the police since the expiry of her period of liberation, but despite the vigilance of the officers it is understood that Mrs Smith had, it seems, effected her escape by a clever ruse. One of her most frequent visitors was her mother, and it is believed that the militant suffragist, 'got up' to look as like this lady as possible, easily passed the scrutiny of the waiting policemen, and that she joined two women who called at the house in a motor on Thursday of last week. The police surveillance, which is estimated to have cost about £10 per week, thereafter ceased.

NUWSS Half Yearly Council Meeting

Barras Bridge Assembly Rooms, Newcastle, 7 November 1913

That the funds and workers of the EFF [Election Fighting Fund] should be devoted to

(a) Returning the largest possible number of Labour members – Amendment, add the words 'who are individually satisfactory on Women's Suffrage'

(b) Removing the largest number of unsatisfactory Liberals

Proposed by Newcastle-on-Tyne W.S.S.

from The Unexpurgated Case Against Woman Suffrage

For the happy wife and mother is never passionately concerned about the suffrage. It is always the woman who is galled either by physiological hardships, or by the fact that she has not the same amount of money as man, or by the fact that man does not desire her as a co-partner in work, and withholds the homage which she thinks he ought to pay to her intellect.

For this class of grievances the present education of woman is responsible. The girl who is growing up to woman's estate is never taught where she stands relatively to man. She is not taught about woman's physical disabilities. She is not told – she is left to discover it for herself when too late – that child and husband are to woman physiological requirements. She is not taught the defects and limitations of the feminine mind. One might almost think there were no such defects and limitations; and that woman was not always overestimating her intellectual power. And the ordinary girl is not made to realise woman's intrinsically inferior money-earning capacity. She is not made to realise that the woman who cannot work with her hands is generally hard put to earn enough to keep herself alive in the incomplete condition of a spinster.

As a result of such education, when influenced by the feminist movement, woman comes to institute a comparison between herself and man, she brings into that comparison all those qualities in which she is substantially his equal, and leaves out of account all those in which she is his inferior. The failure to recognise that man is the master and why he is the master, lies at the root of the suffrage movement. By disregarding man's superior physical force, the power of compulsion upon which all government is based is disregarded. By leaving out of account those powers of the mind in which man is the superior, woman falls into the error of thinking that she can really compete with him, and that she belongs to the self-same intellectual caste.

Summary of the Effects of Feminism

From every point of view, therefore, except perhaps that of the exceptional woman who would be able to hold her own against masculine competition – and men always issue informal letters of naturalisation to such an exceptional woman – the woman suffrage which leads up to feminism would be a social disaster.

SIR ALMROTH E. WRIGHT M.D, F.R.S.

Sir Almroth had previously written a series of articles in The Times *which he published with embellishments as 'The Unexpurgated Case . . .' Even Antis such as Mrs Humphry Ward were outraged.*

Press Cutting 1913

And in those days was Amroth (son of Wasroth), King in Babble-On. And having gathered his great company of Soothsayers, Astrologers, and Physicians together, they did bake a great sacrifice of Cats and Dogs, upon the alter called SI Ens. And when they had made an end of sacrificing, then did Amroth lift up his voice and say, 'Am I not he who is for ever Wright?' And they answered him, 'Yea.'—

And he spake further, saying, 'There are in this land certain wild creatures, having the semblance of Women, being clothed in long hair and sausage skins, very tight. And their voice is as the voice of Sirens, even as the steam-whistle Sirens. But their deeds are the deeds of Men, and their faces are hid by reason of their much smoking—And me, even Amroth, have they defied. Wherefore do I go down into the Land of Tish and Bosh, and will unexpurgate them utterly—For all women are bad and an abomination in the earth; they sew not neither do they sweep, and understanding is hid from them.'

from I Have Been Young

A Lack of Generosity

In one respect the militants were greatly inferior to us: in generosity. They persistently belittled and even abused us, while our people were constantly getting in hot water because of their frank recognition of the courage and devotion of the militants. I will mention here one little instance from my own experience. In a book published by Sylvia Pankhurst in 1931* (when she was old enough to know better) she describes the National Union as 'incorrigibly lazy' in 1913. Well, my record for that year—

210

included speaking at public meetings in [*56 towns in England and Wales are listed*]. Besides these, I spoke that year in London at seventeen public indoor meetings, and four Hyde Park meetings. These last we undertook weekly, because the conduct of the militants was threatening to make it impossible for women to speak in the open air, and we wanted to compel the police authorities to keep order at all meetings which were not guilty of advocating disorder.

Besides these public meetings, I spoke at many private ones, took a full share of committee and organising work, reported a number of conferences, wrote countless reviews, edited a suffrage monthly during the editor's holiday, wrote 50,000 words on *The Future of the Women's Movement* and attended the Suffrage Alliance Congress at Budapest, where I not only reported and spoke, but was on that most arduous of all sub-committees, the Resolutions Sub-Committee, whose job it is every night to wipe up the mess of the day—

Be it remembered that most of these public meetings involved for the speaker not only preparation, but often travel, and nights spent away from home. For the organisers they involved much correspondence, the arrangement of 'hospitality,' the engagement of a hall, the securing of a chairman, the advertisement and stewarding of the meeting, the sale of what is strangely known as 'literature,' the interest of the Press and the footing of the bill—If you take me as one only out of many National Union speakers, you can scarcely agree that we exhibited 'Incorrigible idleness' in 1913.

HELENA SWANWICK

The book was The Suffragette Movement *from which several extracts have been quoted. As Teresa Billington-Greig noted in 1906, Sylvia Pankhurst was sent into 'a form of retirement' to write a suffragette history. Her efforts were originally published in lengthy instalments in* Votes for Women. *The 1931 volume continues the story up to 1928.*

1914 opened with Christabel Pankhurst still ensconced in Paris. Although WSPU membership was dwindling, enough wealthy patrons remained for the arson and bombing campaigns to continue and for Christabel to enjoy a comfortable exile. Her information now came second-hand from a doting mother mentally and physically exhausted by repeated hunger-and-thirst strikes and yet another lecture and fund-raising tour to the United States; or from acolytes who would not dream of questioning Christabel's strategy or tactics, which now included the sexual purity campaign. In a series of articles later published as The Great Scourge *she argued that prostitution and venereal diseases were a direct result of men's failure to match (good) women's moral standards and that none should marry until men 'became as chaste and clean living as women'. In January Sylvia Pankhurst was thrown out of the WSPU. In February despairing dissidents formed the United Suffragists.*

By 1914 the NUWSS had 600 societies under its umbrella and was spending the vast sum of £45,000 per year on the Election Fighting Fund and on creating the groundswell of public opinion that would overwhelm the opposition. Trouble threatened when Eleanor Rathbone, a prominent EC member from Liverpool, led a revolt against the Labour alliance which she claimed had become permanent (true) and could lead to a Tory victory at the next General Election. Miss Rathbone was out-voted and temporarily resigned.

from The Suffragette Movement

The Pankhursts Part Company

For some time messages had been reaching me that Mrs Pankhurst and Christabel desired to see me in Paris. I was loath to go, for as the ports were watched I was likely to be arrested on embarking, and I was unwilling to expend my energy in another hunger and thirst strike except as the price of a rousing struggle—

As soon as we reached Paris the business was opened. Christabel, nursing a tiny Pomeranian dog, announced that the East London Federation of the W.S.P.U. must become a separate organisation; the *Suffragette* [*the WSPU newspaper since the 1912 split*] would announce this, and unless we immediately chose to adopt one for ourselves, a new name would be given to us—a working woman's movement was of no value; working women were the weakest portion of the sex; how could it be otherwise? Their lives were too hard, their education too meagre to equip them for the contest. 'You have your own ideas. We do not want that; we want all our women to take their instructions and walk in step like an army!'—

We drove in the Bois; Christabel with the small dog on her arm, I struggling against headache and weakness, Mrs Pankhurst blanched and emaciated—Christabel was emphatic. 'It must be a clean cut!' So it went on. 'As you will then,' I answered at last.

SYLVIA PANKHURST

from Fire of Life

The United Suffragists

Do what we would, I felt all through the year 1913 that the Movement was weakening, and the prospect of struggle seemed to stretch out to all eternity. The relations between the W.S.P.U. and us who had tried to serve with them so long became more and more strained, until the officials in their new quarters became openly hostile and shut the door against us—Very reluctantly we formed a new society called the United Suffragists – a society comprising men and women alike. We were but a small band, with an executive of twelve members—We had difficult work before us.

HENRY NEVINSON

The membership, mostly ex-WSPU, was impressive. Evelyn Sharp, Lena Ashwell and Nevinson himself – with his colleague Henry Brailsford he had resigned in protest at the first forcible feeding – were on the executive. The renowned scientist Hertha Ayrton, Edith and Israel Zangwill, Dr Louisa Garrett Anderson, the Hon. Evelina Haverfield, Maud Arncliffe Sennett, Laurence Housman and Mrs Bernard Shaw were among the Vice-Presidents. The Pethick-Lawrences soon joined and Votes for Women *became the society's newspaper with Evelyn Sharp its editor.*

Extracts from the Minutes of The NUWSS Manchester & District Federation 1914

March 31, EC meeting. It was reported that Mrs Tozer had done splendid work during the last eighteen months in Accrington. A Labour & Suffrage Club had been formed & had a joint membership of 400. Rossendale reported that Mrs Chew had been working in this very large constituency with great success.

June 15 Organisation Committee: The secretary reported that 50 new members had been enrolled during the Lightning [*recruiting*] Campaign: the service at the Cathedral had been attended by 450 members & friends—It was reported that the Federation Active Service League [*another recruiting scheme*] had held a most successful tour in Whit Week, in the High Peak district, when 400 Friends' cards were signed & many meetings held.

Mrs Pankhurst's Arrest In Glasgow

Metropolitan Police Report
Criminal Investigation Department,
New Scotland Yard.

11th March, 1914.

I beg to report that at 2 p.m., 6th inst. in company of Sergeant Mole, I proceeded to Glasgow, with the object of affecting the arrest of Mrs E. Pankhurst, wanted for failure to comply with the Order of her Temporary Discharge under The Prisoner's (Temporary Discharge for Ill-Health) Act, 1913.

We arrived in Glasgow at 11 p.m. and next morning called and presented ourselves to Mr Stevenson, the Chief Constable, and handed him a letter from the Assistant Commissioner. He at once placed at our disposal Lieut. Trench and Chief Inspector Weir of the Detective Department. Together we made many enquiries in the city and its environs, regarding the whereabouts of Mrs Pankhurst, but we were unable to obtain any definite information.

On Monday evening 9th inst, Mrs Pankhurst was announced to address a meeting at Saint Andrew's Hall, Kent Road, Glasgow, at 8 p.m. On the morning of that date I conferred with Superintendent Douglas who has charge of the division in which the Hall is situated, and it was decided to keep observation on the various entrances to the building.

Before the doors of the Hall were opened, Detective officers wore posted at each entrance, but Mrs Pankhurst was not observed to enter. About 8.15 p.m. Superintendent Douglas received information that Mrs Pankhurst was on the platform. At his suggestion I accompanied him and Lieut. Trench to one of the platform entrances. We were there confronted by several stewards, who demanded our authority. The Superintendent informed them that we were Police Officers, and as the building was the property of the Corporation, he had power to enter.

We forced our way into the passage on the right of the platform, and through glass panels of a door-way I identified the person speaking as Mrs Pankhurst, who had evidently entered the building in some effective disguise. At this time the Hall, which is a large one, was crowded, fully 5,000 to 6,000 persons being present.

Superintendent Douglas at once directed the uniform Police, whom he had in waiting to enter the building by entrances on each side of the platform, and form a cordon in front of it, with a view of preventing Mrs Pankhurst escaping through the audience. Detective officers to the number of about 30 rushed on to the platform from both sides. At this moment about the same number of uniform officers followed them. On Police being observed on the platform there was a general uproar; Mrs Pankhurst rushing with members of her body-guard towards the back of the platform. Other members of the body-guard, who occupied the two front rows of seats on the platform, immediately rose to their feet, and held Police batons, Indian Clubs, life preservers, hammers, Etc. over their heads, and threatened the Police that if they attempted to approach the platform they would act. The uniform officers in front of the platform then attempted to climb on to the stage, which was surrounded with barbed-wire covered with papers and flags, displaying the colours of the Women's Social and Political Union.

On the approach of the Police, Mrs Pankhurst's 'body-guard' at once took up flowerpots, water-bottles, glasses, buckets of water, (which were concealed) chairs, forms and everything they could use, and commenced to assault the Police. During the commotion a revolver was fired, which evidently contained blank cartridges.

Mrs Pankhurst's arrest was effected after a severe struggle between Police, who had to use their truncheons to protect themselves from her supporters, by Detective Lieut. Trench of the

216

Glasgow force. She was then conveyed with great difficulty into the street, where she was placed into a taxicab which was in waiting, by Lieut. Trench, myself and other officers, and conveyed, in company of a woman to the Central Police Office, where she was detained for the night.

A number of the audience followed us to Saint Andrew's Street, and demonstrated in front of the Police Station. Their conduct was such that it necessitated the calling out of mounted Police who eventually dispersed them. Members of Mrs Pankhurst's 'body-guard' then took up picket duty outside the Police Station which they continued throughout the night, having a number of motor-cars waiting in the vicinity.

In company of Lieut. Trench, I went to the London & North Western Railway Station, and made arrangements with the Station Master there to reserve three compartments in a carriage at the rear of the main line train for London, which we joined at Coatbridge at 10.30 a.m., 10th inst. In view of the possibility of an attempt being made to rescue our prisoner, I obtained the permission of Mr Stevenson, Chief Constable of Glasgow, to allow four Detective officers and a matron to accompany us to London.

from Female Pipings in Eden

Mrs Pankhurst's Condition

In April Mrs Pankhurst was once more arrested, and embarked on a hunger-and thirst-strike—This time the authorities were really alarmed at her condition, but none the less, when I went to see her at 'Lady' Pine's nursing home, detectives were on the watch all round it. She was heartrending to look on, her skin yellow, and so tightly drawn over her face that you wondered the bone structure did not come through; her eyes deep sunken and burning, and a deep dark flush on her cheeks. With horror I then became acquainted with one physical result of hunger-striking that still haunts me. It is due, I suppose, to the body feeding on its own tissue; anyhow, the strange, pervasive, sweetish odour of corruption that hangs about a room in which a hunger-striker is being nursed back to health is unlike any other smell. I often hoped that Mrs Pankhurst, the most meticulously dainty of beings, had no idea of this sinister effect of hunger-striking and am glad to believe she hadn't, for she would have minded that almost more than anything.

ETHEL SMYTH

Unpublished Memoirs: 1914

And one fine morning, Tuesday, April 16th, the governor, Dr Paton, instead of the stern official, made his entrance into my cell like a jolly human being, happy as a sand-boy with the joyous, sparkling greeting, 'Well, Ginger!' He had brought my release in a 'Cat and Mouse' licence for 6 days. It would take longer than that to repair the damage His Majesty's Christian Government had done to me. Fourteen weeks and two days, forcibly fed 232 times, for the last 5 weeks and 5 days three times a day. I lost 36 pounds in weight—

Friends who came to see me at Nurse Pine's Nursing Home to which I was taken, were shocked at my changed appearance. An old woman of seventy, they said I looked. My age was forty-three.

KITTY MARION

from Laugh a Defiance

The Rokeby Venus

Law and its application reflected public opinion. Values were stressed from the financial point of view and not the human. I felt I must make my protest from the financial point of view, therefore, as well as letting it be seen as a symbolic act. I had to draw the parallel between the public's indifference to Mrs Pankhurst's slow destruction and the destruction of some financially valuable object. A painting came to my mind. Yes, yes – the Venus Velasquez had painted, hanging in the National Gallery—The fact that I disliked the painting would make it easier for me to do what was in my mind.

I made my plans carefully and sent a copy of them to Christabel, setting out my reasons for such an action. The days, while I waited for her reply, seemed endless. But at last the message came, 'Carry out your plan.'—My axe was fixed up the left sleeve of my jacket and held in position by a chain of safety-pins, the last pin only needing a touch to release it. I walked rapidly and made my way by the side streets through Soho to Leicester Square, and then round to the back of the Gallery and so on to its front entrance.

It was a 'free' day and there were many people going in. I kept with the crowds at first—I studied the landscapes and watched the people who were passing—I felt I would have given anything to have been one of them. I spent an hour like this in utter misery. Chiding myself for having wasted two precious hours I went back to the Venus room. It looked peculiarly empty. There was a ladder lying against one of the walls, left there by some workmen who had been repairing a skylight—As twelve o'clock struck one of the detectives rose from the seat and walked out of the room. The second detective, realising, I suppose, that it was lunch-time and he could relax, sat back, crossed his legs and opened a newspaper.

That presented me with my opportunity – which I was quick to seize. The newspaper held before the man's eyes would hide me for a moment. I dashed up to the painting. My first blow with the axe merely broke the protective glass. But, of course, it did more than that, for the detective rose with his newspaper still in his hand and walked round the red plush seat, staring up at the sky-light. The sound of the glass breaking also attracted the attention of the attendant at the door who, in his frantic efforts to reach me, slipped on the highly polished floor and fell face-downwards. And so I was given time to get in a further four blows with my axe before I was, in turn, attacked. It must all have happened very quickly; but to this day I can remember distinctly every detail of what happened.

Two Baedeker guide books, truly aimed by German tourists, came cracking against the back of my neck. By this time, too, the detective, having decided that the breaking glass had no connec-tion with the skylight, sprang on me and dragged the axe from my hand. As if out of the very walls angry people seemed to appear round me. I was dragged this way and that; but, as on other occasions, the fury of the crowd helped me. In the ensuing commotion we were all mixed together in a tight bunch. No one knew who should or should not be attacked. More than one innocent woman must have received a blow meant for me.

In the end all of us rolled in an uncomfortable heap out of the room on to the broad staircase outside. In the scramble as we stumbled together down the stairs I was pillowed by my would-be attackers. Policemen, attendants and detectives were waiting for us at the foot of the staircase where we were all sorted out. I was discovered in the midst of the struggling crowd, more or less unharmed. They marched me quickly off along a corridor, down some stairs to a large basement—It was some minutes before I was dealt with; then the police inspector came up to me. He spoke breathlessly, 'Any more of your women in the Gallery?' he demanded.

'Oh, I expect so,' I replied, knowing full well that there were none.

'My God!' he shouted and flung his cap down on the stone floor. He at once turned and ran from the room, pushing everybody else out of his way as he did so, in such great haste was he to give the order to 'Clear the Gallery'.

I felt tired all of a sudden and sat down weakly on the floor.

Once again I was taken back to Holloway. The one-time castle home of the Warwick family seemed to have become my home— This time I knew there would be a long term of forcible feeding to face. I was in comparatively good health. I had but two wishes, two hopes: one that Mrs Pankhurst might be benefited by my protest, the other that my heart would give out quickly. It was strange to think that it was our heart that had brought us into the movement and that only its weakness could give us back our freedom.

In prison, of course, I had no immediate news of the public's reaction to my protest. But I had been inside for a week when an elderly tired-faced woman who had come to scrub the floor of my cell told me something. She had to pretend to be scrubbing the floor extra hard while she spoke.

'You ain't half upset everyone,' she said. 'It's going to cost a packet to mend that picture you cut about. My word, you didn't half cut 'er up. Venus! Never 'eard of 'er afore.'

MARY RICHARDSON

Pall Mall Gazette: 20 May 1914

Militants and the King: Big Furze Fire at Aldershot

About midnight last night a large furze fire was discovered a short distance from the Royal Pavilion in the Long Valley at Aldershot, where the King and Queen are at present in residence.

A general fire alarm was sounded, with the result that the 2nd Dragoon Guards, with the 5th Dragoon Guards and the 11th Hussars, with military fire engines, were soon on the spot. The fire was ultimately beaten out by the swords of the cavalry. It is alleged that the furze was ignited by Suffragists, who have been extremely active in the vicinity during the last few days, but this lacks confirmation.

Today as their Majesties left the Royal Pavilion two Suffragists at the entrance held aloft a banner bearing the words 'Votes for Women'.

Belfast Newsletter: 4 July 1914

Beautiful Mansion near Belfast Gutted:
Damage Estimated at £20,000

Ballymenoch House, one of the largest and most stately mansions in Ulster, was totally gutted by fire yesterday—Between five and six o'clock yesterday morning it was discovered that the building was on fire—Although the brigade remained on the scene until half-past three yesterday afternoon, they were unable to do any effective work after the water supply failed, and when they left the whole of the roof collapsed—About four o'clock, when the fire seemed to have spent itself, huge sheets of flame commenced to shoot up from the cellars, and burnt fiercely until everything of a combustible nature had been destroyed—

No explanation can be given for the origin of the fire, but two copies of the 'Suffragette', the organ of the militant women, were found in the grounds, and on the windows of the conservatory, which are painted white, the words 'Votes for Women' had been written—

Flora Murray MD: Memorandum to the Home Secretary

There have been 1,240 commitments of Suffragists to Prisons. 165 of the women prisoners and 3 of the men have been forcibly fed.

Forcible Feeding as practised in H.M. Goals is not the artificial Feeding of Hospitals. *In hospitals* it is regarded as an operation, justifiable only if its object is to save life, or lessen suffering – it is undertaken *with the consent of the patient*, or his friends.

It is resorted to in cases of obstruction, unconsciousness, and insanity. In the first two instances there is *no struggling*, in the third where there may be struggling, the Superintendent sanctions the proceeding and is generally present in person. *Antiseptic Precautions* which include boiling the tube are insisted upon.

In H.M. Prisons the operation is performed upon sane people *without their consent*. Mr McKenna has admitted in the House, that the tube is not *properly sterlised*. Prisoners who are being forcibly fed have to endure *solitary confinement*, and are deprived of Exercise, Chapel and Books, they are usually deprived of baths, and one has stated that she was not allowed to go to the lavatory.

The Prisons in which it has been practised are:

Holloway	Aylesbury	Pentonville	Bristol
Wormwood Scrubs	Newcastle	Liverpool	Dublin
Manchester	Birmingham		

Report by L. Mabel Jones MD Lond. on Miss Gordon

Suffragist Prisoner in Perth for attempted arson, 1914

Released about 5 o'clock on July 3rd having been in prison since June 22nd. On 24th forcible feeding began twice a day. Seen at midnight on July 3rd her appearance was appalling, like a famine victim – the skin brown, her face bones standing out, her eyes half shut – her voice a whisper, her hands quite cold, her pulse a thread – her wrist joints were swollen, stiff and painful – this was not from rough handling but from poisoning. The breath was most offensive unlike anything I have smelt before and the contents of the bowel over which she had no control, smelt the same.

The Suffragette: 10 July 1914

Mrs Dacre Fox's Letter to the Bishop of London

My Lord, I am informed that you will be present to-morrow afternoon in Westminster Abbey, and I shall therefore take the opportunity of attending the service to publicly claim sanctuary from you—As you yourself have compared the militant women to militant Ulster, I am sure you will be the first to protest against the scandalous injustice of such a state of affairs. I shall, therefore, give you the opportunity of registering a protest in a practical manner, and shall appeal to you publicly tomorrow in God's House—I feel confident I shall not appeal to you in vain.
I am, Yours faithfully,
Norah Dacre Fox

Mrs Dacre Fox Re-arrested: Appeals to the Bishop in vain for Sanctuary

When the Bishop of London was preaching in Westminster Abbey at the 3 o'clock Service, the building being crowded to the doors, the Congregation was startled by a woman stepping out from the nave and addressing the Bishop. 'My Lord,' she cried, 'In the name of God stop forcible feeding. I am myself a prisoner under the Cat-and-Mouse Act and will be arrested on leaving the Abbey.'

For a minute or so there was silence in the Abbey, and then she was led out of the building—and was at once re-arrested and taken to Holloway.

Correspondence

Letter from the Bishop of London to Reginald McKenna

Lambeth Palace S.W.
July 15, 1914

Dear Home Secretary

No one can dispute the seriousness of the situation which has arisen, and on which you ask my advice—I can only repeat that forcible feeding is, in my opinion, objectionable in itself, and also that it very largely fails in its object.

In theory it is resorted to in order to prevent the self-starvation of prisoners, and their consequent release from prison. In practice it too often results in the detention of the prisoners for two or three weeks longer than they could otherwise have been detained. And this is accomplished at the cost of physical and mental suffering wholly disproportionate to the end achieved.

The consequence is that the deterrent effect of the punishment is destroyed. Pity and admiration for those who have been forcibly fed takes its place together with vehement and, if you will, unreasonable indignation against the authorities for what is regarded as their cruelty.

If, therefore, your only alternative is a stringent administration of the Prisoners Temporary Discharge Act I should strongly hold that the risk of additional arson and other acts of violence by the released individual is less than the risk of further crime on the part of the comrades of those who are being forcibly fed.

Reply from the Home Secretary

17th July, 1914.

Dear Bishop,

I am much obliged for your letter. I did not intend to put you to the trouble of giving me advice, but merely wanted to understand your position which was left quite ambiguous in your letter to the 'Times'. I now understand that you are of opinion that a woman who has caused explosions in five churches in London should, if she starves herself, be released notwithstanding the practical certainty that she will cause more explosions as soon as she is at liberty, and that you object to the use of ordinary and proper medical measures by which she can be prevented either from committing suicide or from blowing up churches.

May I correct you on one point of fact? It is not the case that otherwise healthy persons who insist on being forcibly fed have to be released in two or three days or in two or three weeks. We now have good reason to believe that the apparent failures of forcible feeding were due to the women drugging themselves.* I must also repeat that forcible feeding is never used in any sense as a punishment. If and when it causes pain, the pain is self-inflicted by the prisoner.

How suffragette prisoners, stripped on arrival, dressed in prison clothes, by then mainly kept in solitary confinement and refused visitors, obtained the drugs was not explained. The relevant 1913–14 Home Office files on Mary Richardson who claimed she was drugged by the prison doctors were destroyed.

After her mother's and sister's rejection Sylvia Pankhurst's life became heroically manic. She was arrested, hunger-and-thirst struck, escaped to Europe to lecture on socialism and suffragism, organised mass rallies in the East End and after another hunger-and-thirst strike, barely able to walk, lay down outside the House of Commons. On 20 June Mr Asquith finally agreed to meet a deputation from her East London Federation of Suffragettes. Wisely, Sylvia herself did not attend. Her comrades' reports convinced her that the meeting with working-class women had changed the Prime Minister's attitude. This seems unlikely. After the NUWSS Pilgrimage Asquith had made similar soothing noises to Mrs Fawcett's deputation. With a General Election looming in 1915 there was some concern about the effects of the mass defection of disillusioned Liberal women (who did the election donkey work) and the NUWSS/Labour alliance. Pragmatism, if nothing else, might have won the suffrage day. We shall never know. On 28 June 1914 the Austrian Archduke Franz Ferdinand and his wife were assassinated in Sarejevo. Balkan crises being a common occurrence, nothing much happened for a month. With Austria-Hungary's declaration of war on Serbia which it held responsible for the murders, the prospect of a European war suddenly became an appalling reality.

Manchester Guardian: 1 August 1914

International Manifesto of Women [to Heads of State]

We women of twenty-six countries, having bonded ourselves together in the International Woman Suffrage Alliance with the object of obtaining the political means of sharing with men the power which shapes the fate of nations, appeal to you to leave untried no method of conciliation or arbitration for arranging international differences to avert deluging half the civilised world in blood.

Signed on behalf of the International Woman Suffrage Alliance
MILLICENT GARRETT FAWCETT, FIRST VICE-PRESIDENT
CHRYSTAL MACMILLAN, RECORDING SECRETARY

Militant Memories

The Last Suffragette Prisoner, August 1914

Well, I was in seven prisons in England, and getting quite to know the difference between them. I was convicted for carrying dynamite and things like that in my case – suitcase, you know. Well, I hadn't been able to find anything to do at that particular time but under the Cat and Mouse Act I was arrested as soon as they suspected me. And then I was put in Birmingham, and there the war broke out. I still had two years and three months to serve, from that and a few other sentences, but the matron was very worried because things were going up in price so much. She told me butter was six shillings, and they couldn't get enough food for the people and her girls were all worn out at having to forcibly feed me three times a day, and she was in tears about it.

So I said, 'Well, it's no good telling me that. Tell that to the Home Office, and they will perhaps arrange food.'

I was being filled with Sanatogen, which had to be brought over from Germany, with the forcible feeding. But, anyhow, on the 12th or 16th of August, I think it was, I was released and later on I got a letter of remission of sentence from the King. That was all I had. But I was the last suffragette that was sentenced and let out.

EILEEN CASEY

The Great War
Years
1914–1918

Lord Curzon is up, ladies, but 'e
won't do you no 'arm

QUOTED BY RAY STRACHEY IN *The Cause*

To live to see the triumph of a 'lost'
cause must be almost the greatest
of delights

EVELYN SHARP
JOURNALIST, SUFFRAGETTE AND TAX RESISTER

When the United Kingdom went to war on 4 August 1914 the majority of women supported their country, if some with reservations. In the chaotic early days the well-organised suffrage networks did invaluable work with the flood of Belgian refugees, in repatriating those stranded in now enemy countries, in setting up a bureau to trace missing soldiers and civilians, and in assisting the thousands of suddenly unemployed women or those left destitute when their menfolk volunteered to fight for King and Country. (Official 'separation allowances' were abysmal.) Initially rejected by the British authorities, the swiftly raised women's hospital units provided desperately needed medical services in Belgium, France, Serbia and later Russia. Emmeline Pankhurst and Christabel – who remained in Paris – immediately flew off on their patriotic broomsticks, but Sylvia was a dedicated pacifist. A few women endeavoured to keep the Cause alive.

from The Office Of The United Suffragists

October 30th 1914

Dear Mrs Arncliffe Sennett,

To keep the suffrage flag flying throughout the war is, we believe, an act of the greatest service to the community as well as to our particular cause—We ask you to remember what *Votes for Women* has been for years past; we ask you to recall the passionate loyalty with which innumerable suffragists have given time, health and money to keep it going and extend its influence. We would remind them how consistently the paper has stood for freedom and progress, for good faith and high ideals. We venture to say that if the continuity were broken, if after the war we had to look back upon a failure to keep our paper alive, we should all reproach ourselves bitterly for having failed in loyalty and courage and faith. We therefore appeal to you to spare something, even at this time of public stress, for the upkeep of *Votes for Women*.

Yours very truly,

Evelyn Sharp

In February 1915 the NUWSS Executive Council agreed that the NU should not 'express opinions about the present war and the part taken by Great Britain'. In April suffragists in neutral Holland organised an International Women's Peace Congress. In the murk of the February non-resolution the NU voted not to send delegates. Only a handful of British women managed to attend the Hague Congress – the Government temporarily closed the North Sea to all ships – but the pacifist issue caused a split, not so heavily in the ranks as on the EC. More than half its experienced, long-serving members resigned. For some including Catherine Marshall who had worked closely with Millicent Fawcett as secretary of the Election Fighting Fund and Kathleen Courtney as Hon. Sec., the breach was never healed.

Common Cause: 4 June 1915

The Split in the NUWSS: Statement by Retiring Members

The real cleavage of opinion in the Union lies between those who consider it essential to work for the vote simply as a political tool, and those who believe that the demand for the vote should be linked with the advocacy of the deeper principles which underlie it—

Do we ask for the vote merely as a political tool, or do we wish the National Union to link it with the advocacy of the deeper principles, the consciousness of which has been the source of so much vigour and impassioned devotion to our workers?—

We believe that the Union cannot survive as a living organisation with the driving power of ideals behind it unless, at this tremendous crisis, it recognises the great principles for which it stands, and continues to uphold the ideal of the supremacy of moral force in human affairs. To this belief the N. U. has indeed already testified in its declaration against militancy.

CATHERINE MARSHALL, KATHLEEN COURTNEY AND OTHERS

By 1916 the Government had decided that manhood suffrage must be implemented. How could the vote continue to be denied to thousands of men willing to die for their country? Available suffragists reacted swiftly – many were otherwise engaged at home or abroad. The climate had already changed. In December 1916 Asquith was ousted and Lloyd George, who had never opposed women's suffrage per se, was the new Prime Minister. More crucially women had become an essential part of the war machine, in munition factories, on the land, in multifarious previously male jobs. There were women police, and women were soon to be serving with the armed forces in the WAAC, WRNS and WRAF.

from Unfinished Adventure

Within the Sphere of Practical Politics

By the time the need for a new Parliamentary Register brought our question at last within the sphere of practical politics, suffragists generally had combined once more into a force that counted; and the United Suffragists were only one of the societies represented on the National Adult Suffrage Society, which was formed in the autumn of 1916 when it appeared certain that manhood suffrage would be the basis of the forthcoming franchise measure and so our claim for equality could no longer be satisfied by the old limited Suffrage Bill. If any special credit was due to our own group for the suffrage victory in 1918, it was for the suggestion made by the United Suffragists through their representative, H.W. Nevinson, at a meeting arranged by Mrs Fawcett between suffragists and M.P.s and held in the House of Commons in August, 1916. This was to the effect that a conference presided by the Speaker should be convened for the purpose of framing a Reform Bill that should include women.

EVELYN SHARP

The Northern Men's Federation for Women's Suffrage

Founder and President – Mrs Arncliffe Sennett

August 10th, 1916

To the Rt. Hon. David Lloyd George M.P.

Sir,

It is not well for the Government to allow itself to be lulled into a sense of security against an uprising of women, should the Register be altered in any way without their inclusion—

We have suffered so abnormally through the cruel administration of Englishmen and their heartless apathy to the
inhuman conditions which they have forced upon our suffering
working woman—that were the Germans to invade this
Country, after the first avalanche of atrocities was over, we
could not see worse things than we behold to-day in our
midst—After all, British women are outlaws in their own land
and they could be no worse under German rule—We don't
desire German rule—but it is impossible to avoid the reflection
that we couldn't be worse off under *any* rule no matter whence
it came.

We will resist with all our might any alteration of the Franchise
without our inclusion and we are rapidly drawing to our side all
the Trade Unions of the country, who are now making our Cause
their own. The Northern men in various Northern Centres have
already done so.

Yours obediently,
Maud Arncliffe Sennett

from The Suffragette Movement

At last the terms of the Speaker's Conference Report were
announced: 'Votes for Women over thirty or thirty-five years of
age who were local government electors or wives of local government electors (i.e. owners and tenant householders and the
wives of both), and University graduates over thirty or thirty-five
years of age.' The Report was widely condemned. Mrs Pethick-
Lawrence wrote in the *Daily News*:

By what grotesque working of the political mind has the
conclusion been reached that the welfare of the community can only be safeguarded by the exclusion of women

from the human commonwealth until they have attained the age of thirty or thirty-five years?—

Yet in spite of such criticism from many sources the only robust determination to struggle for Adult Suffrage was to be found in the Workers' Suffrage Federation—The National Union of Women's Suffrage Society led the way in acceptance. It now held its first public meeting on Women's Suffrage since the declaration of the War, to request legislation on the lines of the Speaker's Conference Report. It also summoned a conference, whereat a large number of Women's Suffrage and Labour organisations were induced to welcome the recommendation to admit women to the franchise which the Speaker's Conference had made, without expressing an opinion as to the terms. This resolution was afterwards quoted as an acceptance of the terms of the report by all the societies concerned.

SYLVIA PANKHURST

NUWSS Executive Committee: 1 February 1917

The Speaker's Conference Proposals

Miss Eleanor Rathbone thought that the recommendations were not at all satisfactory as such a Franchise would be of no use to the factory worker. We had been pressing for the Franchise on account of the industrial dislocation to be expected after the War. This basis would only enfranchise the wives of Trade Unionists who would vote with the men. She thought we might have to yield to it, but it seemed like throwing over the factory worker altogether.

Mrs Strachey thought that the basis was thoroughly unsatisfactory, but that as it had been accepted by the Speaker's

Conference there was a strong presumption that it would also be accepted by the House—We stand a chance of really getting something now, and opposition to it based on however good reasons might wreck the chance altogether.

Trades, Professions & Occupations Represented on the Deputation to Mr Lloyd George, Thursday, March 29th, 1917

Introduced by Mrs Henry Fawcett, LL.D.

Agriculture
Ambulance Drivers
Accountants
Authors
Bacteriologists
Bookbinders
Bus Conductors
Bakers
Civil Servants
Carpenters
Chainmakers
Cutlery
Dentists
Dressmakers
Doctors
Dispensing Chemists
Electro-platers
Headmistresses
House Agents
Infant Welfare
Lamplighters

Pit-brow
Police
Poor Law Guardians
Post Office
Press
Railway-engine cleaners
Railwaywomen
Millicent Fawcett Hospital
  Units for Russia (N.U.W.S.S.)
Scottish Women's Hospitals
  (N.U.W.S.S.)
Sanitary Inspectors
Shipping
Silversmiths
Social Workers
Textile workers (Cotton)
Textile workers (Wool)
Temperance
Town Councillors
Teachers
Tailoring

Munitions	Telephonists
Munition Welfare	University Women
Midwives	Van Drivers.
Nurses I.C.C.	V.A.D
Nurses Norland	Weavers Association
Overseas Dominions	Women's Services
Oxy-acetylene Welders	

from The Cause

The Penultimate Fight: the House of Commons: June 1917

When the second reading of the Representation of the People Bill was taken, most of the discussion centred round the question of Women's Suffrage—Mr Lloyd George could not throw the women overboard, as Mr Gladstone had done, nor could he withdraw his whole Bill, like Mr Asquith; nor did he want to do these things. The tide had turned, and though they hardly dared to say it, the suffragists knew that victory was sailing in.

For all their certainty, however, the women who thronged the Ladies' Gallery on 10th June, when the House was to take the committee stage of Clause IV (the Women's Suffrage clause), were desperately excited. Often as some of them had sat there before, to hear their cause mocked, obstructed, or outvoted in the Chamber below, the scene was still painfully impressive. Through the bars of the absurd little cage* in which they were penned they saw chiefly the tops of the heads of the legislators, but the atmosphere of excitement which pervaded the House was noticeable even so. Members trooped in in unwonted numbers, and more than filled the benches. A dense crowd stood below the Bar, and overflowed into the side galleries. All the well-known friends and enemies were in their places, and there was that irrepressible buzz of sound which arises when the attention of the assembly is really aroused.

The debate went its way, noticeable chiefly for the great number of favourable speakers, and the hopeless tone of the opponents—The tide had really turned, and when the time for the division came there were found to be but 55 opponents in the whole House, while 385 went into the other lobby. The vote was larger than even the most optimistic had expected. It was victory without reserve.

RAY STRACHEY

* *'The absurd little cage' was a small space above the floor of the House, with a harem-like grille through which women peered down. After the favourable vote it was finally removed.*

from The Cause

The Penultimate Fight: The House of Lords: January 1918

The House of Lords had always been the stronghold of the league for opposing Women's Suffrage. Lord Curzon, who was still its president, was leader of the House, and there were plenty of others whose opposition was known to be strong and influential—

On 8th January 1918 the last fight began—As the debate went on, however, the anxious women began to feel more hope. There were speeches of the good old-fashioned type of course, and there were evidences of unabated prejudice; but there was also the breath of the new understanding. The Peers about whom nothing had been known seemed all to be speaking on the right side, and Mrs Humphry Ward, who sat beside Mrs Fawcett through the debates, looked uneasy and anxious. Her society, it appeared, had

241

lost hope in direct opposition and was trying at this late hour to secure the submission of the question to a referendum. She went so far as to ask Mrs Fawcett, as they sat there together, whether the suffragists would not support this course; but she must have known it to be a forlorn hope. The proposal was indeed made in the Chamber, and some discussion took place as to whether it should be a referendum to men only, or women only, or to men and women; but it was an unreal point, and presently vanished out of sight, and the last test came near.

Lord Curzon wound up the debate on the afternoon of the 10th of January, and as he rose to speak there was a hush of excitement. One of the policemen at the door, friendly as the police always were to the women, went along the passage to the committee-room, where a number of them were gathered, and put his head round the door. 'Lord Curzon is up, ladies,' he announced, 'but 'e won't do you no 'arm.' And so it was. For the President of the Anti-Suffrage League was forced to strike his colours. He said indeed, that the passage of the Bill would be the ruin of the country; women were politically worthless and the whole ideal of the Women's Movement was disastrous and wrong; he felt bound to say these things, for he believed them. But when it came to action he could not lead. The majority in the House of Commons had been too big, and if the Upper House rejected all that would happen would be that the Bill would be returned to them again with the clause re-inserted— For this part, he said, he could not take upon himself the responsibility of 'precipitating a conflict from which your Lordships would not emerge with credit and he would abstain from voting, one way or the other, upon the clause'. With that dramatic and wholly expected announcement the discussion ended, and the voting began; and the suffragists, as they waited for the figures, knew that their fight was won. One hundred and thirty-four Peers voted for the clause, 71 against it, and 13 abstained. The Representation of the People Bill was through both Houses; and on 6th February it received Royal Assent and became the law of the land. The fifty years' struggle was over, and the sex barrier was broken down.

RAY STRACHEY

from Unfinished Adventure

Bankruptcy Procedures: 'Everything Is Proper Under the Act'

I was only one among many tax resisters, but the others—had thought it right to pay their arrears on the outbreak of war. I thought they were wrong; for a war fought to save democracy did not seem to me to provide the best reason for supporting the principle of taxation without representation—The Treasury, having waited until the amount claimed, with costs of various summonses, had reached the sum of £50, were able to hand me over to the Bankruptcy Court. I found that the Court did not much like being used in this way to deal with a political debtor who was not in the ordinary sense insolvent; and they sent somebody round to see if I would not come to an arrangement before they took final action. Finding me obdurate, his manner ceased abruptly to be persuasive. I asked him what would happen next.

'An execution,' he replied acidly, and took up his hat and went. His tone could hardly have been more hostile had it portended the immediate erection of a guillotine under my window. So I came home one day, early in 1917, to find a bailiff sitting in my flat. The bailiff was a real gentleman. He obviously hated his job—Under the circumstances it was difficult for him to stay the whole 24 hours in my apartment, although, when I pointed this out to one of the officials who came round, he replied stiffly, 'Everything is proper under the Act,' which gave me an idea for a

French farce that I have never carried out. But the bailiff had finer feelings, and he made it as pleasant as he could for me by getting his meals elsewhere and going home at night and for weekends—and after he went away for the last time I really missed his unobtrusive presence in my best armchair. He was the one uneducated official with whom I had to deal in this business, and he put the others to shame.

I missed his armchair, too; for they came and cleared out everything except my actual clothes and my bed. They even took up the carpets and left me without curtains, and did not heed my repeated requests for my typewriter, without which I could not earn my living, to say nothing of my need as a writer of a table, chair, and books. Even a manual workman is allowed to keep his tools when bankrupt; so it was impossible not to suspect a certain amount of political persecution—For six months my persecutors diverted and opened all my correspondence, returning to me what they thought fit; and I hope they enjoyed some of the scurrilous anonymous letters that, in common with other Suffragettes and pacifists, I occasionally received. They also brought pressure to bear upon the gas and electricity supply companies to cut off my heating and lighting, though both companies afterwards allowed these to be restored under a friend's guarantee; and a final meanness was to cut off my telephone on the pretext of seizing the rent already paid in advance for the branch line—

Four times I had to appear before the Official Receiver at Carey Street, where I saw the greatest courtesy and forbearance being shown to real insolvent persons, who in some cases had flagrantly defrauded their creditors. Then, when my case came on and I submitted that I owed no debt in the world except this one, which I could not pay without violating my conscience, the officer who presided over the inquiry observed coldly, 'We have nothing to do with conscience here.' It was impossible to dispute his statement.

My friends rallied round me splendidly, lent me necessary furniture to render life just possible in my flat, and made representations to Mr Bonar Law, then Chancellor of the Exchequer, so that the worst features of my persecution were by Christmas time relaxed. The furniture was put up for sale and 'bought in' by my supporters, while the rest of the money was seized in the post. But I was not finally discharged until after the passage of the Franchise Bill.

The Mixed Delights of Victory

I think almost the happiest moment of my life was that in which I walked up Whitehall, with Henry W. Nevinson and Bertha Brewster at my side, on the evening when the Reform Bill received the Royal Assent. To live to see the triumph of a 'lost' cause for which we have suffered much and would have suffered everything, must be almost the greatest of delights. That delight was mine as memories crowded into my mind, of women who had been insulted, rolled in the mud, just there, for attempting to enter the House of Commons and present their petition; years of effort diverted from other causes and other interests, of friends lost by the way and friends gained in the struggle, of horrid disillusionment and transfiguring revelation; memories that hurt so much that they had to be buried out of sight, and memories so illumined by fine behaviour and delicious humour that they would remain a precious possession until the end of life. I suppose victory, to a greater or less extent, contains this kind of exquisite if mixed delight for everyone who has fought a good fight; but I cannot imagine that victory could mean all that ours did unless, like ours, it were the bloodless triumph of a fight for human freedom.

I am sometimes asked if the enfranchisement of women has accomplished all that was expected of it by those who worked to bring it about. That seems to me such a queer question.

EVELYN SHARP

245

The Vote: 1 Feb 1918

Congratulations from German Suffragists

Although we German women have at the present time no ground for rejoicing at the progress of our Cause in our own country, we have followed with all the greater joy and with warmest sympathy the great and unexpected success of our sisters in other lands. Not only as successes of the Cause which binds and holds us together beyond all the terrors and sufferings of the world war, but also out of pardonable selfishness because these victories promise us, too, ultimate victory.

MARIE STRITT, PRESIDENT GERMAN NATIONAL WOMAN SUFFRAGE SOCIETY

The Women's Party

Mrs Pankhurst, Hon Treas: Annie Kenney, Hon. Sec: General Flora Drummond, Chief Organiser

23rd February, 1918.

Dear Friend,

We are writing to you as a friend of the W.S.P.U. in the days when it was fighting for the Vote, because we know that you will consider it a privilege to take part in celebrating the wonderful triumph of our cause.

Votes for Women has been won because the W.S.P.U. was blessed with marvellous leadership, which drew to itself loyal and enthusiastic followers. The W.S.P.U. by its pre-war crusade for the Vote, followed by its patriotic stand and national service during the War, has won the greatest political victory on record.

Under its new name of 'The Women's Party', the W.S.P.U. has now even greater work to do, for it has to ensure that the

246

Women's vote shall be of the utmost possible service in protecting the industrial and other interests of women, and in securing the progress and safety of the nation as a whole. Indeed we need not remind you that everything depends on how vote is used, now that it has been won—

The failure to mention other suffrage societies' involvement was characteristic of the Pankhursts and the WSPU. Neither Mrs Pankhurst, nor Annie Kenney, nor Flora Drummond played any part in the lobbying that led to the 1918 victory.

National News: 10 March 1918

Women Voters: Special Interview with Mrs Henry Fawcett

Now that the People's Bill has enfranchised over 6,000,000 women, there is great interest, particularly in political circles, as to how far these new voters will support the existing parties, and what policy they will pursue. Mrs Henry Fawcett, President of the National Union of Women's Suffrage Societies, said that the suffrage movement in the past has always supported the Labour Party, because it was the only party in the House which definitely upheld the women's cause. 'The Labour Party,' she continued, 'has done a great deal for women and is making every effort to organise them to-day. At the next election it will contest a great number of seats, and I know for a fact that it is running several women as candidates. For these reasons it was only logical that women should support the Labour Party. But I am quite unable to say how women will vote at the next election. It is true that most of those enfranchised by the recent Act are working women, but that does not necessarily say that they will support the Labour movement—

'There are a great many evils which I hope to see remedied now that women have secured the vote. The problem of women's employment, both industrial and professional, is one which demands immediate attention—The Civil Service, employing as it does several thousands of women workers, is one of the first Government Departments women electors will insist on seeing modified. Until a few years ago the Government was one of the worst employers of women workers—in fact, many of the most flagrant cases of sweating were found in Government offices—

'The granting of the franchise to women I regard as a very great victory—At the same time, while I am delighted with the vote, I am by no means satisfied. A law which gives a boy the vote and withholds it from a woman until she is thirty cannot be said to be a fair one. We supported the recommendations of the Speaker's Conference because it was a compromise—A very similar procedure was adopted in Norway when women were first given the vote in that country—But in Norway it soon became apparent that any difficulties—were illusory—and I am sure a similar condition of affairs will prevail in this country.'

Daily Express: 2 April 1918

Why Not Women M.P.s? Can a woman become a Member of Parliament?

That is the question which Miss Nina Boyle, of the Women's Freedom League, is testing by putting herself forward as a candidate for the Parliamentary vacancy at Keighley—Miss Boyle, who has arrived in the constituency—contends that there is no specific law debarring a woman voter from nomination and election—She pointed out that common law has gone by the board since the war began, and as there are now women at the War Office, women constables, sworn in with powers of arrest, and women in many other responsible positions, she did not think it right that lack of precedent should be allowed to debar women from their rights when it did not debar them from service.

Manchester Guardian: 20 April 1918

Women as Parliamentary Candidates

The Returning Officer at Keighley has refused the nomination papers of Miss Boyle, the woman candidate, but he has done so on the ground of a technical flaw, and he has stated that had they been in proper form he would have accepted them. This result is all that Miss Boyle set out to achieve, and it is of the first importance. Ever since Whitelock, in Cromwellian times, classed women with peers and lunatics, the common law has deemed them ineligible— Their right to stand should be clearly affirmed, and the presumption bound up with the granting to them of the franchise given legal shape.

An amendment was rushed through Parliament enabling women to stand as candidates in the 'Coupon Election' that followed immediately after the Armistice.

The Problems of Voting

Letter to Maud Arncliffe Sennett

Ashford July 1918

Dearest Old Aunt Maud

Thank you so much for your long letter—Fancy you thinking that I should not trouble to register my vote! You must think me a backslider or 'outsider'! Not only am I doing so, but I am trying to get everyone I know who has the qualifications to register theirs. I have already got two promised, one the wife of a furious & malignant 'anti'. Isn't that lovely?

Miss Smith and I spent all the morning trying to find the place to vote without success—Everyone we asked was so nasty. I can quite understand now how beastly it must have been to have had that wall of insulting prejudice against one in every turn, if they are like this now that it is won! This afternoon I made further enquiries & this is the exact position at present. Ashford voting list has not been altered for years. The Town Clerk is dead & has yet no successor. No one has instructions to deal with the matter yet. Before long they expect instructions to prepare a new register in which both men & women will be included!

Your affectionate niece Milly

Daily Express: 8 December 1918

The First Woman M.P.?

—As things stand now it looks as if Miss Christabel Pankhurst, the patriotic Independent candidate for Smethwick, will be winner among the women candidates—Smethwick is wide awake to the fight and keenly interested in its Christabel. Around her has gathered the brightest spirits of the Women's Party – Mrs Drummond, Miss Phyllis Ayrton, Miss Georgina Brackenbury and, of course Mrs Pankhurst – 'my greatest asset' as Miss Pankhurst prettily said to me today.

Poster and lantern parades, incessant meetings in the open air by day and in halls by night, decorated cars and bicycles are all playing their part in interesting the electors. One of the latest arrivals is Miss Billinghurst, the crippled woman who has been among the staunchest of the Pankhurstites, and already her tricycle, gaily decorated, is a familiar object in the streets. Miss Pankhurst made the following statement to me today:- 'Smethwick is patriotic to the core, men and women. That is one of the great reasons why I chose to stand for this division, and why I believe I shall be returned at the head of the poll. The voters understand that I shall actively support Mr Lloyd George, the Victory Premier, and the Coalition Government in all their efforts towards a victorious peace.'

Daily News: 11 December 1918

A novel feature is being introduced in Chelsea. The supporters of Miss Phipps have fitted up a model polling booth at their committee rooms, 371 Kings-road, where women electors can practise voting. They are also making arrangements to mind the babies of any over-burdened mothers while they are absent at the polls.

Sunday Pictorial: 15 December 1918

Mrs 'Granny' Lambert, of Edmonton, who is on the voters' register for the first time. She is 105 years of age, and says she has never heard of Mr Lloyd George.

1918 Election Results – Defeated
Women Candidates

Miss Christabel Pankhurst (Coalition) Smethwick	8,614
Miss Mary Macarthur (Labour)Stonebridge	7,587
Mrs Despard (Labour) N. Battersea	5,634
Miss Alison Garland (Liberal) S. Portsmouth	4,283
Miss Violet Markham (Liberal) Mansfield	4,000
Mrs Dacre Fox (Independent) Richmond	3,615
Mrs Lucas (Unionist) Kensington	3,573
Mrs Pethick-Lawrence (Labour) Rusholme	2,985
Mrs E. Phipps (Independent) Chelsea	2,419
Mrs How Martyn (Independent) Hendon	2,067
Mrs J. McEwan (Liberal) Enfield	1,987
Mrs Corbett Ashby (Liberal) Ladywood	1,552
Mrs Oliver Strachey (Independent) Chiswick	1,263
Mrs Eunice Murray (Independent) Bridgeton	991
Miss W. Carney (Sinn Fein) Belfast	395
Hon. Mrs MacKenzie (Labour) Welsh University	176

The only woman to be elected was Constance Markievicz, but she was imprisoned for her part in the 1916 Easter Rising in Dublin and as a member of Sinn Fein would in any case have refused to take her seat in the British House of Commons. The once virulent Anti, Violet Markham, had undergone a Pauline conversion to the Cause during the war.

1919–1929

Women's questions are for the moment in the trough of a wave

NUSEC Annual Report 1921

1929 will for ever stand out in the history of the women's movement as the first year in which wmen had the opportunity of exercising the vote on exactly the same terms as men

NUSEC Annual Report

After 1919 no more was heard of the Women's Party, nor in the suffrage context of Mrs Pankhurst and her beloved daughter Christabel. The NUWSS changed its name to the National Union of Societies for Equal Citizenship (NUSEC). The problems it faced are outlined in the first annual report. The women's cause also faced the deepening disillusionment, widespread unemployment and political instability of the post-war years. In 1922 Lloyd George's Coalition Government collapsed. At the General Election the Tories were returned to power with Bonar Law (a dying man) Prime Minister, followed by Stanley Baldwin. In January 1924 a minority Labour Government led by Ramsay MacDonald came to power. Yet another General Election in the same year saw the Tories under Baldwin back in office, this time for a full term – which included the 1926 General Strike. In 1929 Labour was again returned to power. As Israel Zangwill had predicted years before it was a Conservative Government that finally gave women the vote on the same terms as men – at twenty-one, then the age of majority.

NUSEC Annual Report 1919

The first year of the Union's existence after the gaining of a substantial measure of Women's Suffrage has been, not altogether unexpectedly, one of some difficulty. There have been many reasons for this—many societies, once the Representation of the People Act was law, not unnaturally decided to disband. Again the war has opened to many young women all-absorbing and responsible careers in Government offices, QMAAC and other services, and this probably accounts for the fact that recruiting for Suffrage Societies among the younger generation has not been very brisk. Further, the creation of Women Citizen Associations and the like, many of which owe their origin to Suffrage Societies, absorb energy which heretofore went into the Suffrage movement.

It remains true, however, that the cause for which the NUWSS was created has not yet been won, that there is real and imminent danger of many of those careers, professions and trades which have been opened to women being once again closed to them— For these and other reasons it is difficult not to feel that a great future lies before the Union, and that open-minded experiment should lead to the finding of the best method for focussing the demand that undoubtedly exists for the complete equality of liberties, status, and opportunities between men and women.

8th IWSA Congress: Geneva 6–12 June 1920

Mrs Chapman Catt's Address

Since the last Congress, held in Budapest in 1913, the greatest of world wars has devastated the earth. Out of its cruel sorrows and tragedies women of many nations have emerged politically free. The last seven years have witnessed victories for the cause of women suffrage in no fewer than sixteen countries. In Austria, Belgium, Bohemia, British East Africa, Canada, Denmark, Great Britain and Ireland, Holland, Hungary, Iceland, Jamaica, Poland, Rhodesia, Russia, and Sweden women have been partially or wholly enfranchised, and in the USA Arizona, Nevada, Montana, New York, South Dakota, Oklahoma, Texas, Arkansas, and Michigan have been added to those states which have given full and equal suffrage; the Federal Amendment has passed both Houses of Legislature, and has been ratified by thirty-two of the necessary thirty-six states. This triumph of justice is assuredly one of the most definite and positive results of the world war now visible.

NUSEC Annual Report 1921

Another year has passed with practically nothing to show in the way of legislative achievement—It is clear that women's questions are for the moment in the trough of the wave, and that much solid organisation is necessary before anything approaching a real equality can be secured.

NUSEC Annual Report 1922

The year has not been wholly without progress— The British Parliament has granted suffrage to the women of Burmah on equal terms, which have still been denied to British women. For the first time a woman has been appointed a substitute delegate to the League of Nations; the first women barristers have been called and have appeared in court, and the first woman solicitor has qualified in England, a Scottish woman having preceded her by two years.

Your Committee followed with great interest the progress of Lady Rhondda's claim for a seat in the House of Lords, and was delighted at the first report of the Committee of Privileges, which allowed the claim. The disappointment was, therefore all the more grievous when, on the matter being referred back once again to the Committee of Privileges, on which new members had been appointed, the recommendations first made were reversed.

Viscountess Rhondda had inherited the title on her father's death in 1918. Her claim was based on being a peeress in her own right and equality of treatment.

NUSEC Annual Report 1923

The year 1923 shows a chequered history of triumphs and disappointments. The triumphs consist of two actual legislative achievements in the shape of the Matrimonial Causes Act and the Bastardy Act, and the successful return of eight women to Parliament. The disappointments were once again due to the unexpected curtailment of the Session by the General Election, which—left draft Bills which your Committee was either promoting or supporting, stranded and incomplete.

Apart from political events, the successful Congress of the International Woman Suffrage Alliance, held in Rome in May, was the outstanding feature of a memorable year. Mrs Corbett Ashby, who has served the National Union for many years as a member of the Executive, and lately as Vice-Chairman, was elected president to fill the place left vacant by the resignation of Mrs Chapman Catt, the distinguished founder and first President of the Alliance.

NUSEC Annual Report 1926

This year the Government has certainly not sought to acquire fresh laurels in the realm of social reform, and the measures relating to women can certainly not be described as epoch-making—The lack of parliamentary progress with regard to Equal Franchise has been a very depressing factor—In directions other than parliamentary, your Committee can record a year of vigour and growth in the Union, and an increase in the number of Societies.

Acton Women's Citizens Association

Annual Report 1925–26

By far the most successful of our meetings (the audience numbered nearly one hundred) was our At Home of Feb. the 27th when at least we were able to congratulate ourselves on two points: one was the brilliance of Ald. Miss Smee's speech on 'Woman Citizen as Mayor', the other was the excellence of our cakes.

Unfortunately some other meetings were poorly attended. This was partly due to the weather which has been unflinchingly against us. Yet I would like to commend the bravery of this small body of 15 or 20 may be who have dared to walk through fog, snow, rain, storm, to come to those inhospitable rooms of the Priory School—It is true that our programme has no special attraction in itself for we do not say: Come to us and you will see your rates decrease – or join our movement & you will get houses at pre-war rent etc. We simply want to train the women of Acton to make a wise use of their citizenship—We had a successful debate on 'Votes for Women at 21' when the courage and the eloquence of Capt. Tate, Barrister-at-law, proved of no avail before the arguments and caustic wit of Councillor Mrs Moore of Willesden.

NUSEC Annual Report 1927

The chief event of 1927 has been the definite assurance by the Prime Minister [Stanley Baldwin] of his intention to introduce during the following session the legislation to give effect to his election pledge to give Equal Franchise. In the Albert Hall on 27 May he said:

> I, for one, not only look with no apprehension at the enfranchisement of both sexes at the same time. I welcome it. I believe that a Democracy is incomplete and lopsided until it is representative of the whole people, and the responsibility rests alike on men and women.

The harvest of our strenuous effort during the last nine years on behalf of this great cause seems about to be gathered in.

Equal Political Rights Campaign Committee

Chairman – The Viscountess Rhondda
HELP WOMEN TO GET JUSTICE!
VOTES FOR WOMEN AT 21 ON THE SAME TERMS AS MEN!
COME TO THE GREAT DEMONSTRATION
in Trafalgar Square on Saturday, July 16th, at 5 p.m. (1927)
Dame MILLICENT FAWCETT, D.B.E., and Mrs DESPARD
will be present.

Actresses' Franchise League, Association of Women Clerks and Secretaries, British Commonwealth League, Civil Service Clerical Association, Federation of Women Civil Servants, Guild of Girl Citizens, League of the Church Militant, London Young Liberal Federation, National Union of Societies for Equal Citizenship, National Union of Women Teaches, Open Door Council, St Joan's Social and Political Alliance, Six Point Group, Standing Joint Committee of Women's Industrial Organisations, Women's Co-operative Guild, Women's Election Committee, National Guild of Empire, Women's Freedom League, Women's International League, Women's National Liberal Federation, Young Suffragists.

Time and Tide: 16 March 1928

Equal Franchise at Last

The Bill, which is the short and simple measure that the women's organisations have all along demanded, provides that both Parliamentary and Local Government Franchise shall be the same for men and women. The women's organisations are completely satisfied with the text of the Bill—In introducing the Measure in this form the Prime Minister has undoubtedly had regard to his pledge both in the spirit and in the letter.

Time and Tide: 6 April 1928

The papers during the past week have been full of the implications of the change which equal suffrage must bring. The time will come, declares Mr Garvin in *The Observer*, when we shall see a woman as Prime Minister. No doubt it will—

Time and Tide: 11 May 1928

If any person had prophesied two years ago, or even a year ago, that equal political rights between men and women could be so universally accepted within so short a period, that it would be possible to-day for AN EQUAL FRANCHISE BILL to pass its THIRD READING in the House of Commons without division and even without comment, a soul would hardly have believed him—It is still uncertain when the Bill will be taken to the House of Lords, but we understand that it is the intention that the Second Reading shall take place before Whitsuntide.

Time and Tide: 25 May 1928

The House of Lords, as was expected, passed the Second Reading of the EQUAL FRANCHISE Bill by a large majority—Lord Birkenhead wound up the debate for the Government in a speech—(of) amazing inaccuracy in respect both to dates and facts—'My recommendation to your Lordships,' he concluded, 'is to go into the Lobby in favour of this Bill, if without enthusiasm, yet in a spirit of resolute resignation.' And the peers took his advice.

Time and Tide: 22 June 1928

At half-past five on Monday afternoon last, in the House of Lords, the Lord Chancellor formally moved the Third Reading of the EQUAL FRANCHISE BILL. The Bill was read a third time, without discussion, and passed. It now awaits only the Royal Assent, which will, it is expected, be given within the next couple of weeks, to become the law of the land—

By a sad coincidence the day that saw the final passage of the Equal Franchise Bill also saw the funeral of the woman who more than anyone else in the world was responsible for the victory which it embodies. We of to-day stand much too close to the great changes for which MRS PANKHURST was so largely responsible to be able to appreciate their immensity. It was not merely the achievement of the vote that the movement of which she was the leader brought about – it was far more than this, a revolution (or at least the beginning of a revolution, for the end is not yet) in the status of women and in their attitude towards themselves.

Press Cutting: 18 June 1928

Mrs Pankhurst: Impressive Funeral Scenes

Deeply impressive scenes marked the funeral of Mrs Emmeline Pankhurst yesterday. The route from Westminster to Brompton Cemetery was lined with reverent crowds, and behind the coffin there marched a considerable body of old and young comrades who had been associated with her in the campaign for women's suffrage.

One of the most remarkable features of a great demonstration was the number of tricolour sashes worn, reminiscent of the pre-war days of the movement, as well as medals, rosettes, and ribbons, and the broad-arrow badges of those who went to the prison for the cause years ago.

NUSEC Annual Report 1929

1929 will for ever stand out in the history of the Women's Movement as the first year in which women had the opportunity of exercising their vote on exactly the same terms as men. Further as a result of that General Election the largest number of women yet returned to the House of Commons was elected. Among the 14 women elected there was Miss Eleanor Rathbone, our President for the previous ten years—The appointment of Miss Margaret Bondfield to the Cabinet as Minister of Labour, was a matter of satisfaction and congratulation to all feminists.

Time and Tide: 22 June 1929

The First Woman Cabinet Minister

Perhaps the most interesting thing about Miss Bondfield's appointment as Labour Minister is the matter-of-fact way in which it has been accepted by press and public. The appointment of the first Woman Cabinet Minister, the bare idea of which only twenty years ago would have seemed almost as fantastic as a voyage to the moon, has been received to-day with a general quiet approval, and has seemed so much the natural, the obvious thing that it has passed almost without press headlines. Nevertheless, Mr (Ramsay) MacDonald is to be congratulated. The obvious step, if it is a new one, is sometimes a difficult one to take.

Some Contemporary Assessments of the Leaders

A Reed of Steel

There has been no other woman like Emmeline Pankhurst. She was beautiful. Her pale face, with its delicate square jaw and rounded temples, recalled the pansy by its shape and a kind of velvety bloom on the expression. She dressed her taut little body with a cross between the elegance of a Frenchwoman and the neatness of a nun. She was courageous; small and fragile and no longer young, she put herself in the way of horses' hooves, she stood up on platforms under a rain of missiles, she sat in the darkness of underground jails and hunger-struck, and when they let her out because she had starved herself within touching distance of death, she rested for only a day or two and then clambered back on to the platforms, she staggered back under the horses' hooves—She was vibrant. One felt, as she lifted up her hoarse, sweet voice on the platform, that she was trembling like a reed. Only the reed was of steel, and it was tremendous.

The Press loved to present the movement with contempt and derision. Mrs Pankhurst and her daughters were crazy hooligans, their followers were shrieking hysterics, their policy was wild delirium. Nothing could be further from the truth. The movement contained some of the detraqués who follow any drum that is beaten, but these were weeded out, for the Cat and Mouse Act was something of a test for the soldier qualities.

But the movement was neither crazy nor hysterical nor delirious. It was stone-cold in its realism. Mrs Pankhurst was not a clever woman, but when she experienced something she incorporated it in her mind and used it as a basis for action. When she started the Women's Social and Political Union she was sure of two things: that the ideas of freedom and justice which had been slowly developing in England during the eighteenth and nineteenth centuries had grown to such maturity that there existed an army of women resentful of being handicapped by artificial disadvantages imposed simply on the grounds of their sex, and that sex-antagonism was so strong among men that it produced an attitude which, if it were provoked to candid expression, would make every self-respecting woman want to fight it. In both of these suppositions she was entirely correct. The real force that made the suffrage movement was the quality of the opposition. Women, listening to anti-suffrage speeches, for the first time knew what many men really thought of them—apart from general principles, the wicked frivolity of the attitude adopted towards the women by the Liberal Government was the real recruiting-sergeant for the movement—

Mrs Pankhurst never wanted to be old, and her body had been hideously maltreated. As a result of injuries received in forcible feedings, she still suffered from a recurrent form of jaundice. In 1928, shortly after women had received full adult suffrage, she went to church on Easter Monday in the country, was driven home to Whitechapel, took to her bed and, for no particular medical reason, died. She left £72.

REBECCA WEST

Although her health suffered dreadfully from constant hunger-and-thirst strikes, Mrs Pankhurst was never actually forcibly fed. She died in a West End nursing home. Her pathetically small estate amounted to £86.5.6d.

from My Commonplace Book

An Extremist Hero

My own view is that Mrs Pankhurst was born extremist and never well-balanced, that the outbreak of war in 1914 saved her from real mental unbalance resulting from the physical and emotional stresses of the militant suffrage movement, and that thereafter— she never wholly recovered that balance. I think that the outbreak of war in 1914 saved her from herself and saved the W.S.P.U. from an ignominious end. It had shot its bolt, and what an effective bolt it had been.

In March 1928 the National Union, by now the National Union of Societies for Equal Citizenship, organised a meeting in Queen's Hall at which the Prime Minister, Mr Baldwin, was to announce his Government's commitment to the Bill which at last was to give us the equal voting right for which we had campaigned so long. It was a widely representative meeting, chaired by Eleanor Rathbone—Mrs Pankhurst had a front seat on the platform but she was not one of the speakers. I think that many younger members of the audience did not know who she was. She looked very frail, dignified and aloof, almost as though she did not care very much about what was happening. As I looked at her, I wondered whether she recalled the acclaim and hero-worship which had so often surrounded her in that same hall. I certainly recalled it; and when a few months later her death was reported, a bell tolled in my mind for the death of a hero.

MARY STOCKS

from I Have Been Young

I had a great admiration for Mrs Pankhurst, whose eloquence came from the deep heart of womanhood and put into burning words what millions of women must have inarticulately felt for centuries. For – let there be no mistake about it – this movement was not primarily political; it was social, moral, psychological and profoundly religious.

This little woman, not young, with tragic smouldering eyes, a deep voice and a Lancashire burr (I can still hear her cry 'join uzz!') could play upon her audience with untaught art that comes from passionate sincerity and passionate courage. I heard her often, and I never found her dull, until a melancholy night in 1915, when the ghost of the woman she had been talked unbelievable nonsense about Germans at a Queen's Hall meeting.

I felt some admiration for Christabel's impudence and quick wit. She was particularly agile at question time, but her accounts had little relation to facts. She seemed to me a lonely person; with all her capacity for winning adorers (women and men), with all the brightness of her lips and cheeks and eyes, she was, unlike her sisters, cynical and cold at heart. She gave me the impression of fitful and impulsive ambition and quite ruthless love of domination. I used to find her speeches silly; heaven was to come down on earth, sweating was to be abandoned, venereal diseases to disappear, eternal peace to reign. Meanwhile, she created the atmosphere of a dog-fight. There grew up by degrees, the insolence of dictatorship.

Sylvia was more interesting. She was essentially an artist, drawn into the unsuitable and unsympathetic political machine. Martyrdom, in itself, attracted her, and she would go to great lengths in inviting it. She was a very provoking colleague, owing to her habit of going her own separate way, even after she had joined others in hammering out an agreed way. There might have been give and take, and they would, perhaps, loyally carry out the agreed compromise, only to find that, like one of the hoops in Alice's game of croquet, Sylvia had wandered off to another part of the field. She was, however, more lovable than Christabel and her devotion to the people with whom she was later to make her home in the East End was beautiful.

HELENA SWANWICK

268

from We Were Amused

In time, we became known as minor members of that vast army, the Women's Social and Political Union, and knew most of its leaders save Mrs Pankhurst herself. For did *anyone* know her? This aloof, frail woman with her look of wearied contempt shunned the personal touch, probably recognised in herself with that pride, terror and dismay experienced by some women who feel the call to the religious life, that she was an idea rather than a friend and mother, a torchbearer, dedicated and – inevitably – fanatical. (The only perfectly funny thing in connection with her was that when her memorial statue was formally unveiled, the police band volunteered to come and play round it – and did.)

Her perfect foil was Emmeline Pethick-Lawrence, the then treasurer, for Pethums, as we called her, was happily married, childless, temperamentally feminine had times been normal, and could and did blarney and coax with charm, conviction and financial triumph. She was also more acceptable to the mob, her speeches more home-like and therefore reassuring than were the iced but brilliant discourses of Mrs Pankhurst. But all the leaders were remarkable orators, while Mrs Pankhurst had such perfect vocal pitch that she could make herself heard without shouting, above two other mass meetings in Hyde Park.

Of her three daughters, the eldest, Christabel, had, I think, mopped up the lion's share of brains and vitality; in a day of comparative *laissez-aller* where the education of girls was concerned, she had acquired an LL.B. degree. Sylvia was a competent artist, particularly in murals, if her work struck us as being something debilitated and what we call Kensington Flop, while her sister, Adela, I cannot remember to have possessed any extra-militant parlour tricks at all. The only Pankhurst son [*to survive childhood*], Harry, died before his possibilities became apparent.

RACHEL FERGUSON

269

The Death of Millicent Garrett Fawcett

NUSEC Tribute

We trusted her and greatly venerated her balance, her courage, her judgement and her wit. We knew that she was a great leader of women and a great historical figure. We were unspeakably proud of her. But in addition we loved her, her personality, her appearance, her voice, her *self*.

Time and Tide: 22 November 1929

The Fawcett Memorial Service

The memorial service for Dame Millicent Fawcett in Westminster Abbey last Tuesday was a national tribute of great dignity to a national leader whose long political service helped change the course of history. The leaders of the three political parties, each of which had at some time opposed or delayed her work, united in honouring her. Members of Parliament, peers and representatives of women's organisations were present, but the vast majority were women, who whether in mufti or in their academic robes, bore witness to the revolution in their position which has taken place since Emily Davies, staying with the Garretts at Aldburgh, declared that she would have to devote herself to securing higher education for women, while Elizabeth Garrett opened the medical profession to them, and then turned to the child Millicent and told her that she, being younger than they, must get the vote. The vote has been won, though not entirely by the leadership of Dame Millicent. She never failed to acknowledge the part played by her great contemporary, Mrs Pankhust; and now they have both passed on their work to others, and received the homage which it seemed so improbable that their effort would ever win.

from I Have Been Young

Millicent Garrett Fawcett

In spite of her modesty, in spite of her adherence to 'constitutional methods', in spite of her demure and unobtrusive personality, Mrs Fawcett was undoubtedly our most remarkable woman. In an age much addicted to superlatives, in which so many nonentities are 'too marvellous' and people leap into the limelight, and back again, with bewildering rapidity the slow, steady, persistent life-work of such women as Millicent Fawcett, demands of us a soberness of statement in accord with their characters—I quote the following passage from an article of mine which appeared in *Time and Tide* just after her death in 1929:

'Not easily can young women now reconstruct English society in the 1860's and grasp two of its most important conditions for a successful feminist movement. First and foremost the leaders must be lady-like and modest; this, in the very best sense of the words, Mrs Fawcett was. Secondly it was a time when people still believed in the appeal to reason, and there was a very widespread belief that women could not reason; therefore Mrs Fawcett's style of quiet argument, with no oratory and little emotion evident, but with ample store of fact and anecdote and with a self-control which always commanded her nerves and her temper, she was ideally suited to be a pioneer. Moreover she looked nice, dressed becomingly, was married to a heroic blind politician and was to him the perfect wife. I sometimes think that all Mrs Fawcett's art of living so completely concealed its art that people were apt to forget the self-discipline and the public spirit which had drilled her to present such a placid surface, and underrated the steadiness of the moral fibre within.

'Her humour was the salt of life to her and her friends. I remember in particular how she, standing demure and elderly, the very pattern of the cultivated middle-class lady, delighted us by reciting with immense gusto Rudyard Kipling's egregious poem, with its refrain: "The female of the species is more deadly than the male." There was something in it, I believe, about fangs dripping blood and claws that scratched, and Mrs Fawcett would pause now and then and say, "That's me!" On another occasion she teased me to go and see *Medea* with her when I thought I was too busy, and exclaimed, "You must take a holiday sometimes – besides *Medea's* such a good suffrage play!"—'

She accepted people's sometimes provoking differences from herself with admirable calm. 'It's no use arguing with X,' she said, '*She knows*. God has told her.'—When differences of opinion about the war divided us as workers she would not allow it to divide us as friends—The last time I saw her was when we sat together in the gallery of the House of Lords to hear the King's Assent read to the Act enfranchising all women over twenty-one.

HELENA SWANWICK

Time and Tide: 22 June 1928

A Modern Girl to Mrs Pankhurst

I never knew you; never came within the sphere
Of that most radiant personality
I rarely thought of you, nor knew I held you dear
Nor realised for what you stood to me;
For what I breathed in with my native air
For womanhood enfranchised, educated, free.

My career opens, before me rise the heights
Of beckoning high achievement I must scale.
Fear not, oh fighter of a thousand fights,
I am a true woman and I shall not fail.
But, as you pass on your last journey, proud and grave,
I, the heiress of the ground which you have won,
I cry 'ALL HAIL'

Appendices

Acknowledgements
and Sources

The Home Office (HO), Metropolitan Police (MEPO) and Prison Commissioner (PCOM) files covering the militant suffrage years are at the Public Record Officer, Kew, London. Extracts are from: PCOM8/228: HO45/10725 & 11057: HO144/1043/183461: 1045/184808: 1054/187986: 1106/200455: 1107/200655: 1169/214572: 1205/221862: 1254/234646: 1305/248506: 882/167074. My thanks to the always helpful staff at the Public Record Office.

The Collections of the Suffragette Fellowship founded by Edith How Martyn and of David Mitchell (Pankhurst biographer) are at the Museum of London, the Barbican. I am most grateful to Gail Cameron for her assistance and while she was on holiday to Sue Webber and Alex Werner (whose German ancestors were related to Lydia Becker's) for theirs, particularly the loan of the computer when mine crashed! As ever my thanks to David Doughan *et al* at the Fawcett Library in London. The personal recollections of Lilian Lenton, Charlotte Marsh and Eileen Casey are taken from the transcripts of tape recordings made in the 1960s, which the Fawcett Library holds. Maud Arncliffe Sennett's husband donated her Suffrage Collection to the British Museum after her death in 1936. My thanks to the Trustees of the British Library for permission to draw on this treasure-trove. Originally the thousands of her cuttings and letters were stored in cardboard boxes but are now – like the

Manchester Central Library archive – on not always decipherable microfiche.

The Woman Suffrage Collection in the Local Studies Unit of the Central Library, Manchester, houses the papers of Lydia Becker, letters to and from Millicent Garrett Fawcett and other pioneers; the minutes of the North of England/Manchester Women's Suffrage Society; and swatches of the IWSA's and NUWSS's First World War correspondence. Much of the material was preserved by Margaret Ashton – NUWSS activist and Manchester's first woman councillor – who donated it to the library in 1922. I am grateful to the Principal Archivist of the Manchester Central Library for permission to quote from the collection.

My work on the Anthology was nearing its end when Elizabeth Crawford's monumental tome, *The Women's Suffrage Movement: A Reference Guide 1886–1928*, was published in 1999 by UCL Press. Unfortunately, it's a monumental price too (£110), but being able to double-check information and to trust Elizabeth's research for any untraced item was a boon. I extend my grateful thanks and admiration for her diligence.

Permission to reprint copyright material is gratefully acknowledged. Unless otherwise stated the place of publication is London.

Lena **Ashwell** extracts from *Myself a Player* (Michael Joseph, 1936).

Teresa **Billington-Greig** extracts from *The Non-Violent Militant: Selected Writings of Teresa Billington-Greig* (Routledge & Kegan Paul, 1978) by kind permission of the editors Carol McPhee and Ann Fitzgerald.

Helen **Blackburn** extracts from *Women's Suffrage: A Record of the Women's Suffrage Movement in the British Isles with Biographical Sketches of Miss Becker* (Williams & Norgate, 1902).

Doris **Nield Chew** extracts from *Ada Nield Chew: The Life and Writings of a Working Woman* (Virago Press, 1982).

Rachel **Ferguson** extracts from *We Were Amused* (Jonathan Cape, 1958).

Mary **Gawthorpe** extracts from *Up the Hill to Holloway* (Traversity Press, Maine, USA, 1962).

Cicely **Hamilton** extract from *Beware! A Warning to Suffragists* (Artists' Suffrage League c. 1908–9; reprinted by Legjams Productions, 1982) by kind permission of Lady Patricia Bower.

Annie Kenney extracts from *Memories of a Militant* (Edward Arnold, 1924).

Jill Liddington and Jill Norris extracts from *One Hand Tied Behind Us* (Virago Ltd, 1978: new revised edition Rivers Oram, 2000) by kind permission of Jill Liddington and Chris Trent.

Lillah McCarthy extract from *Myself and Friends* (Thornton Butterworth, 1933).

John Stuart Mill extracts from *The Subjection of Women* (first published 1869).

Hannah Mitchell extracts from *The Hard Way up* (Faber & Faber, 1968; Virago Ltd, reprinted 1977) by permission of Faber & Faber.

Henry W. Nevinson extracts from *Fire of Life* (James Nisbet & Co. Ltd, 1935).

Margaret Wynne Nevinson extracts from *Life's Fitful Fever* (A. & C. Black, 1926).

Christabel Pankhurst extracts from *Unshackled: The Story of How We Won the Vote* (Hutchinson, 1959).

Emmeline Pankhurst extracts from *My Own Story* (Eveleigh Nash, 1914; Virago Ltd reprinted, 1979; reprinted by Greenwood Press).

Sylvia Pankhurst extracts from *The Suffragette Movement* (Longman Green & Co. Ltd, 1931; Virago Ltd, reprinted 1977) by kind permission of Richard Pankhurst.

Emmeline Pethick-Lawrence extracts from *My Part in a Changing World* (Victor Gollancz, 1935).

Frederick Pethick-Lawrence extracts from *Fate has Been Kind* (Hutchinson, 1943).

Mary Richardson extracts from *Laugh a Defiance* (Weidenfeld & Nicolson, 1953).

R.J. Richardson extracts from *The Rights of Women* (John Elder, Edinburgh, 1840). Facsimile reprint; biographical introduction by Edmund and Ruth Frow (Working Class Movement Library, Manchester 1986) by kind permission of Ruth Frow.

Evelyn Sharp extracts from *Unfinished Adventure* (John Lane Bodley Head, 1933).

Ethel Smyth extract from *Female Pipings in Eden* (Peter Davies, 1933).

Mary Stocks extracts from *My Commonplace Book* (Peter Davis, 1970) by kind permission of the Hon. Helen Stocks.

Ray Strachey extracts from *The Cause* (G. Bell & Sons Ltd, 1928; Virago Ltd, reprinted, 1978).

Helena Swanwick extracts from *I Have Been Young* (Victor Gollancz, 1935).

William Thompson extracts from *Appeal of one half of the Human Race, Women, against the pretensions of the other half, Men, to retain them in political, and thence in civil and domestic slavery* (Longman, 1825).

Beatrice Webb extracts from *My Apprenticeship* (Longmans, Green & Co., 1926; Penguin reprinted, 1971) by permission of the London School of Economics.

Sir Almroth E. Wright extracts from *The Unexpurgated Case Against Woman Suffrage* (Constable & Company Ltd, 1913).

Every possible effort has been made to trace copyright holders. Inadvertent omissions will be rectified by contacting the publisher. The published material about the British women's suffrage movement is voluminous. Interested readers should consult the Select Bibliography in Elizabeth Crawford's *Reference Guide* which runs to some 250 entries.

Biographical Notes

Laura Ainsworth (1885–1958) Born Northumberland. Trained as a teacher but resigned to work as a full-time WSPU organiser. One of the first to be forcibly fed. Left the WSPU after the 1912 split. Post WW1 worked for the Newcastle branches of the British Legion and the League of Nations.

Louisa Garrett Anderson CBE, MD LOND. (1873–1943) Daughter of Elizabeth Garrett and J.G.S. Anderson. Like her mother qualified as a doctor. A militant until 1912 but never fell out with Aunt Millie (Fawcett). Deep friendship with Dr Flora Murray. In 1914 they took their Women's Hospital Corps to Paris and from 1916–19 ran the Endell Street Military Hospital, Covent Garden. Post WW1 and Flora Murray's death semi-retired. During the London Blitz 1940 returned to serve at her mother's hospital.

Herbert Henry Asquith (1852–1928) Born Morley, Yorkshire. Barrister. MP 1886. 5 children by first marriage, including Violet who became a Bonham-Carter. Ambition spurred by second marriage to the outrageous, deeply devoted Margot (their son Anthony a film director). Deposed by Lloyd George 1916. Never regained power. 1925 ennobled as Earl of Oxford and Asquith. Died a sad figure.

Lena Ashwell OBE, FRAM (1872–1957) Born on board ship in River Tyne. Childhood spent in Canada. Trained as a musician but became an actress and only woman London theatre lessee (the

Kingsway). Tax resister and vice-president of AFL. Second marriage to obstetrician Sir Henry Simson (he delivered Princess Margaret). Inaugurated troop concerts in WW1. Postwar the Lena Ashwell Players developed community theatre. Collapsed early 1930s, semi-retired.

Lucy Minnie Baldock (186?–1954) Londoner. Husband a Labour councillor in West Ham. 2 sons. Genuine working-class socialist and suffragist. Used as such by WSPU but later sidelined. By 1911 seriously ill. Recovered to carry the WSPU banner at Mrs Pankhurst's funeral and the unveiling of her statue in 1930.

Lydia Ernestine Becker (1827–90). Born Manchester, eldest of 15 children. Father of German descent. Ardent botanist – corresponded with Charles Darwin – and talented watercolourist. From 1866 devoted her unmarried life to the Cause. After two decades of ceaseless lobbying, travelling, editing the *Journal*, her health failed. Went to Aix-les-Bains for spa treatment but died in Geneva.

Teresa Billington-Greig (1877–1964) Born Preston. Impoverished Lancashire childhood. Aged 17 ran away to Manchester. Became a teacher. 1903 joined WSPU. 1904 formed Manchester Equal Pay League and worked as ILP organiser. 1905–07 leading member WSPU: 1907–10 WFL: 1911–14 revolutionary critic. Long happy marriage (1907–61) to Frederick Lewis Greig. Only child Fiona born 1915. In 1913 said of ex-militants: 'We shall drop to the level of the commonplace and do our commonplace work.' Believed this to be true of herself. Died of cancer borne with fortitude.

Helen Blackburn (1842–1903) Born off the south-west coast of Ireland where her engineer father was working. 1880 Sec. of the Bristol and West of England Suffrage Society. 1897 on the parliamentary committee of newly formed NUWSS. 1889–1902 edited *The Englishwoman's Review*. 1890 took over editorship of *Manchester Suffrage Journal* from the ailing Lydia Becker. Unmarried. The year before she died published *Women's Suffrage*, her invaluable guide to the pioneer days.

Margaret Bondfield (1873–1953) Born Chard, Somerset, 2nd youngest of 11 children. Worked as a shop assistant. Soon a trade union organiser. Became Chief Woman Officer of the General & Municipal Workers' Union. Sylvia Pankhurst accused her of deprecating 'votes for women as a hobby of disappointed old maids whom no one had wanted to marry'. Perhaps as an advocate of adult suffrage she did, but worked long and hard for women's rights. Labour MP 1923. First woman Cabinet Minister 1929. Remained an 'old maid' herself.

Nina Boyle (1865–1943) Ex-actress, journalist and author. Spent several years in S. Africa where she campaigned for black women's rights. Returned to England c. 1907. Joined the WFL, became its Political and Militant Organiser. 1914 helped found the first Women Volunteer Police. Later went to Serbia but returned to stand at the Keighley by-election. Postwar worked for the newly founded Save the Children Fund and re-campaigned for native rights in S. Africa.

Marie Brackenbury (1866–1946) The female side of the Brackenbury family, mother Hilda, daughters Georgina and Marie all deeply involved with the WSPU (perhaps fortunately for him General Brackenbury was dead). Both sisters studied at the Slade and were talented artists – and vegetarians. All at various times imprisoned, Mrs Brackenbury in her 80th year. Their house in Camden Hill Square, London, was a sanctuary for released 'mice' and became known as 'Mouse Castle'.

Henry Brailsford (1873–1958) Born Mirfield, Yorkshire. Educated Glasgow University. Fabian, prominent radical journalist. 1897 saw him in the Greek Foreign Legion and married to Jane Malloch. WSPU supporter and founder member of Men's League, but had little faith in militancy. Worked tirelessly as Hon. Sec. of Conciliation Committee, then to forge links between the NUWSS and the Labour Party. 1913 separated from suffragist wife Jane (who died an alcoholic). 1918 election stood unsuccessfully as Labour candidate. Later remarried.

Bertha Brewster Born 1887. Educated Bedales College, Germany and University College London. Journalist. Joined WSPU 1906. Resigned after the 1912 split. Friend of Evelyn Sharp and Henry Nevinson. 1914 founder member United Suffragists.

Eileen Casey Born 1886 New South Wales. 1897 family came to England. Did not join WSPU until 1911 but thereafter a super-militant. Earned her niche as the last prisoner to be released. A WW1 land girl. 1923–40 teacher in Japan. 1940–51 back in Australia working as a translator. Then returned to England.

Carrie Chapman Catt (1859–1947) Born Iowa. Teacher and journalist. 1900 chairwoman National American Woman Suffrage Alliance (NAWSA). 1904 president of IWSA, 1915 of NAWSA. Twice married. Brilliant organiser. Postwar founded US League of Women Voters and campaigned for peace.

Ada Nield Chew (1870–1945) Born Staffs. 1894 sacked for publishing a series of highly critical articles by 'A Crewe Factory Girl'. 1897 married weaver and ILP organiser George Chew. Moved to Lancashire. 1898 only daughter Doris born. Excellent speaker. Endlessly toured the north-west banging the socialist and non-militant suffrage drums. Published sketches of working-class life. A vegetarian and pacifist.

Marie Corelli (1864–1924) Of Italian/Scots parentage, adopted as a child by songwriter Charles Mackay. Educated England and France. Immensely popular writer of romantic fiction considered daring in its day. Led an eccentric personal life. Made her home in Stratford-on-Avon where she died.

(Dame) Kathleen Courtney (1878–1974) Born Chatham. Father an army officer. Oxford (non) graduate. 1908 Sec. N. of England Suffrage Society. 1911 Hon. Sec. NUWSS. Managed to attend 1915 Hague Peace Congress but resigned NUWSS on pacifist principle. Re-elected to EC 1918 and then on NUSEC's Executive Committee. 1930s campaigned for disarmament. Post WW2 Chair of United Nations Association. DBE 1952.

Evelyn Baring, 1st Earl of Cromer (1841–1917) Born Cromer Hall, Norfolk. Started his career in the Royal Artillery. ADC to the Viceroy of India 1872–75. Earned his reputation as British Agent and Consul-General in Egypt 1883–1907.

Lord Curzon, 1st Marquess Curzon of Kedleston (1859–1925) Born Kedleston Hall, Derbyshire. Educated Eton and Oxford. The couplet 'My name is George Nathaniel Curzon, I am a very superior person' was penned in his Balliol days. The peaks of his career were Viceroy of India 1898–1905 (where he met his match in Lord Kitchener) and Foreign Secretary 1919–24. Failed to become Prime Minister. Both wives American. Socialist daughter Cynthia married to Sir Oswald Mosley in his Labour Party days.

Emily Davies (1830–1921) Born Southampton. Father a vicar. Moved to Gateshead. 1865 Sec. Kensington Society. 1869 opened a women's college, 1873 moved it to Cambridge, 1874 named it

Girton. Participated in 1906 suffrage deputation and lived to see women enfranchised, but not their graduate admission to Cambridge University.

Emily Wilding Davison (1872–1913) Born London but associated with Northumberland. Educated Kensington High School and London University. First class honours degree. Teacher and governess. 1906 joined WSPU. Thereafter devoted her life – and death – to the Cause.

Charlotte Despard née French (1844–1939) General Sir John French (in 1914 he led the British forces in France) her brother, as newspapers never ceased to mention. 1879 married Maximilian Despard (d. 1890). 1891–1921 variously involved with a settlement in Battersea, the WFL presidency and vegetarianism. Postwar moved to Ireland in support of Irish freedom and a hoped-for socialist state. Known to irreverent suffragettes as 'Mrs Desperate'.

Flora Drummond (1879–1949) Born Manchester, brought up in Scotland. 1898 married Joe Drummond, returned to Manchester. Early member WSPU. 1906 to London. Revelled in the title 'General'. Remained faithful to the Pankhursts. Campaigned for Christabel in 1918 election. Postwar founded Women's Guild of Empire.

Una Dugdale (1880–1975) Educated Cheltenham Ladies College. Studied singing in Paris. Joined WSPU 1907. Accompanied Mrs Pankhurst on her countrywide tours. 2 daughters from 'No Obey' 1912 wedding to Victor Duval. Treasurer of the Suffragette Fellowship. Instrumental in the collection being preserved at the Museum of London.

Marion Wallace Dunlop (1865–1942) Scottish by birth. Studied at the Slade and exhibited at the Royal Academy 1905–06. By 1908 active in WSPU. 1909 initiated the hunger-strike. Organised many suffrage pageants and 1912 window-smashing campaign. Vegetarian and theosophist.

Victor Duval (1885–1945) Founder member of Men's Political Union. Twice briefly imprisoned, not forcibly fed. Served in the Royal Engineers during WW1. Postwar rejoined Liberal Party and three times unsuccessful candidate. All the Duval family were ardent suffragists. Sister Elsie (1892–1919) married Hugh Franklin in 1915. Her early death almost certainly hastened by forcible feeding.

Elizabeth Wolstenholme Elmy (1833–1918) Born Manchester. Father a Methodist minister. Orphaned young, largely self-taught. Ran several schools in Manchester area. 1867 helped establish the North of England Council for Promoting the Education of Women. Hon. Sec. of first Manchester Suffrage Society formed 1865. 'Lived in sin' with Ben Elmy (d. 1906). Aged forty found herself pregnant. Persuaded to marry; only son born 1875. Continued to campaign tirelessly. Supported WSPU until 1912 split. Died Manchester six days after first women enfranchised.

(Dame) Millicent Garrett Fawcett (1847–1929) Born Aldeburgh, Suffolk. Educated at home and Blackheath School. 1867 married Liberal MP Henry Fawcett who had been blinded in an accident. Acted as his 'eyes' until his death 1884. Studied political economy. Helped found Newnham College, Cambridge, of which her only daughter Philippa became a brilliant (non) graduate. Campaigned for Married Women's Property Act but women's suffrage the life-long cause she nobly served. DBE 1925.

Rachel Ferguson (1893–1957) Born Hampton Wick. 1909 joined WSPU. 1911–13 trained at (R)ADA. Acted for three years. Strong sense of the irreverent – not a noted suffragette trait. 1919 onwards earned her living as a writer. First woman on the staff of *Punch*. Publications include *The Brontës Went to Woolworths* and *Celebrated Squeals* (Parodies of Famous Authors).

Hugh Franklin (1889–1962) Born London. Father a banker, uncle Herbert Samuel a prominent Liberal politician. Educated Clifton College and Cambridge. Fabian and ILP member. 1911–13 organiser militant Men's Political Union. Forcibly fed over 100 times. Disowned by father on marriage to non-Jewish Elsie Duval. Remarried after her early death. Twice unsuccessful Labour parliamentary candidate but in 1946 finally elected to Middlesex County Council.

Mary Gawthorpe (1881–1973) Born Leeds. Pupil-teacher aged 13. Later obtained first class teaching certificate. Excellent singer and pianist. Worked herself into the ground in early WSPU days. 1910 collapsed. Returned to the fray but 1916 went to USA. Worked for suffrage and labour movements there until 1921 when collapsed again. 1923 married John Sanders and became an American citizen.

Herbert Gladstone (1854–1930) Youngest son of William Ewart

Gladstone. Educated Eton and Oxford. Taught history. MP 1880. Worshipped his father in whose shadow he lived. Not personally opposed to women's suffrage, unhappy as Home Secretary during the militant years. Created Viscount Gladstone on his return from Governor-Generalship of South Africa.

Eva Gore-Booth (1870–1926) Born Sligo. Family among the largest landowners in the west of Ireland. Constance Markievicz her sister. Met her lifelong partner Esther Roper in Italy. Settled with her in Manchester. Initially influenced Christabel Pankhurst but strongly opposed militancy. Continued to campaign with local radical suffragists. Dedicated WW1 pacifist.

Lilias Ashworth Hallett (1844–1922) Member of the Bright family, Quakers and radical Liberals from Rochdale, Lancashire. Priscilla Bright McLaren (1815–1906) was her aunt; Helen Bright Clark (1840–1927) her cousin; Jacob Bright (1821–99), who took over from J.S. Mill as the women's suffrage MP, her uncle. Signed the 1866 petition and thereafter a tireless campaigner. 1903 on NUWSS executive. Initially supported WSPU but deplored their increasing militancy. Another pioneer who lived to see first women enfranchised.

Cicely Hamilton (1872–1952) Born London. Father an army officer. Unhappy childhood. Educated Malvern College and Germany. Actress, novelist and playwright. Joined NUWSS and WSPU, co-founded Writers' Suffrage League, on AFL executive. WW1 worked with Scottish Women's Hospital unit and for Lena Ashwell concert parties in France. Original director Lady Rhondda's feminist magazine *Time and Tide*. Birth control campaigner. Very good writer.

James Keir Hardie (1846–1915) Born Lanarkshire. Illegitimate child. Worked as a coal miner. 1892 first Independent Labour MP. Regarded as the father of the Labour Party but always a maverick. Had an affair with Sylvia Pankhurst. Alleged to have had one 'with the mother, too' but this seems unlikely; Emmeline worshipped her husband's memory and hardly had the time.

Mrs Frederic (Ethel) Harrison (died 1916). Married 1870, 4 children. Her husband a leading English exponent of Positivism, author of innumerable books on Victorian literature and the meaning of history. She wrote hymns and poetry.

Bessie Hatton playwright and journalist, Joseph Hatton, her father.

Bessie herself wrote romantic fiction. Remained secretary of the Women Writers' Suffrage League until WW1. 1916–18 organised entertainments for patients at the female-staffed Endell Street Military Hospital.

Hon. Evelina Haverfield (1867–1920) Born Scotland, daughter 3rd Baron Abinger. 1887 married Major Henry Haverfield. 2 sons (1 killed in WW1). 1899 remarried after his death but reverted to name 'Haverfield'. 1908 transferred allegiance from NUWSS to WSPU but later joined United Suffragists. 1915–17 in charge of Scottish Women's Hospital transport column in Serbia and Russia. Postwar returned to Serbia to found an orphanage. Died there of pneumonia.

Henry Hunt (1773–1835) Born Upavon, Wilts. Educated Andover Grammar School. 1801 left his wife and ran off with a friend's (they stayed together). By 1806 had been converted from gentleman farmer to radical reformer. A great mob orator, 'Peterloo' the high-water mark of his career. Vain, boastful, bellicose, but genuinely suffered for his causes and remained faithful to them until death.

Alice Kedge (1895–1994) Born London. From pre-war 'service' went into wartime munitions. Postwar realised her ambition of running a guest house in Margate. With interruptions for WW2 did so until in her seventies. Married an Irishman whose health never recovered from WW1 service. One son (the editor's husband). Died Margate.

Annie Kenney (1879–1953) Born near Oldham, Lancashire, 5th of 11 children. Half-timer in cotton mill aged 10. Genuinely working class but from a family steeped in the tradition of self-improvement. 1905 heard Christabel Pankhurst lecture on women's suffrage and her devotion thereafter absolute. 1920 married James Taylor, one son born 1921. After publishing her Peter Pan-style *Memories of a Militant* in 1924 – it was an awfully big adventure – retired into domesticity in Herts. Via sister Jessie became a Rosicrucian. Health affected by hunger striking and forcible feeding. Died after a long illness.

Jessie Kenney (1887–1985) Born near Oldham, similarly a part-timer in a cotton mill. Took a typing course, became Emmeline Pethick-Lawrence's secretary, then a WSPU organiser. Remained faithful to the Pankhursts. Accompanied Mrs Pankhurst on bizarre 1917 mission to rally the fast fading Russian war effort. Post WW1 qualified as a ship's radio officer but as a woman disbarred from practising. Travelled the world as a stewardess. Became a Rosicrucian.

George Lansbury (1859–1940) Born Suffolk, son of a 'navvy'. 1868 family moved to London. 1880 married childhood sweetheart Bessie, 12 children. Briefly emigrated to Australia. Joined ILP. 1910 elected MP. Vociferous supporter of WSPU. Backed Sylvia Pankhurst's East London Federation but joined United Suffragists. 1922 re-elected for Bromley and Bow. Held office in first Labour Government. In 1931, most Labour MPs defeated, became leader of the party. 1935 ill-health forced his retirement.

Mary Leigh née Brown. Born Manchester. A super-militant but like her friend Emily Wilding Davison regarded by the Pankhursts as a very loose cannon. 1912 released from Irish penal servitude, returned to further militancy in England. Visited the dying Emily in hospital and founded a club in her honour. WW1 ambulance driver. Lived to take part in 1950s 'Ban the Bomb' march, carrying Emily's Derby Day flag.

Lilian Lenton (1891–1972) A professional dancer. Joined WSPU 1912. Ferocious militant, famous for avoiding arrest as a 'mouse'. WW1 served with the Scottish Women's Hospital in Serbia. Postwar worked for the Save the Children Fund. 1924–1933 WFL organiser. A vegetarian and campaigner for animal rights.

David Lloyd George (1863–1945) Born Manchester but essentially Welsh. Brought up in Llanystymdwy. Solicitor. 1888 married Margaret Owen. 5 children (Megan and Gwilym both MPs). 1890 Liberal MP. Famed orator and debator. Opposed the Boer War. 1908–15 reforming Chancellor of the Exchequer. 1915–16 Minister of Munitions. 1916–22 Prime Minister. Liberal Party never recovered from its bitter split but he remained a colourful figure. 1943 after Margaret's death married long-time mistress Frances Stevenson. 1945 ennobled as Earl Lloyd-George of Dwyfor.

Lady Constance Lytton (1869–1923) Her father, 1st Earl of Lytton, was Viceroy of India where she lived as a child. Drawn into the WSPU by Emmeline Pethick-Lawrence. Worked with brother Victor, 2nd Earl of Lytton, to promote the Conciliation Bill. Suffered a slight stroke after 1911 'torpedoing' and a more severe one in 1912. Thereafter a valiant invalid until her death, probably hastened by forcible feeding in Walton Gaol.

Jill Liddington (1946–) Born Manchester, now lives with her husband in West Yorkshire. Has worked in television and adult education, currently a reader for the University of Leeds School of Continuing Education. *One Hand Tied Behind Us* was the first book to deal with working-class suffragists. Has since written *The Life & Times of a Respectable Rebel: Selina Cooper; The Long Road to Greenham; Female Fortune*.

Lillah McCarthy OBE (1875–1960) Born Cheltenham. On the stage aged 15. Became leading Shavian actress and London theatre manager. AFL vice-president and treasurer. 1920 married Sir Frederick Keeble. On his appointment to Oxford University, more or less retired to cultivate their garden (he was a botanist).

(Sir) Reginald McKenna (1863–1943) Born London. Cambridge-educated barrister. MP 1895–1918. Home Secretary 1911–15. Retired from political life 1919. Thereafter Chairman of the Midland Bank.

Kitty Marion (1871–1944) Stage name of Katherina Maria Schafer. Born Germany. 1886 came to England. Established herself as a popular, though not top-of-the-bill, music hall artiste. 1909–14 militant suffragette. 1915 after the sinking of the *Lusitania*, threatened with internment or deportation as a German national. Eventually allowed to go to America. Campaigned with Margaret Sanger for birth control. Returned England 1930. Worked similarly with Edith How Martyn. Back to New York where she died. Her memoirs never found a publisher and are in the Museum of London.

Violet Markham C.H. (1872–1959) Born Derbyshire, grand-daughter of Joseph Paxton. 1915 married Lt-Col. James Carruthers 'because he sings in his bath' (of which she was obviously aware). Worked with him for League of Nations in postwar Germany. Her conversion to the Cause absolute, she became the first female Mayor, and later freeman, of Chesterfield. Made a Companion of Honour.

Charlotte (Charlie) Marsh (1887–1961) Born Newcastle. Trained as a sanitary inspector. 1908 joined WSPU. Became a paid organiser. Among first to be forcibly fed. Carried the cross at her friend Emily Wilding Davison's funeral procession. WW1 worked as Lloyd George's chauffeuse and a land girl; postwar for peace organisations and London County Council.

Catherine Marshall (1880–1961) Daughter of Harrow maths master who retired to the Lake District. 1911–14 key figure as NUWSS parliamentary secretary and Hon. Sec. of Election Fighting Fund in support of Labour MPs. Managed to attend Hague Peace Congress. Worked for WW1 No Conscription Fellowship. Unrequited love for its charismatic Chairman Clifford Allen. Collapsed 1917. Remained a dedicated pacifist. Gave Lake District asylum to Jewish refugees from Hitler's Germany.

Edith How Martyn (1875–1954) Born London. Educated University College, Aberystwyth. Physicist and mathematician. 1899 married George Martyn. Member ILP. 1906 joined WSPU but seceded to be founder member WFL and its Hon. Sec. 1907–11. Failed to be elected 1918, but 1919 first woman member and then Chairwoman Middlesex County Council. Birth control campaigner. Emigrated Australia 1939. Died there after a long illness.

Muriel Matters (1877–1969) Australian. Came to England c. 1905 to further her career as singer/actress but joined WSPU. 1907–13 leading member WFL. 1914 seceded to NUWSS and married a Mr Porter. Wartime pacifist. 1924 unsuccessful Labour candidate. Died Hastings.

John Stuart Mill (1806–1873) Political economist and philosopher. 1830 met Harriet Taylor and thereafter committed to women's rights. *The Subjection of Women* remains one of the most influential books written on the subject. 1851 after the death of Harriet's husband they married.

Theodora Mills (1870?–1958) Cheltenham Unitarian family. Sec. local WSPU branch. Apart from composing suffrage verses to well-known tunes she wrote novels, all unpublished, alas. A dedicated anti-vivisectionist.

Hannah Mitchell née Webster (1871–1956) Grew up in rural poverty in the Peak district of Derbyshire. As a child she met Mrs Humphry Ward who 'found her way to our lonely farm' whilst researching her novel *The History of David Grieve*. Hannah ran away from home, worked as a domestic servant and in sweatshops. 1895 married Gibbon Mitchell who drew her into the Labour movement. 1 son. Lived in the Manchester area. 1903 joined WSPU. After recovering from a severe breakdown worked for the WFL. Postwar became a Manchester City Councillor and magistrate. Sadly, her interesting autobiography *The Hard Way Up* did not find a publisher in her lifetime.

Flora Murray CBE, MD, B.SC (1870–1923) Born Dumfriesshire. Father a naval commander. 1903 graduated Durham University. Became a GP in London. 1908 joined WSPU. 1911 with Louisa Garrett Anderson founded a children's hospital. Campaigned against forcible feeding. Tended Mrs Pankhurst and other suffragettes during the Cat-and-Mouse days (see Louisa G.A. for 1914–18 hospital work).

Henry Woodd Nevinson (1856–1941) Born Leicester. Educated Shrewsbury, Oxford and Germany. Taught classics. Radical journalist. Covered Greek/Turkish War, Boer War, Portuguese slave trade. When at home supported WSPU. Founding member of militant Men's Political Union. 1912 split dismayed him. 1914 formed United Suffragists. Postwar helped expose brutality of Black and Tans in Ireland. 1938 President of PEN. His autobiography *Fire of Life* ignores his first wife Margaret but lauds his eventual second wife Evelyn Sharp.

Margaret Wynne Nevinson (1858–1932) Born Leicester. Father a vicar. Worked as a teacher. 1884 married her childhood friend Henry. The artist C.R.W. Nevinson their son. Left WSPU for WFL. Also active in Women Writers' and Tax Resistance Leagues. Unclear when the Nevinsons separated as *she* barely mentions *him* in her autobiography *Life's Fitful Fever*. Postwar became a JP for the County of London.

Jill Norris (1949–1985) Born Newcastle. Taught in primary schools and adult education in Manchester. Co-authored *One Hand Tied Behind Us* with Jill Liddington. Tragically killed in a road accident.

(Dame) Christabel Pankhurst (1880–1958) Born Manchester, eldest daughter of Emmeline and Richard Pankhurst. Political apprenticeship served under Eva Gore-Booth and Esther Roper. Studied law at Manchester University but as a woman unable to practise. Post WW1 led a peripatetic existence preaching the Second Coming of Christ. 1930 adopted a daughter. 1936 DBE. 1939 went to live in California where she died.

Emmeline Pankhurst née Goulden (1858–1928) Born Manchester. 1879 married lawyer Richard Pankhurst, a fervent but impratical reformer. 5 children, both boys died, one aged 4, Harry aged 20. 1885 moved to London. 1889 helped form Women's Franchise

League (soon disbanded). 1893 back to Manchester. 1898 Richard died. 1903 founded the WSPU and the rest is history. Her life undoubtedly shortened by constant arrests, hunger-and-thirst strikes. Least-known daughter Adela also a suffragette, but ended her days as a fascist in Australia. Emmeline's own last stand was as a prospective Tory candidate.

Sylvia Pankhurst (1882–1960) Born Manchester. Idolised her father. A talented artist but devoted her life to socialist and pacifist causes which make her the most popular Pankhurst for latterday feminists (Christabel's and Emmeline's wartime jingoism and postwar activities are difficult subjects). *The Suffragette Movement* remains the only first-hand account of the Pankhursts' and WSPU's early days. As such to be treasured but also treated with caution, Sylvia not being the most reliable or unbiased of chroniclers. 1930s championed Abyssinia (now Ethiopia), hardly a model democracy but it had been brutally invaded by Mussolini's forces. Ended her days in Addis Ababa.

Dorothy Pethick (1881–1970) Born Somerset, younger sister of Emmeline (see below). Joined the WSPU 1906, several times arrested and imprisoned, resigned 1912 when her sister ousted. A wartime volunteer policewoman. Postwar Sec. Rudolph Steiner School, Hampstead.

Emmeline Pethick-Lawrence (1867–1954) Grew up in Weston-super-Mare, one of 13 children. Educated Cheltenham Ladies' College. Fabian and genuine 'do-gooder'. 1901 married Frederick Lawrence. No children. 1906–12 devoted their lives and money to the WSPU. Emmeline a brilliant fund-raiser. WW1 pacifist. Thereafter dedicated herself to world peace until her faculties waned.

Frederick Pethick-Lawrence (1871–1961) Wealthy Unitarian family. Educated Eton and Cambridge. Barrister and socialist. Post WW1 became a Labour MP. Secretary of State for India during the crucial years leading to partition and independence 1945–47. Ennobled as Lord Pethick-Lawrence. After Emmeline's death married ex-suffragette Helen Craggs.

Mrs Henry Davis Pochin née Agnes Heap (1825–1908) Born near Manchester. Unitarian family. 1852 married radical Liberal H.D. Pochin. Her 'Justitia' pamphlet is cogently and wittily argued. Spoke at first public suffrage meeting in Manchester's Free Trade

Hall, chaired by her husband. Severely criticised for so doing. 1874 they bought the Bodnant estate in North Wales, now a favourite National Trust garden.

Eleanor Rathbone (1872–1946) Born Liverpool into wealthy, radical Unitarian family. Studied Somerville College, Oxford. 1898–1913 Sec. Liverpool Suffrage Society. 1900–19 NUWSS Executive member, apart from brief resignation over the Labour alliance. Supported Millicent Fawcett in 1915 split. 1919–29 President NUSEC. Campaigned for wartime separation allowances and then family allowances. MP for Combined English Universities 1929 until her death. Unmarried. Hollywood film actor Basil Rathbone her cousin.

Lady Rhondda née Margaret Haig Thomas (1883–1958) Daughter of Welsh coal owner and Liberal MP. Became Viscount Rhondda. Studied Oxford. 1908 married Sir Charles Mackworth, divorced 1923. Copious contributor to *Votes for Women*. 1913 imprisoned S. Wales. 1915 survived the sinking of the *Lusitania*. Influential feminist. Founded *Time and Tide* – 1928–58 its proprietor and editor – and Six Point Group. Did not live to see women in the House of Lords, though was personally given royal permission to attend sittings.

Mary Richardson (1883?–1961) Canadian. Travelled to Europe c. 1900. Settled in London. Joined the WSPU 1909 but did not become militant until 1913. Her account of Derby Day 1913 has been queried – *was* she present when Emily Wilding Davison threw herself at the King's horse? If Richardson wasn't, she should have written more novels. 1915 joined the United Suffragists. Postwar stood three times as unsuccessful Labour candidate. Then followed Sir Oswald Mosley into the British Union of Fascists.

R.J. Richardson (1808–61) Reginald John. Born Salford. Master carpenter and radical reformer. 1839 arrested for Chartist activities. Tried at Liverpool Assizes and sentenced to 9 months' imprisonment in Lancaster Castle. On release edited the Chartist *Dundee Chronicle* but fell out with Feargus O'Connor (not difficult to do). Returned to Manchester where he died.

Elizabeth Robins (1862–1952) Born Kentucky. 1885 married fellow-actor George Parks who committed suicide 1889. Came to London where she was renowned as an interpreter of Ibsen.

1902 gave up acting (last performances in a play of Mrs Humphry Ward's) to concentrate on writing. 1907 published *The Convert*, her influential and still very readable suffrage novel. 1908 president Women Writers' League. Wrote suffrage plays and lectured for WSPU until 1912 split. Original director *Time and Tide*.

Esther Roper (1868–1938) Born near Manchester. Father a lay missionary. Educated Church Mission School, London. 1891 graduated Owen's College. 1893 Sec. Manchester National Society. Radical suffragist and pacifist like her partner Eva Gore-Booth. After Eva's death edited her poems and the prison letters of her sister Constance Markievicz.

Annie Cobden Sanderson (1853–1926) Daughter of renowned Liberal politician Richard Cobden. 1882 married James Sanderson, 2 children. Joined ILP. Friend of Millicent Fawcett but defected to WSPU. 1906 Liberal Government's arrest and imprisonment of Cobden's daughter caused an uproar. 1907 founder member WFL. Tax resister. Active until the end of her life.

Maud Arncliffe Sennett née Sparagnapane (1862–1936) Born London. Italian father, English mother. Acted under stage name 'Mary Kingsley'. 1898 married Henry Arncliffe Sennett and became main partner and chief designer in Sparagnapane family business (Christmas crackers and wedding-cake ornaments). Flamboyant personality at various times in NUWSS, WSPU and AFL. 1913 founded the Northern Federation for Women's Suffrage based in Scotland. 1914 Vice-President United Suffragists. She and her sister Florence de Fonblanque organised the first women's pilgrimage from Edinburgh. Her Suffrage Collection is invaluable.

Evelyn Sharp (1869–1955) Born London. Cecil Sharp, folk-song enthusiast, her brother. Tutored before establishing herself as novelist and journalist. 1906 joined WSPU. Twice imprisoned. Resigned after 1912 split. Founder member United Suffragists. 1918–23 on staff of Labour's *Daily Herald*. 1933 after his wife's death married long-time companion Henry Nevinson (they first met c. 1903).

George Bernard Shaw (1856-1950) Born Dublin. Came to England 1876. Initial struggle before making his name as music critic and

Fabian socialist propagandist. Staunch suffragist. 1890s onwards the plays poured out. Sir Ralph Bloomfield Bonnington in *The Doctor's Dilemma* (1906) said to have been based on Sir Almroth Wright. 1926 Nobel Prize for Literature. Died Ayot St Lawrence, Herts, where he had lived for decades.

(Dame) Ethel Smyth (1858–1944) Father a major-general. Studied music Berlin and Leipzig. An established composer by 1910 when first met Mrs Pankhurst. Imprisoned 1912. Renowned for beating time with a toothbrush as fellow-suffragettes in Holloway exercised to *The March of the Women*. 1913 returned to music-making. 1914 friendship with Mrs Pankhurst strained, as jingoism not her style. Worked as wartime radiographer with French army. DBE 1922. Campaigned tirelessly for women musicians.

Mrs Saul Solomon née Georgiana Thomson (1844–1933) Born Edinburgh. Emigrated S. Africa. Principal Good Hope seminary. 1874 married Saul Solomon, liberal Premier and Governor-General Cape Colony. 1892 he died in Scotland. Georgiana and 6 children remained in Britain. 1907 member WFL. 1908 joined WSPU. Led deputations to H of C including 'Black Friday'. Resigned WSPU after 1912 split. Daughter Daisy one of human letters posted to Downing Street.

(Baroness) Mary Stocks née Brinton (1891–1975) Educated St Paul's Girls School and LSE. 1913 married fellow academic John Stocks. 3 children. Lecturer at King's College London and Manchester University. 1939–51 principal Westfield College, London. Life peeress 1966.

Ray Strachey (1887–1940) Daughter of Mary Pearsall Smith (American Quaker suffragist family) and Frank Costelloe. Educated Newnham and Bryn Mawr Colleges. Took a course in electrical engineering. 1911 married Oliver Strachey, brother of Lytton. 2 children. 1916–21 NUWSS parliamentary sec. which included the crucial years lobbying for the 1918 Act. Stood 3 times as Independent parliamentary candidate without success.

Helena Swanwick MA née Sickert (1864–1939) Born Munich to Danish father, English mother. The artist Walter Sickert her brother. Studied Girton College. 1888 married F.T. Swanwick, lecturer at Manchester University (d. 1931). No children. Lived in Manchester for 2 decades but did not join WSPU. First editor *Common Cause*. Dedicated pacifist, resigned NUWSS 1915 but retained friendship with Millicent Fawcett. Delegate to League of Nations. Committee suicide shortly after outbreak of WW2.

Harriet Taylor (1807–58) Born London, Unitarian family. 1826 married John Taylor. 3 children. 1830 met John Stuart Mill. 1833 trial separation spent with Mill in Paris. Returned home to preserve the proprieties. Civilised arrangement until Taylor died 1849. 1851 Harriet and Mill married in a register office after he had renounced all marital rights under the existing laws. Harriet died of consumption before *The Subjection of Women* completed.

William Thompson (1785–1833) Born Cork, wealthy Protestant family. By 1820s part of London's radical society. Became involved with Mrs Anna Wheeler, to whom the first suffrage pamphlet is dedicated. She probably wrote much of it – the horrors of the marital slavery she had endured loom large. Lady Constance Lytton was her great-grand-daughter.

Mrs Humphry Ward (1851–1920) Born Mary Augusta Arnold in Tasmania. Her father was Dr Thomas Arnold of Rugby School, Matthew Arnold her brother. 1872 married Thomas Humphry Ward. She the family breadwinner, MP son Arnold as spendthrift as his father. Millicent Fawcett regarded her as 'a social reformer who had somehow wandered into the wrong camp' – she founded what became the Mary Ward Settlement in London – but she genuinely believed in 'separate spheres' for men and women.

Beatrice Webb née Potter (1858–1943) One of 9 Potter daughters. Self-taught social scientist. Lifelong diary keeper. 1892 married Sydney Webb. In a 50-year partnership they were pivotal figures in British left-wing intellectual life.

(Dame) Rebecca West (1892–1983) Born Cicely Fairfield, Edinburgh. Took her pen-name from the heroine of Ibsen's *Rosmersholm*. Brilliant polemical journalist; author fiction and non-fiction books. WSPU supporter. Affair with H.G. Wells produced her only child, born 1914. Original director *Time and Tide*. 1930 married banker Henry Maxwell Andrews. Covered the Nuremberg War Trials. DBE 1959.

Sir Almroth Wright (1861–1947) Educated Dublin. Gold medal for literature as well as medicine. Studied Roman and International Law in Germany. *Was* married – to Jane Wilson of Co. Kildare. 2 children. Principal the Institute of Pathology, St Mary's, Paddington. 1914–18 consultant physician in France where his insistence on preventative vaccines saved many British soldiers' lives.

Israel Zangwill (1864–1926) Playwright and novelist. President Jewish Drama League. His play *The Melting Pot* (1908) popularised the phrase for USA's influx of immigrants. 1903 married Edith Ayrton, stepdaughter of pioneer woman scientist Hertha Ayrton. All staunch suffragists. 1907 joined Men's League, 1913 its Vice-President. Supported WSPU but 1914 switched to United Suffragists.

Every effort has been made to trace the contributors, but the editor will be pleased to hear from any reader with further information.